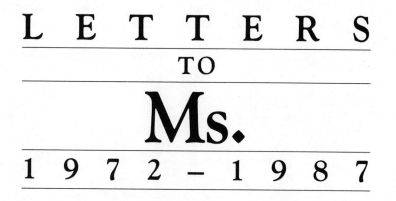

LETTERS
TO
Ms.
1 9 7 2 – 1 9 8 7

LETTERS
TO
Ms.
1972 – 1987

EDITED BY
MARY THOM

INTRODUCTION BY
GLORIA STEINEM

AFTERWORD BY
EVA MOSELEY

HENRY HOLT AND COMPANY
NEW YORK

Published by Henry Holt and Company, Inc.,
521 Fifth Avenue, New York, New York 10175.

Produced by IMG Publishing

Distributed in Canada by Fitzhenry & Whiteside, 195 Allstate Parkway,
Markham, Ontario L3R 4T8.

Library of Congress Cataloging-in-Publication Data
Letters to Ms. Magazine, 1972–1987.
    1. Feminism—United States—Correspondence.
2. Women—United States—Correspondence.   3. Sex
role—United States—Correspondence.   I. Thom, Mary.
II. Ms.
HQ1426.L475   1987   304.4'2'0973   87-8469
ISBN 0-8050-0384-3

FIRST EDITION

Designed by Stanley S. Drate/Folio Graphics Co., Inc.

Printed in the United States of America

10 9 8 7 6 5 4 3 2 1

ISBN 0-8050-0384-3

To the readers of Ms.

CONTENTS

ACKNOWLEDGMENTS

———————— ❧ ————————

In addition to those many readers of Ms. who correspond with us, my special thanks go to the following people.

My colleagues at Ms., particularly Joanne Edgar and Suzanne Levine, for their editorial comments and for their encouragement and friendship in being willing to add to their already onerous workload to give me unlimited time and leisure to read and edit these letters; and Suzanne again and Letty Cottin Pogrebin for skillfully taking care of the business side of this endeavor for Ms.

Angela Miller, my editor at The Miller Press, International Management Group, for her enthusiasm for this project, for her tenacity, and for her many helpful suggestions particularly about the structure and tone of this book.

All of those on the Ms. staff, past and current, who have lovingly read, edited, analyzed, filed, and occasionally answered reader mail, including Margaret Sloan, Rachael Drexler, Ingeborg Day, Susan Thom Loubet, Curtis Ingham, Valerie Monroe, Marcia Rockwood, Jane Bosveld, Betsy Israel, Jill Johnson Keeney, Della Rowland, and the current "Letters" editor, Mary McNamara.

Patricia King, director of Radcliffe College's Arthur and Elizabeth Schlesinger Library on the History of Women in America, Eva Moseley, curator of manuscripts for the Schlesinger Library, and the library staff, for recognizing the historical value of the Ms. letters, for organizing and caring for the collection, and for kindly providing me and others who might peruse these letters with a comfortable and congenial setting in which to work.

A note on style: the letters included in this book that have been published in Ms. carry the date of the issue in which they appear. Unpublished letters carry the date they were written, or if that wasn't noted, the month and year they were received.

INTRODUCTION

by Gloria Steinem

When I look back on the fifteen years of Ms., the letters from readers are what I remember best. More than reporting or short stories, poetry or humor (though the letters contain all of these), I look forward to our readers' continuing gift for putting helpful facts, personal stories, political alerts, article ideas, "clicks" of recognition, accurate criticisms, and sometimes whole life histories into envelopes and sending them to far-off editors as a gesture of faith.

Of course, I have always had an advantage; I get to see the letters there is no room to publish in regular letters columns—and that's a lot. Though we give more space to letters than any magazine I'm aware of—and publish special forums when there are many thoughtful responses on one subject—the real amount of our mail could never be represented in the magazine's pages. Altogether, our monthly mail total is far bigger than that received by magazines with ten times our circulation. That's why I'm grateful for the opportunity to share these letters that this book presents.

Perhaps it was this quantity and quality of letters over the years that allowed me to take them for granted. Like oxygen, much generous letter-writing had become a part of my life. Without the request for our voluminous Letters-to-the-Editors files from the Schlesinger Library at Radcliffe, I might have continued to take these precious letters for granted.

Then six of us made a snowy, pre-Christmas trip to Cambridge to celebrate the library's acquisition of the first files, circa 1972–1980: seven big boxes of letters that archivists had culled from twice that volume by removing, as they explained to us, "routine and nonbiographical letters, photographs and resumes—and moving clippings, articles enclosed with letters and examples of sexist ads to the library's vertical files."

At a dinner given by Radcliffe President Matina Horner, questions about the letters from the feminist scholars and educators there began to turn the whole meal into a Proustian tea cake. I could remember, as I had not in years, the exact sensation of sitting up many late nights after the Preview Issue (Spring 1972), reading at random from bulging mailbags that brought a total of twenty thousand letters into our one-room office.

I remembered a letter from a woman who said she had taken the Preview Issue to a much-feared job interview, carrying it like a badge of courage. The interviewer had been going to offer her less salary, he said. Seeing that she was into this "women's lib" thing, however, he reluctantly offered her the same salary as he gave men.

I remembered many, many women who said they had felt "crazy" or "alone" until they found Ms. on their newsstands; women who didn't have access to bookstores and the few feminist works that were there. Some said they had asked their husbands to read Ms. and felt it helped their marriage. Others said it had given them the courage to walk out the door.

I realized that those moving, thoughtful, intimate letters, much more than the statistical fact of the Preview Issue's success, had given us the courage to keep going. I remembered a seven-year-old who had written in crayon in careful block letters, that the boys got the big part of the playground at every recess, while the girls only got a corner for playing marbles and dolls. "We girls," she explained, "are angry as turnips." (I remember thinking: Turnips! That kid is going to be a writer.) There was a woman well past seventy who wrote that she had been married four times, didn't like any of her husbands very much, and wanted to know how she could get her birth name back legally. (Eventually that and other letters led to an article called, "Give Yourself Your Own Name for Christmas.")

Patricia King, Director of the Schlesinger Library, supplied reporters with a list of catalog entries. *Abortion. Childbirth. Secretaries. Women in Canada.* Each one brought up dozens of voices and personal stories in my memory. *Found Women:* that was a response to the Ms. feature of the same name. How many brave women were waiting in that file? Even *Crackpots* was there as a category, accompanied by a delicate note that letters had been "selected and given this designation by Ms. Magazine staff."

I had kept a copy of a model crackpot postcard above my desk for years; one that was like poetry in its economy of symbols. "Now that I have read your magazine," the writer explained, "I know for sure you are a witch bitch long-haired commie dyke slut—who dates negroids. Isn't that just like a jew?"

I hope the library included it. Such invention deserves reward.

One long letter from a young black woman in the Midwest explained that she had read many issues of Ms. in prison. The first thing she did was to break off with the lover who was also her pimp. The second was to ask why she had been arrested when he had not.

While trying to research her case, she discovered that libraries in women's prisons, unlike men's, had no law books. She made a formal complaint against the prison—and, ultimately, books arrived. After getting herself out on parole, she went to work as a paralegal in a women's law firm and enrolled in law school at night. She had recently passed the bar. "I'm just writing you because I thought you'd like to know," she said.

A more recent letter came from a very active woman from Texas. "I think my feeling for Ms. is something like my feeling for my mother," she wrote. "I wanted her to be perfect, got angry when I perceived a (real or imagined) flaw, but never wanted to be really separated."

I never wanted to be separated from all those letters. I never wanted to stop reading the words of generous, time-giving readers who keep us connected, accountable, and on the cutting edge of change.

So far, whatever Ms. readers are doing at any given moment, a third to a half of American women are doing three to five years later. You can track change through these letters, and even predict the future.

The country couldn't have better leaders and teachers than these thoughtful, compassionate, intelligent letter writers—and neither could I.

THE Ms. LETTERS COLLECTION—A NEW FORUM FOR A LOST ART

by Mary Thom

Letter writing is nearly a lost art in this age of telephones and easy travel—and the receipt of written correspondence that is detailed and witty is a lost pleasure. As a result, when Ms. magazine began publishing in 1972, few of us who were on the staff were prepared for the experience of reading the rich variety of the letters that were addressed to the editors. They allowed us to get to know thousands of our readers on a level of intimacy that one shares with only a few real-life friends.

A young editor of the Letters column in the midseventies, Valerie Monroe, recalls that through the Ms. letters, a whole world of women's experience was opened to her. The job of Letters editor at Ms. is an enviable one. There is a feeling of expectation when, having noted the postmark, you open the envelope. Some information comes from the look of the letter: Is the stationery plain? With a letterhead? A flowered note? Is it handwritten? Typed by a secretary? Fashioned on a word processor? Is it the careful lettering of a child or the sometimes wavering script of the very old?

If the copy deadline for a month's issue is at hand, an editor can get impatient—something about finally sitting down to write a letter seems to bring out the leisurely side of many of us—but it's best when, unhurried, you can take time to unravel an involved story, written across perhaps eight or nine sheets of note paper. Then you appreciate the experience, vulnerability, and wisdom of your correspondent, who has figured out some things about her life that she wants to share.

From the beginning, it was clear that the Ms. readers made up a very special community—mostly sympathetic to us and each other, sometimes querulous, always demanding. Perhaps because the editorial material of Ms. has so profoundly to do with their own life choices, most letter writers are anything but detached observers. (As one subscriber wrote recently, "Ms. is a good old friend. I like to read her before I go to sleep at night. We've been together since her birth.") And they show an astonishing concern about each other that has made the Letters to the Editors column each month probably the most popular feature in *Ms.*

Also from the beginning, readers have claimed the Letters column as a forum in which they can participate directly in the magazine. They use this forum in a number of ways. First, though generous with their praise, they often take us and our writers to task. In this, their letters are most similar to those written to other publications, but *Ms.* readers seem to take it personally when they're annoyed, and their displeasure is more likely to be aimed at the magazine and its editors than a particular author. Second, they use the Letters column to talk directly to each other. They expect, and receive, feedback through letters in subsequent columns as they carry on a running conversation among themselves. Third, they use their forum to help the magazine and each other develop approaches to issues of concern and thus move forward the feminist agenda.

When our readers become critics, it can seem as though we can't get anything right. (See "Critics (and Crackpots) Take On *Ms.*," page 185.) But the depth of their anger generally reflects the real attachment they have to *Ms.* as a national vehicle for feminist thought and experience, so the criticism is easier to accept. In any case, they reserve their most biting sarcasm for the occasional antifeminist fanatic whose ravings we have let enter the discussion.

It is, I'm sure, the desire of *Ms.* readers to speak directly to one another that accounts for the enormous number of letters that begin, "This is the first letter I've ever written to a magazine." As one reader wrote in 1976, adding a postscript to a letter relating a disturbing exchange with her boss, "When the magazine arrives, I sit down with a cup of coffee to read the letters first. I feel sharing the thoughts of others is comforting. It's nice to know what other people think, how they feel, and the personal experiences they have." Or as another wrote in 1984, reacting to an astonishing Letters response to an article by Gloria Steinem on her mother (see "There's No Divorce Between Mothers and Daughters," pages 76 to 77), "I picked up your February issue and turned to what had always been my favorite section, the Letters to the Editors. As I was reading, my train reached its stop, and instead of putting away the magazine and continuing home, I sat on a bench in the station and read all of the letters responding to 'Ruth's Song.' "

The editorial features in the magazine certainly serve as a starting point, but often the readers take over, and the editor becomes somewhat peripheral to the process. And it is a process fueled by intensely personal letters, relating stories to which readers respond with more immediacy than to many an article. Readers share frustration and success, struggle and change. They tell funny anecdotes and report outrageous incidents. They solicit advice and offer solutions.

Over the years, *Ms.* readers have developed their own particular styles of communication as veteran readers of the magazine react to one another. There are the confessional letters that ask, Is there anyone else out there like me? And the letters that share a quick fix to make readers feel better about everyday annoyances, such as comebacks to street hasslers. Then there are the classic "click" letters. The word was coined in a feminist context by Jane O'Reilly in an article for the *Ms.* Preview Issue, Spring 1972, "The Housewife's Moment of Truth," to indicate an instant of feminist insight. Readers enthusiastically adopted the convention as their own, and letters recording clicks, or occasionally clunks, continue to this day.

Ms. was founded to give voice to the concerns of a movement, and the letters help us fulfill that purpose. Often the response to an issue raised editorially will further the discussion in a crucial way. For example, in a cover story on battered women in August 1976, author Judith Gingold made what was at the time a shocking assertion. She said that contrary to what was generally believed, battery took place among all social groups in the United States and that the battered woman was not a stranger; she could be your neighbor next door. The letters in response, which we published as special forum in December 1976, proved her point with an impact greater than the most carefully collected statistics.

The feminist movement had early on discovered the power of a "speak-out" as a way of dealing with issues that were often painful and personal. In the late sixties and the early seventies—before *Ms.* began—activists fighting for reproductive freedom organized speak-outs to share the truth about abortion. In an extension of this tactic, fifty-three well-known American women signed a statement published in the Preview Issue of *Ms.* declaring that each had had an abortion, which was at the time illegal in most states. Readers joined the campaign with their signatures and with their stories.

Following a cover story in November 1977 by Karen Lindsey on sexual harassment on the job, *Ms.* sponsored a speak-out in New York City where women shared stories, tactics, and support in an effort to force legislators to stop thinking that sexual harassment was a dirty joke and start seeing it as a form of job discrimination. Again *Ms.* readers supplied testimony from their own experiences in letters that became a readers' forum. And in an emotional breaking of the silence in the September 1977 issue, readers revealed long-held secrets in a forum responding to an article by Ellen Weber on incest.

Where there was controversy within the women's movement around issues such as the best way to deal with pornography and the question of feminist anti-Semitism, *Ms.* reader mail often served to sort out arguments and air dissension. *Ms.* readers have been particularly ready to use the Letters column for frank talk about sexuality, and this forum, unlike the prototype feminist consciousness-raising session, was one in which men could, and did, participate. (See "Sex: Whose Revolution Was It?" page 3.)

The letters are a continued source of discovery and renewal, and we at *Ms.* are often surprised at the enthusiasm and depth of feeling that coverage of a particular issue can elicit. Sometimes the response alerts us to a constituency that had been neglected in the magazine. In this way, the outpouring of response to special issues on aging (January 1982) and spirituality (December 1985) helped us to define new frontiers and issues for future attention.

In preparing this book, I have read tens of thousands of letters, both published and unpublished, many of them housed as a permanent historical record in the Schlesinger Library at Radcliffe College in Cambridge, Massachusetts. Although most of the characteristics of the earliest letters—the enthusiasm, generosity, and involvement of the readers in particular—carry through to the current letters, there are some differences over time. The language, for example, has changed somewhat. The ambitious campaign to make language more inclusive of women has resulted in changes in national usage. (See "Language: The Great 'Personhole Cover' Debate," page 139.) And with today's wider public acceptance of feminist goals, readers are less apt to use rhetoric to set themselves apart. They are simply more at ease with their feminism.

The letters are a measure of the progress of the women's movement. Some critical problems that readers wrote about over and over again in the early seventies happily have nearly disappeared, such as the most blatant forms of discrimination in employment (employers who blandly would say, or even write, that they didn't hire women, period) and in the granting of credit (see "The Workplace Revolution," page 99, and "Up Against the Institution," pages 158 to 162). Thanks to the womens' health movement, as well as to a national focus on fitness, we've gained a respect for our bodies that has made us smarter consumers of medical care. (See "Woman's Body, Woman's Mind," page 121.) Less happily, some advances, such as the enormous strides that women and girls have made in improving athletic programs (see "Up Against the Institution," pages 176 to 178), are threatened today by a backsliding on earlier legislative gains. And then there are timeless discussions of relationships within families and with friends and lovers that prove over and over again that personal change is at best painstaking and incremental—though definitely worth the effort. (See "Men: Love, Marriage, and Just Friends," page 25, "Parenting: Bringing Up 'Free' Children," page 42, and "Small and Momentous Changes in Everyday Life," page 78.)

Most movingly, *Ms.* readers look to the Letters column as a caring community to share their reactions to national events that affected them, whether it was despair over the defeat of the Equal Rights Amendment, horror at the New Bedford rape trial, euphoria over the tennis Battle of the Sexes between Billie Jean King and Bobbie Riggs, or excitement over the vice-presidential campaign of Geraldine Ferraro. And on the occasion of our anniversaries, particularly the fifth (July 1977) and the tenth (July/August 1982), readers joined us in assessing their own personal progress as they struggled to make change in their lives. For the fifteenth anniversary celebration in 1987, readers also helped us look forward through the next fifteen years into the twenty-first century. (See "Milestones: Readers Live Fifteen Years of History," page 207.) And always, letter writers felt a strength in community with other readers. As one wrote us in 1982, "In 1972, I asked 'What's wrong with me?' Now, at thirty-three, I ask 'What the hell is the matter with them!' "

I

Sex
Whose Revolution Was It?

Feminism in the late sixties and early seventies unleashed an exhilarating and frank exchange of information about sexuality. Women could be informed by the sex experts—from Kinsey to Masters and Johnson—but we would trust to our own authority when it came to sexual tastes and pleasures. And we could share this information, in consciousness-raising sessions with other women, in our bedrooms with lovers, and in the pages of Ms.

In early issues, Anselma Dell'Olio wrote about how the sexual "freedom" associated with the sixties didn't necessarily satisfy our needs (Preview Issue, Spring 1972), and Del Martin and Phyllis Lyon wrote openly and movingly about lesbian love and sexuality (July 1972). Barbara Seaman reported from her own informal sex survey that "the liberated orgasm is an orgasm you like, under any circumstances you find comfortable" (August 1972), and Carol Rinzler bemoaned the shortcomings of sex manuals (July 1972).

The Ms. *readers who generously joined this exchange were spontaneous and honest. Surprisingly, quite a few were men, who found in the* Ms. *Letters column a forum open to their voices, where, as in the following exchange, they might get an answer or two. The letters were a welcome reality check. With all this frank talk about sexual pleasure, were things really any better in bed?*

Much enjoyed "The Liberated Orgasm," but where, may I ask, are men supposed to acquire all this knowledge (it may surprise some sexually frustrated women that we are not born with a Casanova's know-how)? From women who don't openly discuss sexual problems, don't tell their men where things feel best on their bodies, don't use their mouths and hands freely, and don't generally initiate new techniques—yet still

3

expect full sexual satisfaction? Any good male lover—no matter how much he thinks he may have contributed to his present level of sex-pertise—will remember at least one especially good woman who taught him "a thing or two."

Lawrence Schenker
Fort Leonard Wood, Missouri
November 1972 Issue

I wish to reply to the man who wrote that "we are not born with a Casanova's know-how." I confirm his accusation that we women have kept silent in bed too long—but I trust he understands that for many of us, our silence was due to fear of offending a man's pride, his sense of machismo. When I finally found the courage to ask for what I wanted in bed, I had a (only one, so far) surpassingly beautiful experience, both sexually and emotionally. This particular man opened up like a flower. He smiled from head to toe with the happiness I had given him because of the happiness he had given me.

Sheila Walker
Brooklyn, New York
January 1973 Issue

I am now twenty-five. From the age of seventeen until rather recently, I lived as a sexually impotent male, in college, in the army, and in law school. Were it not for the women's movement, I would still be such today.

The problem was that I believed the locker-room theories of sex: that women are "scores"; a sexual encounter is a "conquest" by the male; and a man's part is "to perform." When I encountered a woman who had a fully developed sense of herself as a person with needs, desire, and imagination, in a situation in which making love was for each of us a means of pleasing and expressing appreciation for the other, the word *impotence* became just a word for me, and not a central fact of my life. I suggest that as long as we keep telling young men that women are not really people, a lot of them are going to face the same frustrations I did for so long, without ever knowing why.

Name Withheld
May 1974 Issue

One woman used a little nonverbal communication to introduce a man to a feminist view of sexual rights and wrongs.

Recently, I was at a party. As usual, one male neighbor patted my fanny. Not wishing to be unsociable, I swallowed my anger and impulsively, playfully, patted his genitals.

His surprise was something to behold. Needless to say, he backed off for the rest of the evening. How's that for a turnabout?

Marilyn J. Hauser
Cranbury, New Jersey
May 1975 Issue

Coping with the attitudes of the conservative Texas panhandle as a lesbian is difficult, but as an underage lesbian, even more difficult. Not only are we not accepted by "straight" society, but looked down upon by our lesbian sisters.

I am so tired of the word *jailbait* when all I want is a lesbian friend. The concept of the woman as sex object is as prevalent in gay society as in straight society. The worst pain in the world is the sensuous pat on the ass from the so-called friend.

Why must a person be judged by chronological age instead of being accepted as she is? I am a proud, young lesbian-feminist who is angry and hurt, needless to say.

Name Withheld
November 7, 1976

A male reader shared his theory about the sexual preferences of street hasslers.

That American men are frequently hung up about sex is not a particularly startling observation. But today, working at a construction site, I was once again exposed to my fellow workers' idiocy, and I paused to consider it for a bit.

A woman cannot appear on the horizon of a construction site without occasioning some sort of remark about the sexual possibilities of her presence. Hurrying to prove their fragile potency, men vie for the distinction of making the first, funniest, or dirtiest comment. Between the guttural outbursts comes a litany of whistles and gestures. What is it that has so many men convinced that it is important to establish their amorous skills in the eyes of other men?

It seems evident that the only person with any reason for interest in one's sexual prowess is a potential bed mate. Thus we are faced with the logical conclusion that the reason for loud and obnoxious references to penile size and erotic behavior is a sort of mating cry from repressed homosexuals one to another. Unable to direct their lust at the people for whom they really feel it, they make a great to-do over the women strolling by.

Not that I am yet convinced that the construction industry is peopled by closet queens, but it did make me think that there must be some explanation for the garbage

I am exposed to every day. Seeing this sort of posturing in my male acquaintances makes me grateful I'm not a woman.

Best wishes for the ERA!

Cecil L. Bothwell III
Dover, New Hampshire
November 1976 Issue

I'd like to share the best women's graffiti I've found yet: Let Him Sleep in the Wet Spot! (in a bathroom stall, the University of Wisconsin, Madison).

Name Withheld
January 18, 1976

In a June 1976 article, Angela Wilson and Shalmon Bernstein posed the question "Does a Forty-Year-Old Woman Find Happiness With a Twenty-Nine-Year-Old Man?" Judging from the response, Ms. *readers had shattered that particular age barrier.*

I have been actively dating men for two years since the end of my five-year marriage. During this time, I have been involved with men twenty-seven years my senior and ten years my junior. I'm twenty-eight.

I have found older men are *consistently* hung up about the following things: their masculinity, their superiority and dominance, and their intellect.

Older men are very easily threatened by the most incredible things! Paying my own way, for example, gives them anxiety attacks. When I convince an older man that my time is important to me, that I will only see him at prearranged times, and that I resent his "dropping by" when I have other things to do, he comes unglued. Many older men still hold on to that old stereotype of the single girl waiting breathlessly by the phone.

Of course, sex is invariably a problem. Older men view women as potential notches in their belts. They equate liberation with promiscuity and find it completely incomprehensible that you don't want to go to bed with them. Sexual freedom to me means not only the freedom to say yes but the freedom to say no!

And the games older men play! All that nonsense is so far behind me now that I don't even remember how to come back with the "helpless little me" response.

If we agree, however, that the basis for a good relationship is open communication, then younger men are the only way to go! They know how to talk, how to get in touch with their feelings. For one thing, their more recent education has included the latest discoveries in psychology and human interaction. They're not afraid of who they are.

They're freer of sex-role stereotyping; they're able to express emotion; they're not afraid of feeling. They're more able to consider women as equals. The whole macho tradition has been so little a part of their experience that in short there are fewer years of social conditioning to have to combat. And these are just some of the reasons why the answer to your question is *yes*, it *is* better with a younger man!

Sue Clarry
Sunnyvale, California
October 1976 Issue

Hah! You call a forty-year-old woman "older" in a relationship with a twenty-nine-year-old man? Phooey! That's a piddling eleven-year difference.

Show me a seventy-two-year-old woman married to a twenty-eight-year-old man, and I'll show you *real* happiness!

Colleen N. Vetter
Piedmont, California
October 1976 Issue

Carol Tavris's article "The Sexual Lives of Women Over 60," July 1977, brought more revelations about age.

Reading Carol Tavris's article had an effect on me that I did not anticipate: it made me horny. I am thirty-four years old. Bravo.

Karen Petrovich
Traverse City, Michigan
November 1977 Issue

While reading the article "Vintage Sex—Does It Get Better?" [by Sara Mandelbaum, January 1982], I was reminded of a story about my great-great-aunt Annie (now ninety-four years old).

At one of the many family gatherings we've had, a woman asked Aunt Annie (then in her late seventies) how old a woman is when she starts losing interest in sex. That spry little parakeet of a woman deadpanned, "Well, honey, you'll have to ask somebody older than me."

Priceless . . .

Cecilia M. Barfield
Ocala, Florida
May 1982 Issue

The over-sixty set may have had things all worked out, but young readers reported plenty of misunderstandings.

I hope you get a good laugh out of this anyway:

Why don't you give some time to the embarrassed virgins as well as the people who want to ——— around freely? That's what I'd love to know. If I seem paranoid, it's only because I believe there is a conspiracy to make people (all of us now instead of just men) feel ridiculous if they don't *get rid* of their virginity by the time they are sixteen at most. I am (get this, kiddies) nineteen years old and have yet to go out on an official "date," let alone lose my you know what. (Personal hygiene most probably isn't it. I brush my teeth and wash regularly and am not the ugliest person you've ever seen.) But now, I am sorry to say, I feel almost barred from having a sex life, since I'm afraid people will laugh at me. I feel like a criminal sometimes. I have no friends who are virgins. They don't respect me as a sexual person. People make jokes about virgins and I feel stupid. Now I don't mean to say (folks, are you still with me?) that I have any moral obligations to remain a virgin. I'd rather not, but as it works out, some people are inhibited, and people laughing at them sure as hell doesn't make them feel any less inhibited. There must be some other nineteen-year-old virgins out there!

Help!

Name Withheld
July 9, 1974

Isn't it a shame that *love* and *sex* seem to mean the same thing to so many people in America?

I've got a close friend, another woman, with whom I've shared a feeling of sisterhood since long before we were aware that the feminist movement existed.

When we met, as freshwomen in college, we both really needed someone to care about us, to be supportive. Our mothers and fathers thought this was just fine up to a point. Then they started to drive us apart; each set of parents was sure that their daughter was being corrupted by some strange and evil person.

We were young and vulnerable to our parents. They won. For nine years, we did not even know what had happened to each other. We both got married, and our families moved, and we lost contact with each other.

Last month my friend remembered my parents' telephone number and called to persuade them to give her my address. Luckily, I was visiting them, and I took the call. I was afraid, because for nine years I'd been convinced that my friend *had* been a "bad influence" on me. After a minute or two of conversation, we exchanged addresses and found ourselves saying, "I love you," meaning it, and knowing that we're not the least bit interested in sex with each other—just in committed sisterhood.

Our husbands tell us we are at last on the right track, being open and happy and free—thank goodness *they've* got the sense not to feel threatened.

Mary Watson
Austin, Texas
March 1977 Issue

Readers, working to find and define their own sexual identities, appreciated a June 1974 article by Kate Millett, "The Pain of Public Scrutiny."

Bravo, Kate Millett. So little has been said and written about bisexuality. The time has come for this subject to be discussed openly and understood.

I have always believed that bisexuality is the most natural and normal way of expressing one's spiritual and physical love for another person. The ability to love both sexes and to share sexual enjoyment regardless of one's sex is a true indication that one loves a person, not just a specific sex type.

While the idea of homosexuality is being accepted more and more, bisexuality is still being condemned by homosexuals and heterosexuals alike. If society could accept the idea of loving and sharing with a person regardless of sex type, there would be a more natural inclination toward acceptance of interpersonal relationships and a healthy and sensitive attitude to sexual and spiritual fulfillment.

Name Withheld
October 1974 Issue

I have realized that when I am attracted to people, their sexuality is entirely secondary. I have made the decision to become sexually involved only with other bisexuals. I feel most comfortable with them. It is so refreshing to have my male lover turn around and say, "Look at that man's eyes, aren't they beautiful?" Believe me, people like us are hard to find.

Name Withheld
February 1979 Issue

One constituency definitely felt left out of the discussion.

Sexwise, why are we never, in your publication, offered an alternative? I mean chastity. It's not absurd—it's practical, and it works. I'm in my thirties, and I haven't had sexual intercourse for four years now. No, I'm neither ugly nor frigid. I love members of both sexes deeply and openly.

Chastity has made me feel as if I'm my own woman—I have power, and I'm in charge—at last.

Name Withheld
September 1974 Issue

Our November 1976 issue asked the question straight out—"How's Your Sex Life?"—and suggested three answers the reader might check: "better," "worse," or "I forget. . . ." It turned out the third possibility was no joke.

The November issue was great, fun, relevant, and reassuring. I concluded that I'm not the only woman who's not getting much sex. I used to be a prom-queen type and scored great with men, but I didn't like them a lot. Now I know many men who are making an impressive effort to look at themselves and sex roles. I like these men, and they like me—in a genuine way I never experienced ten years ago. But they don't invite me to sleep with them. I don't invite them, because I'm not really positive that I want to sleep with them.

Maybe today single people know each other too well to sleep together. I used to go for macho types who ask you out right away after meeting you and ask you to bed on the first date. That way you can get involved sexually before you find that you don't like each other very much. And the resulting sexual satisfactions will keep you from noticing—for months—that you don't like each other.

The result of the change in attitude is that men and women are getting to know each other. And like each other. And a lot of people complain that they aren't "getting any." Is it because we are conditioned to domination-submission games and must unlearn that? Or because our biological makeup decrees that we are only turned on by fear and rage?

Believe me, it matters which. I miss sex a lot.

Name Withheld
March 1977 Issue

Picture me on the cover of a hypothetical *Today's Woman.* Thirtyish, bright, and pretty, smiling confidently; I wear three-piece suits and carry a briefcase. My job is a challenge and pays well. My six-year-old son is delightful. I can share my soul with a few close friends. Brimming with health, I have never looked better.

But damn it, I'm lonely.

Most of my clients and colleagues are men. We joke, we share anecdotes, we commiserate; sometimes we flirt. The talk gets intimate. They perspire. Bantering sputters to a stop.

I meet men at parties, in bars. At first they are eager. They want to make love to some woman they have seen in a commercial somewhere. "Wait a bit," I say. "Know me a little first. I am honest, funny, intelligent, *like you*. I have a kid and a tough, demanding job, *like you*." They fold up. Is equality so frightening?

Some men are not scared. They are (1) gay, (2) married.

I protest! I like men. I like sex. If anything, I am a humanist. Are equality and sexual intimacy mutually exclusive?

Name Withheld
February 1979

The response to a September 1976 article by Bette-Jane Raphael—"Sexual Rejection: When He Says, 'I Have a Headache . . .' "—revealed that it wasn't only single women who were dealing with such frustration.

I saw the article on sexual rejection and quite honestly was afraid to read it. Then in the January (1977) issue I read a letter from a woman who seemed to share some of my feelings. I often feel alone and too embarrassed to speak of it.

Sex is on the bottom of my husband's list of things to do—somewhere after feeding the cat. If I suggest sex, you can bet we won't have it. He uses as an excuse our age difference (I'm thirty-three and he's forty-nine). Sometimes we go a month or six weeks. He's very involved with his body, but not mine. He says for him there's little difference between masturbating and intercourse! Then I feel devastated, even though I know it's his problem.

I do love him, but sometimes I wonder why . . . I stay with him partly because I keep hoping. In the meantime, I masturbate a lot, cry sometimes, and often get outrageously angry.

Name Withheld
January 1977

I am fifty. Last year I became a tenured professor. This was a great satisfaction, coming as it did after thirty-two years of hard work, during which I could pursue the studies necessary to my career only while supporting myself, helping my husband financially, and raising two children. It was also a great relief, for at the time of the good news, my husband's business was clearly on the road to bankruptcy. But it brought me no joy. My husband's response to my success was to become impotent.

Today he is broke and unable to find employment because of his age. I support him and do a lot of moonlight work in order to compensate for his lost income, but mostly because activity seems the only way to relieve, to some degree, the anxiety engendered by sexual rejection. Of course, I could leave him—just send him money—and look for someone else. But there's the rub. At fifty, a sexually hungry woman is a frightening object to most men . . . and other women as well. They stop inviting her socially "with the men," thus depriving her of much-needed opportunities to meet new people.

I am aware that sex can be enjoyed as long as there is life and that, for women especially, sexual pleasure tends to increase with age. But this is only a case of increasing expectations leading to greater frustration and bitterness.

As long as our society does not change some of its patterns—males having to marry younger females or risk ridicule; men having to bear the burden of excessive professional competition and as a result dying younger than women; girls and women being all but forbidden to make the first move in approaching men—older women will continue to suffer the anguish of sexual loneliness.

Name Withheld
November 1977 Issue

Another reader in her fifties seemed to manage quite well, thank you.

Speaking as a woman who was divorced after twenty-five years of marriage and who is now well into her fifties, I have made it a point to make sure that my lovers are free from disease before contact. When I have discussed this with women younger than myself, the reaction has been astonishment—"I wouldn't dare"; "How unromantic!"

My experience over the past seven years has been most enlightening. First of all, no man has expressed anger at my suggestion that he be examined for VD (blood test *and* smears), though most have been surprised. I, of course, also go for the necessary tests when I decide to accept a new lover. The attitude of the men, after thinking it over, has generally been that it was a good idea and well worth doing.

Name Withheld
May 1978 Issue

It was in the Preview Issue of Ms. *that Anselma Dell'Olio had exploded the myth about the Sexual Revolution and feminism, explaining that it was a "misconception that the Women's Liberation Movement was in some way a continuation of the Sexual Revolution, also known as the More-Free-Sex-For-Us Revolution." A misconception certainly, but a persistent one, as readers continued to try to sort out the confusion of sexual attitudes and politics.*

Not too long ago, my husband accepted an invitation for an affair outside our relationship. I feel I have chosen freely to be monogamous in our relationship at this point in my life. His contract assumed the same. Upon finding out about my husband's secret arrangement, I felt emotionally ripped off. (Unwittingly, I had been supporting the two of them.)

Although I feel my husband was the most to blame (because it was his breach of our contract), I was especially angered by the fact that the woman used the women's movement as a cover for her actions. So often today it seems that the "Sexual Revolution" is mistakenly confused with women's liberation. I could hardly call this sisterhood-brotherhood, as it infringed upon my rights.

My husband and I are beginning to rebuild our relationship. Because of his deceit, it will be a long time before I trust him again, although he claims he has learned from this experience.

Name Withheld
March 1977 Issue

After talking with my man friend and house mate of six months about my doing most of the housework, I finally presented him with a bill today for "domestic services": approximately four hours a week at three dollars and fifty cents an hour. This so-called liberated male (he talks a good line) thought about this for two minutes, then drew up his own bill. "Sexual services": approximately four hours a week at five dollars an hour. He even thinks his sexual services are worth more than mine! Click.

Name Withheld
July 1977 Issue

A November 1980 article by Judith Brackley reported on a relatively new phenomenon: "Male Strip Shows: What Women See in Them." Brackley observed that in comparison to men watching women strippers, the audience of women seemed to be having good, clean fun.

Not long ago I went to see such a show with friends. I felt sexually stimulated, and I am certain others in the audience reacted similarly to the erotic movement of attractive male bodies in this place where there was public acknowledgement of women's sexual feelings. Thus, I challenge Brackley's conclusion that women don't get turned on by male strip shows.

Could it be that she and the women she talked to are suffering the legacy of Victorian morality? True sexual liberation will occur when a woman feels completely comfortable with her sexual response no matter what it is. We all must continue to work toward this goal.

Brenda Wiewel
Lakewood, California
March 1981 Issue

In a March 1982 article, "Report on the Sex Crisis," Barbara Ehrenreich, Elizabeth Hess, and Gloria Jacobs confronted what seemed to be a growing controversy about whether there was a feminist orthodoxy about "politically correct" sexuality. Readers joined in the discussion.

I can see why as feminists we reject the pornography of today, because through words and pictures it displays the attitude that men are in control of women. I regret, though, that there isn't more literature, written and visual, that displays the whole range of our sexuality without the usual stigmatism of male dominance.

There has to be some middle ground, where our sensuality doesn't have to be so quickly labeled. I, for one, run the gamut in my sexual feelings—sometimes I like to be the aggressor, sometimes the passive partner, sometimes I like to cuddle and be gentle or quiet, sometimes I like to be kinky and scream, sometimes I want to make love on the supermarket floor, and sometimes I want to make love tucked away in front of a fireplace in a mountain cabin. I might entertain a thousand fantasies and any *one* is probably not consistent with the person I am in real life. But I *am* all those things—I am not *always* any of those things. And I think there should be room in all our lives to dispense with the need to stereotype ourselves to dispel the guilt we feel over our own ambivalence, and to accept that we are all partly "clitorally centered and potentially insatiable" and partly "wimmin holding hands, taking their shirts off, and dancing in a circle."

Name Withheld
September 1982 Issue

Another reader commented on how the public viewed expressions of lesbian sexuality.

I was not able to tell anyone what *I* received on Valentine's Day from my lover nor to tell them what the significance of the little diamond ring around my neck is. It has always irked me that we, as lesbians, are accused of "flaunting" our sexuality but are subjected to hearing stories of live-in boyfriends and husbands every day of the year.

Name Withheld
February 22, 1984

In a memorably sensible article of November 1976, "The 2,000-Year-Old Misunderstanding," Molly Haskell explained the difference between imagining Paul Newman coming along to sweep you off your feet and a "rape fantasy." Robin Morgan returned to the discussion in June 1977, drawing on "mytho-history" and metaphor in "What Do Our Masochistic Fantasies Really Mean?" Both articles opened up a forum for our readers to discuss fantasy and reality.

I have just finished reading Molly Haskell's article, and I am filled with relief to have some understanding, finally, of my own fantasies. I am a feminist, and I have had rape fantasies ever since I began fantasizing but always with the knowledge that I had absolutely no desire to be raped in "real life."

A couple of years ago I *was* raped. It was the most terrifying experience I have ever had. I stopped my rape fantasies after that and became more confused about how this kind of fantasy could turn me on. Haskell superbly explained how it was possible—there was no fear in my fantasy—only a situation in which I could enjoy being overwhelmed, with no responsibility, by a man I found attractive. My fantasy has no relation to the reality of rape. A few months ago I decided to resume my fantasies, because I felt that if they turned me on, it was right for me somehow. Haskell's article really clarified it for me!

Name Withheld
March 1977 Issue

It is probably more natural for feminists than for other women to have masochistic fantasies. We can easily become exhausted by our constant fight against societal norms and by our consistently antisocial postures. Humans are social animals. When in our fantasies we act out the roles of acceptors of "norms" we abhor (be they sexual or social), we are taking much-needed rest (that our bodies insist upon), and we are unconsciously allowing ourselves to be emotionally succored by the society we are consciously rebelling against. Fantasies function positively. They should not be regarded as occasions for guilt—*especially* when they are not understood.

Gloria Kaufman
South Bend, Indiana
October 1977 Issue

Some time after we published the discussion of feminist "sexual ortho-doxy" in "The Sex Crisis," March 1982, one reader felt free to talk about sadomasochism that went beyond fantasy to reality. In her extremely thoughtful letter, she expressed the hope that she might find some answers from her sister Ms. *readers.*

What I want to say is so subject to misinterpretation that I have postponed writing it for months. I am in my midthirties, a feminist. I hold graduate degrees in my field and am successful professionally. I have two children. My husband is highly educated and holds a position of considerable civic importance. He has done a great deal in our community toward advancing the rights of women and has been instrumental in the success of a shelter for battered women. Two or three times a month my husband turns me over his knee and applies a paddle, hard.

This well-kept secret could be used to show that all men are brutes, no matter how holier-than-thou they may appear publicly. It could be used to prove the point that all women love to be beaten. Or it could be yet another statistic on sadomasochism. I am convinced that the truth is far deeper and more elusive.

This element of violence, or whatever it ought to be called, was introduced several years ago as we both grappled with the pressures of our changing roles. Intellectually, we knew that sharing child care and household responsibilities was right and fair, and we both wanted it. Sexually, it was a disaster. One night a mock slap during foreplay escalated into a convincing spanking. It was sexual skyrockets. The sexual success carried over into the rest of our relationship. Our marriage, in its twelfth year, has never been better.

We are both happy with our relationship, but I wish I understood it. I would be appalled and humiliated if anyone knew about this. I would also hate to add credence to any of the fallacies I mentioned above. Why do I, a feminist and an intellectual, who loathes bullies and professional machos, thrive on having my husband paddle me? It seems to have roots deeper than fantasy fulfillment or the conditioning that our society subjects all of us to. I wonder if some women like myself may possess something akin to the "memories" mentioned in Jean Auel's *Clan of the Cave Bear.*

Do we, in the far recesses of our minds, have male dominance so imprinted that— our intellects to the contrary—we need reassurance on the sexual level in order to function happily in our new society, the one in fact that we ourselves are trying to forge, in which male and female coexist as loving equals?

Name Withheld
March 1983 Issue

The responses ranged from a relieved shock of recognition to outrage— and a few attempts to answer her questions.

I read with shock the letter you published from a "professional" and "feminist" whose husband regularly paddles her.

But my shock came not from righteous indignation but from recognition. In fact, following the shock was a flood of relief; someone else shares my guilty secret. I have found that spanking produces the same "sexual skyrockets" reported by your anonymous letter writer. Unmarried, I have shared this desire with only one boyfriend, and the results were consistently terrific. Sharing this secret with a man is scary and risky; sharing it with even my closest, most trusted women friends, impossible.

Predictably, when my boyfriend and I tried a role reversal of this particular activity, it turned on neither of us. The turn-on is limited, for me, to spanking. My own explanation has more to do with my own completely undisciplined childhood, with a need for limits and "discipline" in a constructive sense, and even with the pain of living in the chaos of modern America, where even this element of the "escape from freedom" can be inviting.

I can't bring myself to sign this letter, but I hope that you can print it, or others like it, if they turn up. Maybe that other woman and I are the only ones; but her presence, and the laws of averages, make me wonder. And if there are more of us, that makes me wonder all the more.

Name Withheld
June 1983 Issue

In response to the "spanked wife" who loves it, I have several feelings all at once. Here are a few of them.

1. Gross me out!

2. I don't believe it. This must be a copy of a *Penthouse* fantasy letter. (Read *white, male adolescent.*)

3. This must be what the feminists mean when they say "internalized oppression." (One must be constantly vigilant.)

4. Even if this is real, why on the goddess's green earth would feminist women think that it's a good idea to print it. Will we have to read twenty-five more stories of degradation in the sex lives of women in the only feminist magazine in America?

5. Gross me out!

Diane F. Germain
San Diego, California
June 1983 Issue

Being a woman is tough enough without our having to worry whether our sexual impulses are "politically correct." As a close friend told me, "As long as we're stuck with these kinky feelings, we might as well enjoy them."

Or are all our fantasies supposed to read something like this:

Alan Alda (whose wife has left him to attain complete self-actualization and Mike Farrell) falls sexually, emotionally, and intellectually in love with me. I come home from work to find that Alan Alda has dinner on, the table set, the house immaculate, the laundry done, soft music playing, a bouquet of fresh flowers in the bedroom, and a stack of new paperbacks for me to read on the commuter bus. Alan Alda torridly kisses me hello, then *insists* I lie down so he can rub my tired head, neck, shoulders, back—uh—uh—lover—*there*—

Excuse me. Back in a minute.

Name Withheld
February 16, 1983

I am the public-education coordinator for the local shelter for battered women and a former battered woman myself, as well as being the daughter of a battered woman. Because of this, I have felt much concern, bewilderment and shame at my most frequent and intense fantasy, which deals with spanking. I know that being spanked for sexual pleasure is certainly much, much different from being a battered woman, yet I have been unable to justify my fantasy to myself, let alone share it with another human being.

My husband and I have enjoyed a marriage based on the dynamic of equal power for ten years. He, too, is a crusader for the rights of women, specifically, battered women. Although he supports every person's right to their own sexuality, I have been afraid of his reaction if I were to share my fantasy.

This letter gave me the vehicle to share my own well-kept secret with him. I was pleased and surprised at his nonjudgmental, supportive attitude. At this writing, I haven't yet found the courage to act out my fantasy but am feeling as though a great burden has been lifted from me just in the sharing. It has certainly opened the doors to greater communication and sexual experimentation.

Given the complexities of human sexuality, it's interesting that we as feminists tend to force ourselves into sexual stereotypes that are almost as rigid as conventional mores. We cannot be truly free until we are allowed to accept and feel comfortable with our delicate balance of dominance-submission that is part of all human nature.

Name Withheld
June 1983 Issue

I can't believe you all are not sophisticated enough to recognize a pornographic theme when you get one (a wife who likes discipline). What's so mysterious to her about where it came from? History is filled with the glorification of spanked women.

As for her puzzlement about being a feminist, she can call herself a fire hydrant, but that doesn't make her one. She needs to read Andrea Dworkin's book *Pornography: Men Possessing Women.*

Doesn't anyone remember "the Personal Is Political"?

Name Withheld
June 1983 Issue

Your enjoyment of occasional paddling by someone you can trust to stop hardly denotes masochism in you, nor does it suggest some deep, universal vein of masochism in woman as a group.

And many happy paddles, if I may say so.

Name Withheld
February 1983

I am a certified and licensed massage therapist in the state of Ohio. I wish to assure these women who are good feminists that there are sound, physical reasons for the [fact that] *voluntary* spanking or paddling stimulates a satisfactory sexual response— and no guilt is necessary.

Very briefly, males have their sex organs exposed on the outside. By the time males are "ready" for sex, they are well aware of the "feeling" and the tremendous emotional release that sexual orgasm can give. Females, on the other hand, have their sex organs internalized. Physical stimulation of the clitoris can be avoided.

There is a very important "reflex action" that goes on between the surface parts and the internal organs, so that the body can react immediately without the brain having to react on a conscious level. Stimulation of the skin at any level stimulates the muscle, bone, and organs beneath.

One of the seven procedures for massaging is called percussion. This procedure, *when properly administered,* can be a powerful body stimulant from head to toes and very beneficial for the health of the body. Dr. Kellogg (in *The Art Of Massage*) tells the little-known fact that the ancient Romans practiced whipping of the buttocks for relief of impotence in men and sterility in women.

Other professionals may know their anatomy and physiology, but only one trained in the art of massage therapy can offer the simplest *physical* answer to what might become a very difficult emotional problem.

Name Withheld
May 19, 1983

The next year a reader's questions about sexual fantasy brought another remarkable exchange of experiences and perception.

I need to bring up an aspect of child abuse that seems, so far, to be overlooked: the effect on the sexuality of the adult female who was molested as a child. Before the age of eight, I was sexually abused by five different males. After being accused of lying regarding the earliest incidents, I kept the others to myself. My parents, however, treated me thereafter like a sexual time bomb, likely to explode into uncontrolled wanton behavior at any moment.

As a woman, going beyond my inner barriers to physical and emotional sexual pleasure has been a lengthy and agonizing process. I have achieved levels that I believed beyond me, thanks mostly to my intense wish to be whole. Now, in my midforties, I am sufficiently liberated to tune in (for the first time) to sexual fantasies—with the shocking discovery that the fantasies that arise spontaneously and succeed in turning me on center on child abuse. In the fantasies, I sometimes am the victim: a little girl, often myself, innocent, frightened, silent, powerless, inwardly resistant, outwardly passive, but in spite of all this, eventually, and with great shame, coming to orgasm. Other times I am the abuser: a man, often one who abused me, ashamed but excited by my power and by the emotions of the child and my ability to manipulate her.

Intellectually, I am not surprised by these fantasies—and can even find rational explanations. My understanding, however, is far from complete. Emotionally, I am disturbed by them. I feel dirty and degraded. I do not believe that I am a "pervert," though that conclusion came only with a lot of painful soul-searching. Am I to be stuck always at this point in past time? How do I move on and dump these fantasies in the nearest garbage can? Are there books I can read, therapies designed for adults who were sexually abused as children? What is the experience of other women in similar situations?

Name Withheld
October 1984 Issue

I am the mother of two girls who were sexually abused. When the man who was my husband was arrested for molesting them, my life changed a lot. He had been violent to me for most of our marriage, but I did not know the extent of his violence toward them. For a year or more after I found out, I had sexual fantasies that I felt were "perverted." These fantasies are not bothering me as much now that I feel I have more control over my life.

Your fantasies are reenacting your past to give you a *chance* to move on. I don't think we need to interfere with our fantasies. It's our *lives* we should try to improve.

I recommend reading books on nonviolent resistance, such as Gandhi taught. I recommend this because it will take you out of the cycle of violence and violent values that the molesters impose on us. You will see that, hard as it is, it is possible to direct our energies to nonviolent, constructive goals and away from hurting ourselves.

Name Withheld
January 1985 Issue

Raped at twelve, after a year of gentler warm-ups by a man eight years my senior (my sister's boyfriend, living under our roof, trusted by the family), I too have spent years trying to recover my sexual self.

After a "promiscuous" adolescence, some of my lovers chosen, others easier submitted to than argued with (that now has a name: date rape), I felt burned out at eighteen. My parents' separation left me at devastating emotional loose ends. My oppressor became my rescuer, swearing repentant love over drinks and romantic dinners. By my nineteenth birthday, we'd been married four months.

I wonder now at the high incidence of childhood sexual trauma in lesbian women I have met. Surely, my own coerced or violent experiences had something to do with my postdivorce retreat to the "safe" world of womanlove.

A year of soul-splitting psychotherapy with an outstanding therapist finally got me to weep for the child I had been, so badly brutalized; to name the act itself and call the attacker by the rightful name of rapist (instead of discreetly referring to "my ex"); to feel the pain caused by such seriously humiliating encounters.

Opening such old wounds had a curious and frightening side effect. Not only was it exciting to imagine myself as victim, child or not, but the power produced in seeing myself as aggressor was overwhelmingly sexual. As a feminist and politically aware woman, I was uncomfortable with these separate compartments. As a lesbian, I found it doubly shameful to flush at a domination scenario, especially if a male person figured.

A planned, controlled, safe fantasy or sensual exploration is as far from actual rape as erotica is from pornography; there is no victim where there is shared trust. To "move on and dump these fantasies in the nearest garbage can" may not be the answer. Fantasy is exactly that: safe, unreal, and private.

Name Withheld
January 1985 Issue

I am writing primarily to the contributor to your January Letters column. I, too, am a lesbian and am very disturbed by several aspects of your letter. You are quite right: S-M fantasies cannot be "dump[ed] in the nearest garbage can." The process of acquiring them is much too complicated and damaging for such a cavalier dismissal of their consequences. It is a terrible mistake, however, to rationalize the acting out of

S-M rituals as merely a "consensual exchange of power." If you have come to believe that the giving or receiving of *humiliation* (and this is the key word) can ever be okay, you have been duped once again. Political arguments and pain-pleasure definitions aside, we are not talking about stimulation level or minority rights here. We are talking about addictive behavior—addictive both on emotional and chemical levels.

An ex-lover of mine is one such victim. But I am not writing simply out of the shock and hurt of finding that the one you love most in the world needs to hurt and be hurt in order to feel purged and gain a temporary peace of mind. I studied the subject rather intensively in order to understand her needs and the progress of her therapy—which, unfortunately, did not progress very far.

As I understand it, the acting out of S-M rituals gives a false sense of security that comes from a person's attempt to expiate her sense of shame as if it were guilt. Most people don't know the difference. Guilt is a function of what you *do* ("You're a bad little girl for doing that"). Shame is a function of what you perceive yourself to *be* ("You're filth"). This is a very important distinction. You can "do penance" for guilt. You cannot expiate shame. Therefore, masochistic rituals give only a temporary sense of relief.

In addition, there frequently develops, with time and S-M experience, an ability to achieve a chemical high (possibly due to the release of endorphins, naturally produced opiates given off under stress, which lessen physical pain and give a high just as potent as that experienced from smoking pot). Functioning when "drunk" on these chemicals is no safer than driving while drunk on alcohol.

What was done to you as a child is tragic and deeply damaging. The attraction you feel to S-M behavior should serve as a warning. Treatment that seeks out the sources of humiliation in our lives can be terrifying. My lover left therapy for such reasons. Please don't shortcut the healing process. Stick with it until you can exorcise your personal demons. If your lover needs to humiliate you and be humiliated in return, ask yourself—is she really relating sexually-affectionally to you, or are you just a stand-in? Is it you she needs, or will any S-M partner do just as well? It's easy to tell yourself comforting lies. Remember—you did it for years.

One last word. Many people like to link homosexuality with S-M or, as you seem to do, assume homosexuality is caused by the inability to relate to an abuser of the opposite sex. Such mistaken ideas are unfair and damaging to gays of both sexes. If you are with women in order to avoid men, you won't last very long.

Name Withheld
April 1985 Issue

Lack of understanding and public knowledge about sexuality was also a dilemma for disabled women, as this reader explained.

I'm twenty-five, paralyzed from the waist down, and use a wheelchair for my mobility. My sexuality, like that of my able-bodied sisters, has always been of concern to me.

Two years ago I began dating a man my age whom I had met rather casually. We spent our first three months together getting to know each other as friends and sometime thereafter became lovers.

It was during one of the most beautiful autumn weekends that he asked me to go away with him to the lake. Although I was really excited about getting away for a while, I was fearful at the same time. For this would have been the first time that he would have a real opportunity to get to know the real me: my incision-covered hip, which looked as though it had gone to Vietnam and back, my unpredictable bowel and bladder, my thinning, immobile legs, and my distended stomach. After some thought, I decided that the only way I could go with him was if he first read one of the books I had on sexuality and disability and then if we discussed any questions he might have. A day or two later I brought up the subject and handed him the book.

As he skimmed through the pages, I waited nervously for his reaction. Finally, after what seemed like an eternity, he closed the book and looked straight at me. "I'm really glad you gave me this book to read," he said. "I thought that you might be nervous about this weekend, and to tell you the truth, I was a bit nervous about it, too. I went to the library the other night looking for a book like this, but I couldn't find anything." From that day on I knew that this sensitive, caring, total man was a "keeper." This September he'll be my husband.

Name Withheld
July/August 1982 Issue

In response to a July 1983 feature on teenage sexuality, biologist and health activist, Ruth Hubbard took us to task.

The entire discussion of adolescent sexuality was embedded in two assumptions: that sexuality means heterosexuality; that sexual pleasure and indeed sexuality don't exist until adolescence. Sexuality was equated or linked with reproduction. Hence, the central problem: how to help our daughters enjoy their sexuality while protecting them from becoming pregnant.

But there are years before age twelve or so, during which our daughters can explore their sexuality in the company of boys without risk of pregnancy, and all through life they can experience pleasure by themselves and with female friends without pregnancy being an issue.

If we want to help our daughters enjoy their sexuality, we will encourage them to discover their clitoris and what gives them pleasure. Your articles ask that girls must reach adolescence as sexual innocents who depend on boyfriends to help them fulfill their sexuality (which is what usually happens in this culture). But if girls learned early to acknowledge sexual needs and to enjoy fulfilling them, they would be better equipped to make the choices they *want* to make in order to satisfy their desires, as well as those they *need* to make in order to avoid becoming pregnant.

Ruth Hubbard
Cambridge, Massachusetts
October 1983 Issue

Men
Love, Marriage, and Just Friends

———————— ❧ ————————

Judging from the response to the Ms. *Preview Issue in the spring of 1972, the institution of marriage was badly in need of adjustment. Articles such as "The Housewife's Moment of Truth" (in which Jane O'Reilly asked, "What sort of bizarre social arrangement is post-industrial-revolution marriage?"), Judy Syfers's "I Want a Wife" ("It suddenly occurred to me that I, too, would like to have a wife"), and Susan Edmiston's "How to Write Your Own Marriage Contract," unleashed a torrent of complaint, confusion, and wry comment on the state of the matrimonial state. Here one reader asks the fundamental question: Can marriage exist come the feminist revolution? Others report methods for an almost peaceful coexistence and nontraditional routes to marital bliss.*

————————————

What type of man would accept the totally liberated woman? I am sure the answer is one who has complete confidence in himself and sees a woman as no ego threat. What percentage of men are like this? If a woman totally liberates herself, can she remain married? Will there be someone left to marry her with such liberation? I assume this would then lead to having no marriages.

I still have to go along with the opinion (though it may be a learned, stereotyped role) that a woman desires to be a wife and a mother and teacher to her own children. This is truly where the conflict lies—how to be a wife and mother and retain a semblance of liberation. Can you have true liberation with motherhood, marriage, and the corporate state? Or must they all see their demise?

Name Withheld
July 1972 Issue

It all comes right down to homemade bread. A lady who makes bread is not only *real*, but she's right there in the kitchen, proving to her husband's friends that he is to be envied. Right? The glory doesn't go to her; it goes to him. He's *got* something. And he pays her with the most subtle viciousness of all. He says, "I love you," for the *bread*.

Parenthetically, I have conducted an experiment on homemade bread and determined that of twenty-one men who have come in here regularly over the course of a year, none of them can tell the difference between real homemade bread and the kind that can be found in the supermarket as a lump of frozen dough (white, rye, or whole-wheat). None of them! But they all think that "good old Bruce" (my husband) has just a perfect gem of a wife because she makes bread while their wives won't. (The trick is, of course, to get it into the oven while they're out hunting, and out of it just before they're expected back. That way the bread is hot when they come home. Cold—you can tell the difference.) I don't make bread anymore. And I miss it. I don't get cuddled for my poems.

We can't *all* solemnly and sadly step out alone; it's just no fun. And love is. And reordering the priorities, the conditions under which love is exchanged, has got to be one of a housewife's main concerns. If she is ever going to break free, it's gonna be a pisser.

Name Withheld
July 1972 Issue

In the middle of sewing a seam at my golden Touch N' Sew and waiting for my bread to rise, I started thinking about you. Your concern with human rights sets the mind abuzzing.

I've eliminated a lot of injustices in my home. As a mother, I don't clean my plate at every meal—why should my children? If I'm moody and upset, I don't want to be banished to my room, alone. When I sometimes get home late through no fault of my own, why should I be punished and lose privileges I hold dear?

Injustice prevents understanding and mutual trust. Just listening to my children, I've learned that it is awful to go to bed by your "lone." If girls have long hair, why can't boys? If long hair is beautiful on women, why isn't it beautiful on men? If God said, "Thou shalt not kill," why are there wars? Why can't boys make cookies and girls work in the garage with their fathers? Why?

Right now, my husband and I are facing a family decision. He's been laid off after six years. Maybe I should go to work and spend six years contributing to the family. Both children are in school now. They are doing very well, according to their teachers. Independent, resourceful, friendly, responsible, intelligent, and kind to others. My husband would like to develop his abilities—make furniture, plan a future in the country, learn about alternative life styles, spend more time with the children, get into cooking. . . . Why couldn't we try to solve our dilemma by letting the person who can get a job go to work? What counts is the family—not necessarily who brings home the money. Perhaps we could share the responsibility with part-time jobs for both of us. It has been so wonderful seeing him at home during the day, talking with him more, and seeing his personal growth since he has had more time to read and think.

You have given me the courage to question all the old rules of society.

Mary Doering
Perkasie, Pennsylvania
February 1973 Issue

My husband says I used to be a bitch once a month but, since I subscribed to *Ms.*, now I'm a bitch twice a month.

Claudia N. Heller
Los Angeles, California
June 1973 Issue

I had just put the kids to bed, the house was a wreck, and I still had the dinner dishes to do. But this month's *Ms.* had just arrived, and I couldn't resist sitting down with it for a minute.

Well, one article led to another before I realized that any minute the door would open on the shambles around me. What would I say?

The door opened. It was time to practice what I'd been reading. "I left the dishes for you for a change," I said, cool as a revolutionary. Click!

My wife, home from her graduate-school class, was flabbergasted! I hope she doesn't cancel our subscription.

Mike Tighe
Davis, California
July 1973 Issue

After working full time and attending ten hours of evening classes each week, I can't begin to describe the rage I feel when performing 100 percent of the household duties—not to mention being zoo-keeper for an overly energetic Great Dane and a cat—while my husband leisurely reads.

Because numerous discussions on this matter have not changed the situation, I am continually searching for new tactics to help him see the folly of his ways.

In the meantime, I have found that the occasional lacing of his dinner with the cat's food has done wonders for my spirit. *Bon appetit!*

Name Withheld
December 1976 Issue

I am enclosing this letter to let you know that I, as a man, do not feel threatened by your magazine or by women as some males do. I am buying the person I dearly love a renewal subscription. We are both aircraft mechanics in the air force stationed in New Mexico, and Debbie (my lady) is better at the job than most of the men. I hate to sound so possessive, but that is the way our society is.

Name Withheld
January 1977

Amid the lively debate were stories of loneliness and alienation, as women coped with their rising feminist sensibilities in hostile territory.

I am writing this on a day when I could not possibly feel any greater depression, alienation, or isolation. I am writing to you because I have no one, male or female, to talk to who will not try to push, cajole, threaten, even beg me into accepting my "proper" role and "duties" as housewife and mother. I live in an area where marriages thrive not on mutual consideration of each other as equal human beings but on the Biblical "man is the head of the house" myth. I am probably the only woman in the county in which I exist (*not* live) who receives your magazine. I have been told I am stubborn, selfish, domineering, hate men, and crazy because I talk about that "women's lib" thing. I have been called unnatural because I don't want any more children. I am the mother of two beautiful daughters whom I have been accused of not loving because I think there is more to life than motherhood alone. Yet it is these very accusers who were "disappointed" when I did not give birth to a boy!

I had grown weary of fighting everyone and anyone, I had been losing courage and had started to believe there really was something wrong with me, until I began to receive your magazine. It has been literally a "lifesaver"; it has been the only friend I've had; it has given me the courage to go on believing that women were not put on this earth to be the handmaidens of men. I intend to go on believing that need and dependency, not love, are what will grow in a "king-queen," "master-slave" relationship. Only one in which each partner realizes the right of the other to have an individual life outside of the home and children, one in which each partner assumes daily responsibility for home and child care, one in which each accepts the other's differences of opinion with respect for that opinion, one in which two people stay married not because they need each other but because they like each other as people will there be a chance for the closeness, intimacy, and communication which we call love.

Name Withheld
December 16, 1973

Along with the questioning of traditional marriage came the revolution-
ary suggestion that being single might even be a viable choice for an adult
woman, at least for the time being. One reader responds to "The View
from My Bed," another evocative story by Jane O'Reilly, in the April 1973
Ms.

I have visions of sisters everywhere choosing the warmth and aloneness of their
electric blankets rather than the warmth and loneliness of just another body.

Being a single parent, career person, student, and sexually active female, the
thought of coming home to my queen-size womb—even though it's usually strewn
with empty cups, filled ashtrays, half-written pages, and half-read books—is the
highlight of my day. It will continue to serve as my haven, my conscience, my office,
my entertainment center—the springboard of my life until a real mutuality of love
comes along and displaces my bed.

> Barbara Treen
> Westbury, New York
> July 1973 Issue

Men who were trying to adjust to this new state of affairs were having
their own epiphanies. Here, as was often the case, a father comes to a
feminist understanding through his love for his daughter. And following,
a "liberal" man struggles with his own conditioning.

I am writing from the viewpoint of the father of the bride.

Bill, the husband of my daughter Janet (not their real names), is a highly talented
artist of superior intellect—knowledgeable on many subjects, politically aware and
well-informed. But there is one subject he will not talk about: women's liberation.

Bill and Janet have a ten-month-old boy—intelligent, good-natured, happy, inquiring, and mischievous. Janet, under thirty, is also an artist with as much talent as her
husband. But since the birth of Davie, she has almost entirely given up practicing her
art. She has been unsuccessful in selling some beautiful and original fabric designs,
chiefly because this would require her to be away from home and would take more
time than she has.

When they got married, Bill said he wanted a large family, and I think he was
sincere, without fully understanding all the responsibilities involved. He loves his son
and enjoys playing with him, but when the baby cries, Bill gets a pained expression.
Bill gets wild-eyed if Janet suggests leaving the baby in his care for an hour or two so
that she can shop or visit.

Bill struggles to make an inadequate living by teaching. He spends much of his time working at his art, the income from which is practically zero. Bill's inability to achieve some recognition is, of course, very frustrating and demoralizing. He sometimes becomes moody and angry, which terrifies Janet; yet when she was a child and a young, unmarried woman, she had a noticeably independent spirit, which her mother and I did nothing to thwart.

Nevertheless, as far as my wife and I can tell, Janet and Bill seem to get along most of the time, at least while they are within earshot of us.

No doubt this kind of situation is common enough, even with highly educated people. But now when Bill is having an intellectual discussion with me, or any of his male friends, neither Janet nor any woman present is drawn into the conversation, even if I attempt to steer it that way. I have talked to my daughter, who appears to stand in some awe of Bill's mentality. It is difficult to know what her inner thoughts are. I think I am not biased in believing that *her* mentality is every bit the equal of his.

I suppose it should be my duty to give Bill a talking-to, but I fear that would only cause friction between the couple and get me labeled as a domineering and meddling in-law. I have a strong desire to remain friendly with Bill because he is a worthwhile person, and I do respect his talents. But it looks to me as though trouble is brewing; Janet's spirit will not be broken, but will reassert itself sooner or later.

Name Withheld
May 1973 Issue

As a liberal activist in most of the movements of the past decade, I began teaching a course on modern American history at the local college several years ago. Being middle-aged, I began to do my own research into the social mores of college-age people. I had expected some males would have taken some of the points of the women's movement to heart. Instead I discovered that most of the subject males were not only more sexist in their attitudes but much more insecure.

What is more disturbing is that so many young men seem not to really like women. This sexist backlash seems to be rather like the white backlash connected to the civil rights movement.

I can attest that, even with the best will in the world, it is almost impossible to remove sexist feelings. My wife is the local leader of the feminist movement, but regardless of my intellectual sympathy for her cause, which includes her personal fulfillment, I cannot rid myself of a deep feeling of bitterness toward her activities. It does seem that, as she herself has said, our marriage is at the end of her list of priorities.

In some ways this is strange, because I never could imagine marriage with a person who was not my intellectual equal and a person who was fully capable of creating her own career. Our marriage began as an equal partnership. It was from its start an open arrangement. But no sooner were we married than we slipped into conventional roles, imitating the relationships of our parents.

All of this indicates that the new feminist movement will have to remain valid for a long period before meaningful change does take place. Liberated women are going to have to be both strong and aware enough to deal with basically sexist male creatures before conversion can come about within family relationships. Men, after all, do dwell in a separate world, no matter how liberated they may strive to be.

Name Withheld
June 27, 1974

Even with well-meaning husbands, it was all but unquestioned that it was the wife's responsibility to effect whatever changes were needed. And in the early seventies Ms. readers were just beginning to see that it wasn't only dishes that needed tending, but the emotional and social fabric of a marriage.

While my husband cleared the dishes after dinner, he mentioned going out to a restaurant someone had recommended and that maybe some friends would like to join us. When I suggested that he call them while I attended my tennis class, he paused, started to speak, and then stood silent.

I left the house and mused that in twenty years of marriage I had made every date we'd ever had as a couple, including those with customers and suppliers of my husband's business. The few rare times I'd suggested he make the call, his answer had always been, "That's what I married you for," or "That's women's work."

As I hung up my coat later on, and was putting away my racket, he came over to me, smiling broadly, and said that our friends were really excited that he'd called to ask them to join us and that we had an eight o'clock reservation at the restaurant.

Name Withheld
December 5, 1973

Even seemingly small changes and challenges could seem enormous when a woman's identity was at stake.

The census taker came to our door today, counting noses as he went. Having established that we were a married couple, he was required to ascertain who was the "head of the household." First, he asked if I, the husband, were the head of the household. My wife politely explained to him that we do not believe that a household needs a "head," or that the husband, by virtue of male genes, is somehow naturally endowed as head of any household, or that his wife is naturally subordinate to him.

Our determined census taker scratched his head awhile, considered our answer, and then asked my wife if she were the head of the household. My wife answered no, for the same reasons. Undaunted, he tried again: was it that she was the head of the household but let me *think* that I was?

An immediate protest call to the local Census Bureau office produced the explanation that someone must be designated as "head of the household," or else the computer won't know how to relate the various members of a household to one another.

The net result of the whole matter was that, somehow, my wife was listed as "head of the household," and I as "other relative."

John Michael Brounoff (other relative)
Patricia Seed (head of household)
Madison, Wisconsin
March 1975 Issue

"Give Yourself Your Own Name for Christmas" [December 1973] provided me with the final assurance I needed: I really wasn't so weird for wanting my original name back. On December 26, I went to court and in a few short minutes was once again Teresa Manning.

I have found the experience to be totally exhilarating. With my husband's name, I felt tied to roles I didn't want and social expectations I could never live up to. With my own, I am my own person again—free, independent, and happy. Changing my name back was the best thing I've done since I gave it up.

I have included a copy of the announcement I sent out. I have since had my consciousness raised even further and regret that I used the term *maiden name* instead of *birth name* or *original name*. Indeed, consciousness-raising is a continuing process—with new discoveries every day. That's what's so great about the women's movement—one cannot stay involved in it and not grow.

By order of the
Superior Court of the State of Washington
King County, Washington
Teresa M. Shoemaker resumed
the use of her maiden name
Teresa Mary Manning
on December 26, 1973.
This action in no way affects the
validity of the marriage vows
she exchanged with Dean Shoemaker.

Teresa M. Manning
Eau Claire, Wisconsin
May 1974 Issue

"Give Yourself Your Own Name for Christmas" gave me the idea to change my name—and it really worked!

After being a widow for fifteen years, I married an older gentleman who had been an acquaintance for many years. The marriage didn't work out for us, and I divorced him. Having this strange name of his in the late years of my life just didn't seem right after the divorce.

Then along came *Ms.*, and I decided to do it myself. The real digging came when I went to the courthouse, to find there was no probate court to plead with. I wound up in the state law library, where a young attorney helped me find the right books to "do it yourself" in our state. He told me which things to copy for the judge's signature, and to be filed with the court. The next day I went back and presented the paper to the judge. He signed it right then and informed me it was legally my name from that moment forward. The cost of the entire process was eighteen dollars and fifty cents.

N. B. Keller
Austin, Texas
August 1974 Issue

Name change was a topic we often returned to in Ms. *throughout the years.*

I laughed out loud reading Jeanne Desy's article ["When Your Name Is His, and You're Not," December 1983]. As a thrice-married woman, I have undergone many of the same agonies of decision regarding which name to use. My first married name was Rabinowitz (later legally changed to Rabb). Next came Mr. Epstein, by whom I have two children. And now, finally and forever, Mr. MacFarlane. My birth name was Weisberg, and so my children have great fun introducing me as "my mom—Marcia Renee Weisberg Rabinowitz Rabb Epstein MacFarlane"!

I had, as a dutiful child of the 1950s, used each husband's name, as a good wife should. By the time Mr. MacFarlane came along, I said "Enough is enough." And so I continue to use Epstein, which after all, *is* my children's last name. (I must also admit that ethnically I just don't feel like a MacFarlane!) I've simply created myself as a new Epstein, unrelated to the children's father. It is now "my" name, and that's that!

Marcia Epstein
New York, New York
March 1984 Issue

Whatever their problems in working through relationships, readers were seldom without hope. To the question posed in our February 1978 cover story, "Is There Love After Liberation?," most readers agreed with author Barbara Grizutti Harrison that the answer was a qualified yes, though some wondered if we were turning into another "silly 'women's maga-zine.' "

I am now in the process of reevaluating my "love life" and relationships with men. I went through the "longing of the heart" in adolescence: reading romance comics and romantic novels and searching for the fireworks of meeting the right man.

Several months ago I found love letters that my grandfather had sent to my grandmother during their courtship. His love for her was very great, and from his letters, I feel it was the kind of all-encompassing love that I had been searching for. My grandmother left her job as a schoolteacher and followed him wherever he led, and she gave her entire life and being to him. I know now that I could never do that, and have no desire to give myself in that sense to any person.

At the ripe old age of twenty-one, I am involved with a person a year younger than I. There is affection, passion, fun, and we both have our independence and each other. I am thankful that I need not give up my being or my independence to be in love.

Linda A. Hart
Rockville, Maryland
June 1978 Issue

My friends and I are enthusiastic about nearly all of your issues, but I'm afraid that "Is There Love After Liberation?" was a real disappointment. Is *Ms.* going to turn into another silly "women's magazine," with the ultimate emphasis on romantic love?

Sharon Diehl
Highland Park, Michigan
June 1978 Issue

Until the end of 1978, though we'd hardly neglected the topic of love, Ms. had never reported on a wedding. When columnist Anna Quindlen described her own in "Ms. Goes to a Wedding," December 1978, there were several readers who took issue with her report, including one with inside information.

Anna Quindlen says that she "didn't want monogrammed cocktail napkins . . . or an umbrella with streamers on it. . . ." She must have substituted other amenities, for as her dad, I paid a bill that didn't reflect many do-withouts."

Robert V. Quindlen
Lawrenceville, New Jersey
December 1978 Issue

With feminist friends suddenly rushing to the altar like so many lemmings, we figured it was about time the feminist community addressed itself, once again, to the question of marriage. While we applaud the trend toward tolerance in the women's movement, we cannot forget the dangers inherent in such a trend. We no longer believe there is one "correct line" which all "real" feminists must follow, and no, we don't view married women as the enemy. But we *do* feel that feminists who marry betray themselves, us, and the movement.

Marriage is, above all else, a contract with the state. This state has never been overinterested in equality between women and men within the given structure, much less in a tearing down and rebuilding of that structure.

We who are engaged in fighting the establishment order can't have our cake and eat it too. If a woman feels she must marry in order to satisfy her own needs or wants, she should see it as the contradiction it is and not attempt to defend it in the name of feminism.

Dena Rollo
Ellen Bialo
Douglaston, New York
April 1979 Issue

What probably deserves the prize as the most-often-repeated anecdote in the Ms. *Letters has to do with the official side of marriage.*

While trying to complete the endless errands necessary to get married, my fiancé and I dutifully arrived at the county clerk's office with the items needed to obtain a marriage license. The woman behind the desk filled out several forms and then handed a large legal sheet to us for our signatures. My fiancé got to sign on the line marked Principal, and I got to sign on the blank line underneath.

Next the woman handed me a suspicious-looking plastic bag marked New Homemaker's Kit. It contained the following items: (1) a can of Spray 'n Wash; (2) some Bon Ami polishing cleaner; (3) a bottle of Fantastik; (4) a bottle of Bufferin; (5) coupons for *TV Guide* (so I know when the soap operas are on?), panty hose, and a long list of recommended magazines (*Ms.* was not on the list).

Saving the best for last, the kit included a paperback Harlequin Romance! Inside the front cover were comments from satisfied readers. One summed up the attitude of the New Homemaker's Kit beautifully: "Harlequins help me to escape from housework into a world of romance, adventure, and travel."

Phebe Duff Kelly
Little Rock, Arkansas
September 1978 Issue

The debate on marriage as an institution continued in the eighties. On at least one occasion, Ms. *served as matchmaker but other readers remained critical.*

A year ago the August issue, "Love Among the Classifieds," persuaded me there might be a way to take charge of my social life in a constructive way. Through my ad, I began a casual relationship with one of the respondents, who had also read your article and responded because of it. Much to our mutual amazement, we married in April, and we framed the cover of that issue.

> Robin Bennett
> Fayetteville, Georgia
> November 1984 Issue

Lindsy Van Gelder's "Marriage as a Restricted Club" [February 1984] took the words out of my mouth. It is so important to let our heterosexual friends, married or unmarried, know how this institution oppresses gay people. What hurts most is the fear that my lover and I "can't take care of each other," not only because of homophobic attitudes, but also health-benefit laws and hospital regulations. Income tax and insurance laws are added expenses. We recently found that renter's insurance on the contents of our apartment recognizes only one owner, a law that, like many of the ones mentioned, also discriminates against heterosexual couples.

I recently participated in my brother's wedding, as bridesmaid. My lover of ten years was not welcome at the event, but my sister-in-law asks when we are getting married. I will always be considered "single" by my parents and my parents' friends. Even if my heterosexual friends don't have a wedding ceremony, the law recognizes them as a legal couple if they live together long enough. The choice we've made to live together forces us to expose ourselves in ways that jeopardize our career choices and sometimes our friendships.

> Name Withheld
> June 1984 Issue

An April 1979 article by Emily Prager, "Roommates, But Not Lovers," elicited a number of stories from readers who found that just about the hardest thing for people to understand was simple friendship between a man and a woman.

For the past year and a half, I have lived with not one, not two, but with three male roommates. The first thing that people naturally assume is that one of them is my lover. None of them am I intimate with. The man in my life is rather amused by my living arrangement. When I moved into the apartment there were female roommates, and several months later the vital statistics changed. We have our own friends, and our outlooks coincide more often than not. We share food staples, utility bills, records, movies, trials and tribulations. I still get a big kick when I tell people about my house situation. "Three men?" someone would gasp. "Four bedrooms," I'd reply with a smile.

Name Withheld
May 2, 1979

About a year ago I started working at a factory in my home town. I met and became very close to a young man at the plant. We had a great deal in common, and since we worked the same shift rotation and lived within a few blocks of each other, we began to spend a great deal of time together.

I am married, and my friend is single. At first, everyone "knew" that my friend and I were lovers. We've never been lovers, and we've tried to convince our co-workers. He and I spent a lot of time with my husband, so everyone "knew" that we had some kind of *ménage à trois* going on. My husband knew exactly what was going on, and never once objected to our friendship.

The worst thing is that the young women I was closest to at the plant were the first ones to accuse me of having an affair!

Name Withheld
April 1979

Every once in a while I try to talk to a man about something serious, but I usually give it up. Which is too bad, because they are cute, and they do turn you on. But the trouble is, they don't seem to be able to follow ordinary logic. Sometimes you meet a man who sounds like he can think, but as soon as you get into something that involves a pretty woman—or actually any woman, when you think about it, or anything that gets them riled up and competing with each other—they're off. They pick up an idea and stay with it; it doesn't matter what you say to them.

The problem is, they have too many hormones. And they have this trouble all the time, not just ten days a month, like a woman does.

Sally Dustin
Contoocook, New Hampshire
April 2, 1982

I'd like to bring up a grudge peculiar to my situation as a retiree and a sexagenarian. After some eighteen jobs in New York, on almost all of which I worked more closely with men than with women, I hear with fair regularity from eight former women co-workers. Not too bad for New York . . . and my age. But only one man is interested enough in me as a person—or perhaps I should say "brave" enough or "unconventional" enough—to call me up and chat, or go to lunch or for a walk. That's one more than any former woman colleague can boast of. Yet I know that the men I have worked with get together regularly. It's a minuscule matter, of course, but one indicative of the prevailing attitude.

Name Withheld
July 28, 1984

Sometimes a reader's long-term relationship underwent surprising adjustments—and the notion of family, if sufficiently flexible, proved impressively resilient as the reader changed her life in other ways.

I am a woman of fifty-three who "came out" to myself at the age of forty-seven, to my own shock. I have been married to my present husband for twenty years now, and we share our home with my lover, a widow of fifty. We will celebrate our third anniversary in April and are deeply committed to and love one another. It is *not* "sexual chic"!

My lover and I (we do not have a word in our language that connotes a full lesbian relationship, so I have to use *lover*) do not threaten my husband. Indeed, my relationship with him has improved tremendously *because* I am not demanding from him the love that I unconsciously knew I needed, and which he could never give. In fact, I have more to give him as a result of experiencing the healing and reinforcing of myself that loving and being loved by a woman has given me. Thirty years in therapy didn't do it!

We (the three of us) are friends with another family—gay husband, "straight" wife, and his lover. The six of us are all responsible adults, having raised—or still raising—teenagers, who have positive role models who are not conforming to the cultural "norm."

I feel that human sexuality has too long been seen in such simplistic, heterosexist terms and that it *is* a positive result of gay and women's liberation to have the full range of human relating to choose from.

Name Withheld
October 1, 1981

Adjustments within long-term marriages weren't always so smooth. Letter writers told stories of loneliness, of emotional and physical abuse, and of the abandonment of older wives that came to be known as "wife dumping."

It is with much regret that I must ask you to cancel my subscription. I believe it's in effect for another year. If possible, donate my copy to a library or school. Over the years I have enjoyed *Ms.* immensely, but for the last two months I've had to *hide* the magazine in my dresser drawer. My supposedly "liberal and understanding" husband believes the magazine is changing my personality, making me less flexible to his demands. In an effort to "save" my marriage, I am canceling the subscription. I feel like crying. Should you print this, please do not use my name or address.

Name Withheld
September 1980 Issue

Young ones, beware! Do not wait until you are seventy. We of the past raised families in all good faith and were abandoned by our husbands for younger women.

Now at seventy we are asked to be independent without ever having the opportunity to set aside the monies we now need.

They asked us for sacrifice and we gave it.

Watch what you give!

Don't be kidded by what really constitutes self-fulfillment.

One who learned too late.

Name Withheld
June 5, 1981

While traveling in Nova Scotia this summer, I was browsing in a rather nice gift shop when a sort of double click occurred. I noticed, among the expensive items, a tourist gimmick—a wooden mallet with the words Wife Tamer printed on it. In a polite but assertive manner I carried it to the proprietor, a friendly and helpful gentleman (who had given us advice on where to stay, eat, et cetera). I suggested he return this item to the manufacturer, as it was an overt message suggesting women be abused. Said he, "Maybe some women need taming." Click!

Outside the shop, my traveling companion, a single career woman like myself, told me my behavior was uncalled for and that the tourist item was only a "joke." I was disappointed in her and angry with myself for not being able to convince even one of the two people involved that this was more than a trivial point.

Ruth M. Stern
Decatur, Georgia
April 1982 Issue

I feel so alone! I decided to write and ask what *anyone* else thinks about my situation. My husband is so hard-nosed. I think he loves me. But how can I always be wrong?

All I wanted to do was view Halley's comet—I've waited thirty years for this, and he said I could go outside to look at it all I wanted to. I hope I'll be able to see it with my eyes because I have no telescope. I suggested to him that I might go to the Huntsville, Alabama, observatory to see it, and he said, "You might as well pack your clothes to take with you." It really shocked me, and I told him how I was a grown woman and I have had the dream all my life. He said I was a *fool*. He made me feel so bad—I told him if I were a fool, then there were a million more like me. And he agreed—but I wasn't going to Huntsville—the end.

He is so good to me in every way, and he expects me to do as he asks. But now I'm going to miss probably something I'll always regret not seeing. We always end up asking ourselves if it's really worth losing everything in order to do one thing. So I'll stay home and try to see my dream Halley's comet from my front yard. I have a big field and no trees; maybe I'll be lucky.

Name Withheld
March 1986 Issue

Despite the dark tales, by far the most common story told by Ms. *readers concerning marriage and other long-term relationships was of working it through—sometimes with patience and humor, sometimes simply with perseverance.*

My husband ordered "you" last fall from a high-school senior who was raising funds. It took me six months to get used to having a magazine of my own to read. I am writing this during my only "quiet, alone" time—five minutes before I dash off to teach fourth grade.

I have raised three daughters, aged twenty-two, twenty-one, and seventeen. My twenty-four-and-a-half-year marriage is as typical as a 1950s romance can be! As we try to change the roles of a male-dominated household, you can hear the creaks and cracks (or is it screams?).

Louise Bement
Lansing, New York
October 5, 1979

I wish Barbara Ehrenreich hadn't reminded one of the 1950s ["The *Playboy* Man and the American Family," June 1983]. It's taken me thirty years to recover from the humiliation! We wives were the laughingstock of the male-bonded buddies. We had coffee klatches every morning to counteract the put-downs. One woman's husband had told our husbands that "his wife didn't like to do it." We listened to her sorrow at being married to a man who was a premature ejaculator. Another woman who was beautiful enough to put any *Playboy* bunny to shame had a husband whose greatest joy at parties was to run after the rest of the women. She wondered whether if she did her hair a different way, he would pay more attention to her.

As for my own husband, I told him it wasn't fair that he got to bowl, golf, and hang around with his buddies when I needed a change from taking care of our four children—even if it was only once a month. Instead of taking me out once in a while, he gave up his buddies and games and twenty-five years later was still angry at me for "making him give up his fun." And I was still feeling guilty.

Name Withheld
September 1983 Issue

Whatever its troubles, the institution seemed safe enough in some quarters. Several readers wrote in response to a wonderfully satiric article in February 1981, in which Caryl Rivers described the drastic differences she and her husband had over socks in bed—and asked, "Can This Marriage Be Saved?"

Tonight in Nebraska, as usual, the temperature is minus five degrees and the wind chill is unmentionable. With the thermostat set at an approved energy-conservation level, I am reading in bed, under two blankets, a quilt, a comforter, and an afghan. I am wearing my flannel nightgown, a sweater, and, of course, wool socks. My husband is enjoying his favorite January recreation. He's out on the lake, hoping to catch fish though a hole hacked in two feet of ice. This marriage has endured for almost eighteen years.

Neva L. Pruess
Lincoln, Nebraska
June 1981 Issue

Like Caryl Rivers, my wife is not Jewish. Like her, my wife hates cold, while I like it.

After thirty years of marriage and disagreement about climate, I have come to the end of my rope. If my wife doesn't shape up in ten years time, I shall consider leaving her.

Since, however, Ms. Rivers is considerably younger than my sixty-eight, I suggest she increase the trial period proportionately, to, say, twenty years.

After all, how can monogamy last without monothermality?

Name Withheld
January 24, 1981

Parenting
Bringing Up "Free" Children

❦

In May 1973, we put a perfect-looking Gerber-type baby on the cover of
Ms. *with the line "Up With Motherhood." The cover story's author, Letty
Cottin Pogrebin—who had initiated the* Stories for Free Children *feature
in* Ms. *and had worked with Marlo Thomas, developer of the* Free to Be . . .
You and Me *record, book, and television special—felt it time to explode
the myth that "the women's movement is rabidly antimotherhood." Of
course, anyone who attended a women's movement meeting knew that
lots of feminists were also parents, but Americans had already begun to
change the pattern of parenthood. The birth rate had been declining since
the midsixties, and women were having their children later in life; as
John Naisbitt and Patricia Aburdene reported in a July 1985 article
("Here Come the New Megatrends"), among the baby-boom generation, 24
percent of the women are choosing not to have any children at all.*

*Through all these changes, bringing up children remained a primary
concern of* Ms. *editors and readers. In one aspect of parenting, the issue
of working parents and child care, the* Ms. *offices served as a laboratory.
Alix Matty Langer had been coming to work at* Ms. *with her mother,
Phyllis, since she was six weeks old, and we decided to tell her story, "Alix
at* Ms.," *in March 1975. Some readers were less enthusiastic than we were
about the experiment—among them Dr. Benjamin Spock.*

I'd enjoy having Alix around too—an unusually appealing, sociable, yet independent
child, which surely means loving, calm parental care.

But plenty of your children—fundamentally sound ones included—would be demanding and disruptive.

You can't count on parents to recognize when their child is unpopular, either; that's
their narcissism. I remember a proud mother who just kept smiling when her baby

dropped a large BM on the carpet during a Saturday-afternoon office visit. I waited anxiously for several minutes for her to start to recover it. But then I realized I had to do the job myself, on hands and knees at her feet, while she continued to beam and talk about her child. I don't think she was being hostile to me, either.

If one worker's child is brought to the office regularly, why wouldn't others demand the same privilege?

I don't see how multi-employee offices could generally be turned into day-care centers without creating all kinds of hard feelings; unless there was a nursery under a skilled person—that's a different story, with pros and cons.

Benjamin Spock, M.D.
New York, New York
July 1975 Issue

Your article about children in the office reminded me of stories in old women's magazines about mothers of six children, great home-cooked meals and immaculate houses, who turn out three best sellers a year on the side. It ain't always that easy.

My baby was born in July, and in September I started taking him to my office a few days a week. (I'm a teaching fellow in linguistics at the University of Michigan.) Everybody—my office mates, employers, and students—was cooperative—except the baby. Unlike Alix, Tony did not "mostly sleep and eat for months." Even at the age of one month, he slept very little during the day. Being in the office, with all that activity, disrupted what little schedule he had, so he didn't sleep at all, and I got no work done.

In addition, the office turned out to be an unhealthy place for babies. It was drafty, dirty, and full of people with infections, all of which he caught. Perhaps the worst effect was the anxiety I felt when he was noisy, which was often. People assured me that they didn't mind, but I certainly did, and they soon would have as well. Certain kinds of babies and offices just don't go well together.

Gail Raimi Dreyfuss
Ann Arbor, Michigan
July 1975 Issue

Alix did thrive, as did a number of other Ms. *babies and numerous small visitors, but we heard about other institutions that were not receptive to the idea—even when the baby was willing to cooperate.*

The March 1975 article reminded me of the time I brought my son, Karl, to work with me three or so years ago. I was teaching at a small college in Minnesota, and the baby sitter canceled out twenty minutes before one of my classes. I put Karl in the front pouch of the baby carrier and wore him on my chest for the two-hour class. He slept, and I lectured, and everything was fine—or so I thought. The department head heard about the "incident" and wrote me a letter of reprimand for unprofessional conduct.

The course I was teaching? Sociology of the family. Click!

Jack Sattel
Eugene, Oregon
July 1975 Issue

Just how welcome kids were in public places continued to be a question. In response to a November 1979 essay by Sandra Thompson, "Children Welcome—If They're Neither Seen Nor Heard," a reader reported feeling uncomfortable even among her sisters.

Sandra Thompson is right on! The last straw was reached by me when I wanted to bring my month-old nursing baby to a party for my C-R [consciousness-raising] group. The hostess said no, she wasn't "into crying babies."

Meredith Phillips
Menlo Park, California
March 1980 Issue

Two other reader responses to the Thompson essay, particularly to her proposal for government-sponsored child care, opened up a debate.

I'm afraid Sandra Thompson isn't going to get any sympathy from me regarding her dilemma as a mother.

Evidently, motherhood was not a well-thought-out choice, since she seems to have ignored its realities.

Of course children have to be watched every minute. *Of course* people will look none too kindly upon a child throwing a tantrum in public, especially in a restaurant (where some people are trying to escape from their *own* screaming kids).

It appears that Thompson wants the rest of us to support her choice of life style, not to mention her offspring.

Pam Palmer
Los Angeles, California
March 1980 Issue

Sandra Thompson makes an excellent point with her question on child-care facilities at places of employment, and I agree that private companies could provide them. But to ask the government to pick up the tab is unfair. Why should part of my taxes go to caring for someone else's child, or worse, why should I have to pay more tax to accomplish this? I am childless by choice, and part of this decision is based on my financial situation. She is a parent by choice, and should have based her decision partially on her finances. Anyone who has a child should be capable of providing the proper care for that child.

Children are children and should be allowed to be, as Thompson states in her "restaurant" section. But has she never been to a restaurant and had to sit through a meal made unbearable by a screaming or crying child? Children in restaurants are comparable to campaign loudspeakers cruising the streets—an invasion of privacy!

Laura Lynn Nelson
Killington, Vermont
March 1980 Issue

Someday we will grow old; we'll make inappropriate remarks, we'll lose control of our bladders, we'll spill our food, we'll get in the way of "real" people, that is, competent adults. Then all those important people, who were the noxious children of a few years ago, will shut us out of society because we have taught them that only one phase of life has value. A society that has lost all love for its children is hopelessly corrupt and deserves the self-annihilation it breeds.

Jane Jelinski
Bozeman, Montana
July 1980 Issue

I am childless by choice, but I was very sad when I read the responses from some *Ms.* readers to Sandra Thompson's article. Sure, I'm annoyed by crying children in a restaurant, but I am also charmed and amused by those children who are not crying. If I want to eat undisturbed where children are unlikely to be, I pick the restaurant and the time carefully. And, if it turns out that there should be a cranky child there, I'd still rather suffer the "noise" than outlaw young children and their parents from any place that I have a right to be.

I really don't relate well to children, but I have the greatest admiration for a woman who chooses to become a mother. It's a hard decision, and who am I to judge if her finances are adequate to raise a child?

Name Withheld
February 28, 1980

I was in a restaurant reading the Letters column in my copy of *Ms.* A few tables away was a couple with a little girl about eight, who was disabled, very quiet, and very frail looking. I think even Palmer and Nelson would have been overjoyed if this little girl could have been turned into a rambunctious, energy-filled, loud, growing child.

Sally Harms
San Francisco, California
March 11, 1980

The issue of affording children was raised again in a letter responding to an article on women and children in poverty, "The Nouveau Poor," by Barbara Ehrenreich and Karin Stallard, in the Tenth Anniversary Issue of Ms., *July/August 1982. That letter in turn brought a response from Carolyn Chute, who must have been at work on her 1985 novel, 'The Beans of Egypt, Maine.'*

If women are to free themselves from the ranks of the "new poor," they must stop having children until they have the ability to support them *on their own.*

Diane L. Loos, M.D.
Phoenix, Arizona
November 1982 Issue

Dr. Loos is putting her advice in the wrong place. Instead of telling low-income women that they "must stop having children until they have the ability to support them *on their own*," which means a low-income woman may *never* be able to have a child, Dr. Loos *could* instead advise the government to raise the minimum wage (perhaps with subsidies to small businesses and farms that cannot compensate for the difference). And Dr. Loos *could* have advised the public schools to change their ways, to concentrate on the students' self-confidence *first*, skills *second*. She is, much like blaming the victim, advising the victim. With advice given to the appropriate party, living conditions and the ability to support one's own family could improve for both sexes.

Otherwise, what I hear Dr. Loos saying is only one step away from sterilization of the poor.

Carolyn Chute
Gorham, Maine
October 28, 1982

The lack of societal support for parents was one of the conditions that led Letty Cottin Pogrebin to ask, in her November 1983 cover story, "Do Americans Hate Children?" A number of readers agreed that there was some evidence that we do.

Here was the scene last night—about 8:00 P.M., into the restaurant where my family was dining came a family of six, grandparents and two daughters—one with her husband and one with her toddler son. The child was cranky and probably tired and hungry. (My own eleven-year-old was tiredly wolfing down her much-delayed meal.) During the course of the twenty minutes before we left, that baby was threatened with a belt, cursed at, and given chocolate pudding, then Jell-O, and never once offered any of the real food from the buffet available. As the child rapidly became more active, the adults became more and more abusive, spanking, scolding, et cetera.

Do I notice more of these incidents these days because I am more aware, or are they happening more often? For a number of years, I've done my grocery shopping at night to avoid the child abuse scenes that panicked me in college— once I grabbed the hand of an adult who was smacking the face of a small child in a grocery cart, and I ended up being arrested for assault (the judge dropped it). That toddler last night was threatened more times in one meal than I have been in my thirty-five years! What can be done? What can I do?

Theresa Cook
Goodview, Virginia
October 21, 1983

I was traveling by plane with my seventeen-month-old son. A man who was assigned the seat next to us took one look at Daniel and said, "I won't sit by a baby!" As it happened, I was flying home for my father's funeral. I've often recalled that incident with sadness, remembering my dad's love for children. A nurturing man and a public-school teacher, he never lost a basic appreciation for and enjoyment of children. How he would have enjoyed sitting next to his little grandson, or anyone's grandson! Where are the people like my dad, who value children and their lively spirits over a more orderly, controlled existence? I often wonder if there will be anyone to mourn the death of that prejudiced, insensitive airline passenger the way that I grieve for my father!

Jeannie Alford Hagy
Oklahoma City, Oklahoma
April 1984 Issue

Most Ms. *readers thought that they should be accepted nursing their babies in public—some were ready to insist on it.*

On a recent visit to New York, I went to see a photography exhibit at a gallery. When my child let me know she needed to eat, I asked if I could sit on the patio or in a restroom while nursing. I was told both these alternatives were closed. I sat down in a nearby chair and proceeded to feed my baby. A man then asked if I would stop, since I was in an art gallery. When I explained the necessity of my nursing there, he showed my husband a clock and threatened to call the police if I did not leave in two minutes.

I was not about to interrupt my child's meal, so I waited a minute or so until she finished. I really wanted to stay longer to see if the police really would arrest a woman for breast-feeding.

Name Withheld
June 15, 1976

The more private side of breast-feeding was explored in Ms. *by the actress Viva, in an April 1975 article, "Hooked on Weaning."*

The story of Viva's breast-feeding caper made my day. My daughter, Sarah, a beautiful, pink, plucky child of four, still climbs onto our bed every morning to nurse. At birth she clamped on like a barnacle, and only after three years did she show any sign of weaning. Naturally, having been thus nurtured, she loves her mother's breasts. Whenever she's tired or wants company and I'm around (I teach at a college fifty miles away), she sticks her hand down inside my T-shirt to fondle my breasts, touching home base, as it were. Like Emma, she talks and sings and coos to them and nurses her dolls. My son occasionally nurses his teddy bear.

Luckily for us, my pediatrician knows that although parents may be stiffly overcivilized, babies keep coming out the way they have been for thousands of years, needing prolonged breast-feeding—the best way to help them grow into strong, loving, independent people.

Harriet Turner
Wooster, Ohio
August 1975 Issue

Eight years later Elizabeth Stone wrote about her own doubts in a February 1983 article, "Breast-feeding—A Feminist Fad?" It hit a responsive chord in a number of readers.

In the hospital, my baby absolutely refused to take the breast, and even at home he always needed a supplementary bottle. My frustration was increased so much by the "helpful" advice of friends, relatives, hospital staff, and strangers that I was driven to tears many times, a situation which I'm sure did not help my breast-feeding attempts. After weeks devoted exclusively to trying to get the baby to suck (each feeding simply ran into the next one), I was deeply hurt by people telling me that I was taking the easy way out by giving the baby a bottle. The current literature on the subject consistently enforces the view that breast-feeding is the *only* healthy way to feed your baby and that anyone who "really" wants to breast-feed will eventually succeed. It does not acknowledge the fact that sometimes it just doesn't work.

Anita S. Cohen
Staten Island, New York
May 1983 Issue

When it came to giving birth, there was much for readers to discuss, as the promise of high-tech hospital facilities vied with the trend toward natural childbirth, birthing centers with midwives, and for some, home birth.

My experience with natural childbirth was wonderful. Our local hospital has a birth center, which is a room just like a bedroom—plants, pictures, a double bed, low lights and privacy. When I started my classes, I had no coach—my husband didn't think he would be able to do it, and I didn't want to be worrying about him when I needed to be devoting my attention to the birth. So my twelve-year-old daughter decided she wanted to do it. She went to classes with me.

I started labor at 6:00 A.M., got to the hospital at 7:30, and by 9:00 I was in transition. My daughter helped me with my breathing, rubbed my back, and when the baby's head crowned, she was right there ready to help the doctor. My husband cut the cord, and I think he wished he'd joined us in the classes.

The doctor had many compliments for our daughter. She was the youngest coach the birth center had ever had, and the doctor said he knew within the first ten minutes that she was very aware and very much in control.

Name Withheld
December 1978

The response to the September 1984 cover story, titled "The American Way of Birth," included so many different perspectives and additions, we named the Letters column "What Ms. *Didn't Tell You About Childbirth." Some readers thought it was time to reassess certain accepted ideas.*

I am becoming resentful of the tyrannical notion that there is only one "correct" way to give birth, i.e., "natural" childbirth. When I become pregnant, I will eat right, sleep well, exercise, and abstain from alcohol, drugs, and even my beloved coffee. But, by God, when the delivery time comes, I will take anesthesia, and gratefully, too. I do not need to feel myself being ripped open by an eight-pound baby to stir my "motherly instincts" or to "stimulate bonding." So what if the baby is groggy for a few minutes? It won't undo the previous nine months of good prenatal care, and the risk is low enough to make it worth it for me. My mother had me under anesthesia, and somehow I managed to become a National Merit scholar in spite of it, thank you. So what's wrong with "Wake me when it's over"?

Martha Barry
Gorham, Maine
December 1984 Issue

After a generation of protest and question about the role of women in the modern world, the archetype of motherhood is on the rise again. Every time I pick up a newspaper or magazine, I see articles on having children after thirty-five or on single motherhood.

In one of the September "birth stories," a woman states that going through labor and giving birth to a child is an act of complete courage. I say that it takes an act of complete courage for a woman to choose *not* to give birth to a child. It takes an act of complete courage for a woman to explore other ways of being in the world besides motherhood. It takes an act of courage for a woman to give birth to a book, a painting, a business, an idea, a dance. Giving birth to *oneself* is an act of complete courage.

Nancy Wakeman
San Francisco, California
December 1984 Issue

In the eighties, medical advances were making it possible to treat sick and disabled newborns who previously would have had no chance to live. But along with the technical miracles came a moral issue: Were desperately ill babies being helped to live or were doctors simply prolonging their deaths? Biologist and longtime health activist Ruth Hubbard, in a May 1984 article, "Caring for Baby Doe," explored the issues raised by proposed government regulations that threatened to take the decision about a newborn's treatment out of the hands of the parents.

As the single parent of a three-year-old born with an unidentifiable, ongoing catastrophic illness and severe developmental disabilities, I've lived through and witnessed every type of heartbreaking challenge Hubbard's article describes. In my own case, my son is easy prey for myopic, scientifically oriented physicians who rarely run across an "undiagnosable" case in these days of high-tech medicine. It is a never-ending battle for me to judge whether a suggested course of treatment or diagnostic intervention is truly in my son's best interest. Choosing at the present time to withhold active treatment (other than what makes him more comfortable) and diagnostic procedures, I regularly feel the pressure from outside sources to change this decision.

Over the years I have become better at making decisions in the middle of a crisis, but I never really *know* that what I am deciding for my noncommunicative son is what he would choose for himself. Most of us, however, are able to live with such a responsibility when we are able to believe in our loving instincts that tie us to our children in ways no outsider could possibly understand.

Name Withheld
March 4, 1984

A particularly moving essay in 1982 by Donna Moriarty, on mourning her unborn child, lost in a late miscarriage, brought much response from readers who'd had similar experiences—and met with little understanding from friends and relatives.

My husband brought me the November *Ms.* along with the other mail, our address book, and stationery. About fourteen hours earlier, our son, David, had been born. The labor had begun so early (I was five and a half months pregnant) that when we left for the hospital, I hadn't packed the items on my take-to-the-hospital list. In fact, I hadn't even written the list yet. Our David died soon after his birth.

Later that day I discovered "The Right To Mourn," and I wept again—this time with some feelings of relief. Donna Moriarty offers useful advice for friends and family, but I think there is another item that is important. The *life*, however short, of the unborn or newborn child who dies has meaning to the parents, and they may want or need to tell you about their baby. Very few people are willing to listen to me talk about our David's life—his beautiful fingers, how much he looked like his older sister Kathleen, how wonderful it was to hug, snuggle, greet our tiny little David while he lived. Family and friends need to remember that the baby who dies so young did live. Please be willing to acknowledge that life to the parents.

Susan Frederick-Schector
Colfax, Wisconsin
February 1983 Issue

Our Mexican heritage told us that the child who dies will be with you forever, guarding the family as an angel, touching your mind with her love. We had begun writing a journal to our daughter from the moment of suspected pregnancy, hoping to leave it as a legacy to the child. Instead, our daughter left it as a legacy to us, a book of her presence, gleeful pregnancy, joy, and our loss. It was only one of many, many gifts that she left.

Name Withheld
December 1982

Another kind of loss at birth was suffered by mothers who gave their children up for adoption. A reader talked about that experience in a plea that her feelings deserved understanding, as did those of women who had abortions.

I was sixteen last April. Three days before my birthday, I delivered a beautiful seven-pound, twenty-one-inch, brown-eyed little boy. I had decided way back in December not to have an abortion but to give my child to clients of my obstetrician who were unable to have any children of their own.

What happens to a woman who carries a child for nine months, then watches a real baby of *hers* being born, and holds the infant in her arms while the father coos, and then the child is gone?

The only thing I had to show for my labor was three days out of school and a mighty sore crotch. The feeling of emptiness that engulfed me on Mother's Day, just twenty-two days later, was unbearable. Now I've gotten to the stage where I don't think about my son much. I'm not his mother now. But I feel that the many women who have given their child up need support and understanding. I feel that a woman should have the right to an abortion, and we are recognizing that women who choose abortion need support. Why not lend support to the woman who is criticized for giving her child away?

Name Withheld
January 1976 Issue

Later women wrote of similar experiences. By the eighties, they had named themselves birth mothers and had organized support groups. Their stories led to an extraordinary dialogue in the Letters column between birth mothers and adoptive mothers.

I would like to voice my agreement with your pro choice position and suggest that there is an untapped resource for more support within the ranks of American womanhood that has traditionally been a *very* silent minority.

We are those women who carry a secret just as painful as those who cannot admit to having had an abortion. We are the birth mothers of adopted children. We rarely speak out because we have been personally and publicly embarrassed, ridiculed, and patronized for having made the ultimate mistake. In the eleven years since I relinquished my child, I have not met one woman who has admitted to having a similar experience, yet there are many thousands of us out there.

I was one of the unwed teenage mothers "epidemic" in 1969, when abortions were all but impossible to obtain. In order to be referred to a doctor who would even consider examining me for the feared operation, I had to visit a pastor who required from me a release form stating that I had seriously considered suicide (which I had not), ingested quantities of LSD and other dangerous drugs (which I had not), and was mentally, emotionally, physically, and financially incapable of caring for any child (which I was not). I was, in fact, a desperate first-year college student on the dean's list, who wanted very much to continue in school.

As abortion negotiations wore on, it became clear that the safest method of terminating the pregnancy (and the most lucrative for the doctor) was similar to that of a caesarean procedure, although a saline injection method was offered with the dour comment that it was cheaper but more dangerous. The only viable solution in my opinion was to drop out of school and deliver the child, wrestling with relinquishment and adoption along the way.

Don't *ever* let anyone fool you into thinking that the answer to an unplanned pregnancy is to carry a child you cannot love. There is nothing holy about the experience, nothing satisfying. Anti abortion supporters use this argument frequently in response to the pregnancy problem, but as one who has been through it, it is *not* an option preferable to termination.

I deeply resent the treatment I received in a self-righteous society that turned a potentially beautiful experience into a horrid memory. It will not happen again.

Name Withheld
June 1981 Issue

I am a strong advocate for a woman's right to control her own reproduction. "Keep your laws off my body" perfectly expresses my reaction to those who would outlaw abortion. I am, however, also an adoptive mother. And to those of you who have suffered the pain of relinquishing a baby for adoption, I must say this: You did not simply contribute a product to the adoption market. You created a unique and beautiful human being, who in all probability is loved and cherished.

I will be forever grateful to the strong woman who gave birth to my, to *our*, child, and I am doing everything in my power to be deserving of the trust placed in me when I was given the privilege of becoming his mother. I know that his first mother suffered and probably still suffers the pain of losing him, but knowing him and loving him as I do, I cannot help but feel he is worth it.

Liz Barnes Abernethy
Tallahassee, Florida
February 1982 Issue

As divorce rates soared—passing the one million per year mark in 1975 according to author Elizabeth Dancey's report ("Who Gets the Kids?" September 1976)—Ms. readers were dealing with difficult issues of child custody. A September 1976, article by Marcia Holly "Joint Custody: The New Haven Plan," outlined what would seem in theory to be an equitable solution. Some readers were not so sure of its practicality.

I was reading the article by Marcia Holly. It really struck home, as I have been hassling with that very same arrangement. I could not believe that anyone else in their right mind would agree to Sunday, Monday, Tuesday, one parent, and Wednesday, Thursday, Friday, and alternate Saturdays, the other. My divorce-decree custody agreement must have been three pages, and as I read it now I almost laugh.

My daughter, three years, talks about Daddy's house and Mommy's house but never her own house. She cries when Daddy picks her up from Mommy's and vise versa. She's bound to be mixed up. She asks, "Who will pick me up tonight from nursery school?" Holidays are a nightmare, with both of us arguing who gets her when. Yesterday I finally returned to my lawyer after six long months to attempt to retain full custody, which will entail more money, time, and hassles.

So please, any mother considering this, please think twice.

Name Withheld
October 13, 1976

By the eighties, many feminists had thought twice and were questioning whether the courts' predisposition toward joint custody might place a woman at a disadvantage during a financially vulnerable point in her life. An April 1983 article by Gail Scott—"Joint Custody: Does It Work?"—aired these doubts. Another reader suggested that American families were complicated enough as it was.

I was very glad to see in Gail Scott's article that someone else had realized that joint custody is not a panacea for divorced parents and their children.

I am married and have custody of my two children from a previous marriage. My ex-husband is married to a woman with one child from a previous marriage, and they have had a child together. My husband's three children from his previous marriage live with their mother, who is married to a man who has two children from a previous marriage. (It sounds bizarre, but it is getting to be more the norm all the time.)

If one or more of these ex-couples had joint custody, the children would never know who was to be where when. Although all three of these re-created families have had their problems, we've adjusted, and the children are happy people.

Name Withheld
July 1983 Issue

Custody was a particularly wrenching issue for lesbians and gay men, as one reader pointed out in response to a March 1983 news note about a study, "Myths About Gay Parents Disproved."

Last week I sat through a nasty twelve-hour custody hearing. My fourteen-year-old brother wishes to live with my father, where he is loved, valued as a person, and where his opinions are considered. Unfortunately, my father is homosexual and lives with his lover of eight years. My brother will be awarded to my mother simply because she is his mother and heterosexual.

My brother has been beaten by his stepfather, but it seems, according to the courts, that it is better to live in a home where you are physically, verbally, and emotionally abused than to live with your gay father, where you are loved.

Name Withheld
June 1983 Issue

A November 1982 essay, "Stepmothering—Am I Ready for This?" by Lois Lovett, was reassuring to a number of readers.

What a relief to read about the very real problems of being a stepmother! I became a stepmother in January 1979, when I married a man who had three children by his first marriage.

I especially responded to the statement "Little things become enormous." How true that has been for me! I sometimes feel overwhelmed by pettiness: my anger about the monthly support payments, college expenses for my eldest stepdaughter, the payments for braces, contacts, music lessons, and so on. I feel deprived of the things that we could have if only we didn't have to spend so much money on his children.

And yet I am not usually a mean, ungenerous person. Does stepmothering bring out the worst in me? I somehow feel threatened by my stepchildren. They share memories and experiences with their father that I will never share. And no matter how long we are married, he will always have known them longer. They have an emotional precedence over me and that I find uncomfortable.

Name Withheld
February 1983 Issue

Some mothers were voluntarily giving up custody—although never as many as the media's fascination with "runaway wives" would have led you to believe. The experience could be confusing and isolating, but the stories Ms. *readers shared reflected a truly amazing resiliency on the part of that supposedly threatened institution, the American family, in all its variations.*

I am wondering about an issue, important to me, that I haven't seen covered, or I missed it. This is: women who leave homes and families. I am one, having left November 4, 1971. My children were one-and-a-half and four.

Having just ended a visit with them, the longest I've been with them since 1971, I am very interested in other women like myself. Why did they feel they had to leave it all (I'm still not sure of all the answers)? Do they feel remorse or guilt? How are the children? What kinds of people are we—these runaway mothers? What has happened to us since?

I returned to school (B.A., 1974; finished as art-ed. teacher). I became a hippie. Frequented the hippie nightclubs—worked in a deli in one for six months. Then found a job as a teacher under a very good supervisor of art education here in Charlotte, North Carolina. I took the job, changed my lifestyle some—bought clothes, wore makeup—fitted into my more or less straight work scene. Remarried Christmas 1974.

It was not easy. I came close to a breakdown when the divorce was finalized. I had given up the two human beings who had unselfishly loved me. But I was poor in mind, heart, and money then.

Now, after this last visit, I can see my strength has grown. They don't overwhelm me. Their love is very much still there. It still is not easy.

Name Withheld
July 16, 1975

While I was reading the articles on single moms, I became aware of the smell of steaks cooking and the sounds of my husband (number 2) bustling about in the kitchen. I grinned and thought of my daughter safely ensconced in her father's home across town, being cared for by a very nice lady who somehow got conned into taking on the supermom role so that my former husband could get custody—his revenge, I suppose, for my refusal to make our marriage my number-one priority.

When I lost the custody battle, because, presumably, I was "emotionally unstable" (he drove me crazy), I felt as if half of me had been snatched away. I struggled with that judgment of me as the "lesser parent," and I plotted and calculated ways I could fight for a reversal. Two years later I have come round to the truth: I have the best possible situation any feminist mother could hope for. The weekend relationship I have with my daughter is basically a friendship; I am her favorite confidante. We giggle together over things she would never tell Dad or Stepmom because *they* would get upset. I listen to her problems, give her emotional support, offer suggestions for solutions, let her know I have faith in her ability to solve her own problems.

I have a triple blessing: a second husband who is fully supportive of my commitment to writing and is no stranger to a kitchen or toilet-bowl brush; a mother-daughter relationship that enriches far more than it consumes; and five days a week completely free of parenting responsibilities for which I pay not one penny. (Daddy makes over thirty thousand dollars a year.)

With all these riches, I feel guilty. But not too guilty. One of these days Stepmom is going to wake up and dump the kid back in my lap. Gotta make hay while the sun shines.

Name Withheld
March 23, 1981

One of our most popular features on parenting was an annual end-of-the-year selection of toys, which ideally were nonsexist, nonracist, safe, sometimes educational, and fun to play with. One reader's child found a recommended toy fun anyway.

As a follow-up to "Toys for Free Children," I'd like to tell you the good news: my two-year-old daughter is playing with her Playskool Tool Bench today. . . . The bad news: she's using it as a stove.

Lavonne Peck Bergman
Berkeley, California
April 1974 Issue

It was my turn to choose the Christmas present that my brother and sister and I collectively buy for our young cousin. After much debate about whether my aunt and uncle would see my choice as trying to radicalize their daughter, I went ahead and bought her the present I had always wanted when I was young—a children's tool set.

I sent the present off by mail and after Christmas received two notes. The first was from my aunt. She thanked me for the gift and remarked that the youngster "thought she was being nice by sharing her tools with her brother."

The second note was from the child. In her large, uneven lettering she, too, thanked me for the gift. Then, in her truthful manner, she told me what had happened when she (with her father's and younger brother's help) attempted to put her gift to work. "I tried to use the tools, but I only got in the way." Sometimes giving a nonsexist gift is not enough.

> Jennifer Abromowitz
> Mount Kisco, New York
> August 1981 Issue

Parenting children reasonably free of stereotypical sex roles was a complicated business, as Letty Cottin Pogrebin discussed in an October 1980 article, "The Secret Fear That Keeps Us From Raising Free Children." Elizabeth Rommel returned to the subject in a January 1984 essay, "Grade School Blues."

Letty Cottin Pogrebin's article really spoke to me and to issues I have been struggling with for years.

My twelve-year-old son is interested in cooking, building toy houses with very elaborate kitchens, and playing the female part in puppet shows. Most recently, he has built a doll house and furniture to go with it. Although he has studiously avoided team sports, he has exhibited lots of other interests, many considered traditionally masculine. But because I worried about what Pogrebin dubbed the "secret fear," I only paid attention to his feminine interests.

I blamed myself of course and tried to seek help. When I expressed my worries to the pediatrician, he said, "Don't worry, but if it continues . . ." The nursery-school teacher and later my therapist, both women, said, "Explore your feelings about it." I already knew my feelings. I was scared to death I had ruined my son somehow.

What Pogrebin gave me was information, a new perspective that fits my reality, and a sensible rationale to drop my attempts to make my son fit into a mold. The article laid to rest many of the ancient fears rattling around inside me. I feel I can finally "stop worrying about gender and love my child."

> Name Withheld
> February 1981 Issue

I deal with both racism *and* sexism in my children's lives. I thought a lot about the experience Elizabeth Rommel's daughter, Lizzy, had when she saw her friend Daniel. She said "Hi." Daniel ignored her, and Daniel's mother explained, "Daniel doesn't speak to girls anymore." Not many mothers of white children would dare make such an explanation if their child snubbed mine because she was black. Rommel wondered whether to tell Daniel's mother her son was rude or let it pass. I would ask Lizzy if being ignored by her friend hurt her feelings—right on the spot, so that the children could get it straight right there.

When children behave rudely, they don't need adults to explain their behavior to another adult, but they do need adult guidance to understand the effects of their behavior on others and to communicate directly for themselves.

Kay Lieberknecht
Oakland, California
April 1984 Issue

In the early seventies, author Madelon Bedell recognized the absurdity of trying to do it all in "Supermom" (April 1973). Eight years later, in an April 1981 cover story, Lindsy Van Gelder asked the question "Are Single Mothers the Last of the Supermoms?" Our readers had plenty to say in response.

It's almost midnight, but before I sack out, I just had to write you a note. I could identify very much with the super-single-mom cover story.

After I made breakfast this morning and got my daughter off to school, I dashed off to my local community college. I delivered a time sheet for some part-time work I had done (slinging beer at a Friday-night dance for five hours). Paycheck may or may not be typed up tomorrow.

In the meantime, I'm living on air until my next student loan comes through, am also still waiting for my scholarship money, which was recently awarded to me, and am planning to go on to the University of British Columbia in May.

I went to my morning classes, came home in midafternoon for a hasty lunch, studied some more for an upcoming English final, went jogging for a half hour, returned home, and started supper.

The out-of-school day care phoned. Some man had been taking pictures of my daughter and her girlfriend playing in the schoolyard. I dash off to the day-care—police . . . teachers . . . upset children. The police nabbed the creep and discovered he had a record of child molestations. Dash back home with daughter. In the meanwhile, one of our cats has eaten part of our supper, which I'd hurriedly left on the counter.

My daughter wants to take a bath and wash her hair. She has supper after, and we discuss her experience in as calm and rational a manner as possible. Every night I have to give her an hour's extra help in math and reading, as she's been having learning problems—tonight we decide to skip it, though, and just relax, reading bedtime stories after the lunches for tomorrow are made.

I talk to a friend on the phone after—am feeling calmer. Spend an hour on my English essay and study Coleridge and Shelley; plan tomorrow and look over the rest of the week's agenda (allergy shots, dentist appointments, shopping, et cêtera); take a shower, wash my hair, watch the news, do my exercises, make coffee and tuck myself into bed with a late night mystery. This is a typical day in the life of a super-single-parent mom!

Name Withheld
April 8, 1981

In response to your article, I felt so acutely the feelings of Claire, the lesbian mother of sons. I, too, am a lesbian mother, living with my lover, and raising my two young sons.

I have given up membership in many so-called support groups, because boys are simply not acceptable for a lesbian to have! Where does my support come from?

I work full time and have a college degree, yet I find it very difficult and downright frustrating at times to find myself always alone with my sons. It's indeed very hard being a single mom!

Name Withheld
March 20, 1981

One reader made it clear that stories about European vacations and advertisements that featured glamorous superwomen didn't quite relate to her life.

Please, *Ms.* magazine, one more article about two women vacationing in Europe, complaining about sexual harassment, and I'll give up! Vidal Sassoon is beginning to get on my nerves, too. It's difficult to explain. I mean, I'd like to bring home the bacon, fry it up in a pan, and never, never let him forget he's a man, but there are days when I can't find a match to light the pilot.

Rosy-cheeked, polite, straight-A-student kids with summer jobs are making me sick. Are mothers allowed trade-ins?

I'm thirty-two years old, twenty pounds overweight, I have completed Rhetoric 101 and 102, Basic Design, and Introduction to Typing over a one-year span at the junior college. I am happily divorced; I have Angela, who is thirteen, and Richard, who is ten, a cat that goes into heat every three months. They all live with me. I have Lou, who doesn't live with me, a sales job at a country music radio station, where hanging above my desk is a small newspaper clipping that says, "I don't feel like a token." I have nine payments left on a 1972 Ford Maverick. It's true! I rent a three-bedroom duplex. And having my very own bedroom is a real rush. Good friends supplied the mattress, box springs, and frame. My bedroom is located downstairs between the living room and kitchen. It's the thought that counts.

My son has flunked fifth grade. It took me two days to understand that the Band-Aids covering Angie's neck were not covering up cat scratches. The "cat" that "scratched" her heaved a rock at Richard's head. One trip to the hospital, three stitches above the right eye. The next day Lou called, and he decided he wanted to end the relationship. Too much stress.

I was planning to buy a new nineteen-inch color TV with my income-tax refund. Before the bill arrived for the TV set, the tax refund did. Angie needed a new coat. We found a pair of heels that matched the plum flowers on her dress. She likes her new Nikes. Richard needed boots. He looks great in his three-piece navy suit and the new jogging outfit keeps him outside a little longer. At fifteen dollars per month, the TV will be paid in full by April 1983. I pay my rent the fifteenth of every month, and I have bought a new bedspread. I can retire in thirty-three years. I have lost ten pounds and applied for a scholarship. The children and I visit the family counselor weekly.

Angie cleaned up her room last week, and the Band-Aid tin is empty. I had a long talk with her and her boyfriend.

Richard can attend summer school for thirty-four dollars, and the stitches come out tomorrow. I suppose it is a well-arranged plan of survival that kittens are so cute.

Lou and I have reconciled. A weekend in Chicago, some talking, some quiet, a lot of touching, a lot of space, tacos and beer.

Next April, it is a sewing machine for sure!

Name Withheld
May 1981

Over the years, Ms. has published almost as much about fatherhood as we have about motherhood. And fathers, both single and married, shared their stories with other readers.

It never stops. The beds each morning and endless breakfasts. Pigtails and squabbles and stomach acid mixed with slugs of juice and coffee. And midday calls from the school nurse, rescheduled business meetings, half-assed excuses, and even a tyke as company on a last-minute flight to a Chicago meeting.

I'm a thirty-three-year-old, 100 percent of the time, single-parent father nigh on two and a half years now. My daughter is six, and the hair ties always have to match. And it's been a hell of a day. But, you know, I wouldn't take a trade. I know the scut work can't last forever. I have love and hope, and I'm finding out I can be a good mother. I finally understand it all. I finally, really understand it all. I'm home free!

Name Withheld
November 3, 1978

As a male single parent, I haven't run into the "superdad" expectation. As a matter of fact, I have been let mostly off the hook because of the male stereotype: namely, "men can't cook, sew, change diapers, or vacuum."

In the eyes of society (though not my three children), the combination of soup and water in a pan is somewhat of an achievement. While Van Gelder has had trouble leaving work to attend to her children, I have actually received strokes for announcing "I've got to go feed the kids."

Skip Branch
Salt Lake City, Utah
August 1981 Issue

Is the "new" Ms. a father? If so, when did this sex-change operation take place?

"Equal-opportunity fathers"—in a pig's eye! The day they take off from work and take on the complete running of the household so that *mothers* can have time to "be involved in the lives of their children" at play—that's the day I'll concede equal-opportunity fathering. Until then, the "discovery" of fatherhood is only another grab for the goodies . . . the "joys."

Name Withheld
June 1982 Issue

Despite the skeptics, it was hard to ignore the fact that a lot of fathers were indeed taking this job of parenting seriously.

In my fervor to become "the father I wish I'd had," I unknowingly started to lose perspective on my responsibility as a husband. If the present state of motherhood had deteriorated to becoming a burdensome flight for mothers to journey alone, then there I was to the rescue. The caped crusader in surgical greens, ready, from the moment of our daughter's birth, to tackle her every need. Interceding with diapering, comforting, midnight feedings, and so on, little did I know that what I thought was a sharing situation was viewed instead by my wife as an overzealous imposition, depriving her of the joys and challenges she so much wanted to be part of. She was feeling as though she was losing her husband and child—and gaining a nanny—

while I was becoming overwhelmed by the enormous emotional and physical involvement, especially since I had a full-time schedule at work.

Once our feelings had an opportunity to surface, our only alternative was to sit down and set up guidelines to help balance our respective involvement, which to this day needs continual reassessing. While some spontaneity may be forsaken, the gain in the "self-discovery" inherent in fathering is tremendous.

Steven H. McCormack
Newton, Massachusetts
June 1982 Issue

I run a church nursery (for fifteen children ages two to three), and two years ago I didn't know one father by sight. This year I know all the fathers. Why? Because the fathers bring the children, give me the necessary instructions, and later come to pick the kids up, stuffing them into coats and (thank God) car seats.

Name Withheld
January 21, 1982

Noting it's the sixth anniversary of *Ms.*, I fondly recall what happened while I was reading your charter issue.

Our daughter was just a few weeks old, and my husband came into the kitchen to announce Lori had a dirty diaper. I looked up from my *Ms.* and said, "So change it." "Well," he said, "*you* don't mind dirty diapers as much as *I* do." I closed my *Ms.* and took a deep breath. "I *hate* changing dirty diapers!"

Ever since then, we've been sharing child-raising joys and woes. Our children are six and a half and ten and a half. Our marriage is nearly fifteen years old.

Irene Sanders
Vacaville, California
June 26, 1978

There's No Divorce Between Mothers and Daughters

——————— ❧ ———————

"In search of my mother's garden, I found my own," wrote Alice Walker in her famous essay on black women's creativity, which appeared in Ms. *in May 1974. She and other poets, writers, and scholars, notably Adrienne Rich* (Of Woman Born), *Dorothy Dinnerstein* (The Mermaid and the Minotaur), *and Nancy Chodorow* (The Reproduction of Mothering), *explored the complicated experience of being daughters and being mothers—in the pages of* Ms. *and in major books in the seventies and early eighties.*

Rich wrote about "the girl-child still longing for a woman's nurture" and looked forward to "a world in which strong mothers and strong daughters will be a matter of course." Dorothy Dinnerstein described a mother's burden when "the overbearing intimate *authority the child must defy is female" and explained, "When men take an equal part in early child care, men will no longer represent uncontaminated humanity." Nancy Chodorow described, on the one hand, how "children have a hard time distinguishing their mothers' . . . wants and needs from their own" and feel "overwhelmed" by mothers and, on the other hand, how "women gain, from their mothers, a very valuable sense of self in a relationship, a sense of nurturance and caring" that "allows women to bond with and support one another." **

Ms. readers, as they explored their own roles and relationships, found both inspiration and warning in their mothers' lives. Often they discovered a new appreciation for their mothers' struggles and accomplishments, a new intimacy with a parent now viewed as a friend, and an ironic shock of recognition as they began to mother their own daughters—and sons.

* See Adrienne Rich, "A Challenge to All Your Ideas About Motherhood and Daughterhood," October 1976; Robin Morgan, "The Changeless Need: A Conversation With Dorothy Dinnerstein," August 1978; Judith Thurman, "Breaking the Mother-Daughter Code: An Interview With Nancy Chodorow," September 1982.

One reader, in response to a February 1974 portrait of working-class women, "Measuring Thirty Years by the Yard," by Agnes Schipper, describes her own life in sharp contrast to her mother's.

Marion Gray, in the sketch of her job at Woolworth's, reminded me of my own mother, who packs tea in a spice factory. She, like Ms. Gray, works hard, sees her children go their separate ways, and finds it difficult to grow old. My mother's life doesn't seem very colorful; she never had the opportunity to go to high school. She wraps herself up in her family and job, while I am wrapped up in myself.

It's not that my mother's life is so drab; it's that mine seems so colorful. A freshwoman in college, I am becoming aware of the world, what I want from it, and what I am capable of giving it. I have aspirations of learning German and Russian; and I daydream about becoming a farmer, and I revel in notions of traveling up and down America and Europe.

Both my mother and Marion Gray think of themselves as "too old to start something else again." They've given family and job their best years, and now they want to relax. I hope their ships come in; as for me, I am just setting out.

Marian Klymkowsky
University Park, Pennsylvania
June 1974 Issue

Another reader, writing in response to a July 1975 excerpt from Florynce King's Sex and the Good Ole Boy, *now appreciates a mother who seemed just a little too colorful for comfort when the daughter was a self-conscious teenager.*

My mother was one of the exceptions to the Southern-belle stereotype. She never learned that a woman's place was in the home, with her mouth and brain both shut. Being a typical teenager growing up in the fifties, I found her behavior to be a constant source of dismay. How I then wished she would stay at home and wear an apron and be like all other mothers.

One of her finest hours came as a result of having four children attending local schools at the same time. Every spring we came home from school complaining that the school milk tasted of wild onions, and we refused to drink it. Her Scots-Irish ancestry could not tolerate such waste. My mother solved the problem by running for the local school board, an unheard-of thing for a woman in North Carolina in 1954.

She was elected and proceeded to use her "moxie" to set standards for all supplies purchased by the school system. For the first time, the school board asked for sealed bids on a milk contract, a contract that for many years had automatically gone to a "local boy." His milk was not fit to drink, but it took my outspoken, unbashful, unladylike mother to prove it.

Now, twenty years later, I can appreciate her struggle to stay out of the mold that produced Southern belles. And, of course, I still cringe when I remember how she threw spitballs at . . . but that's another story.

Barbara L. Carrubba
Baldwin, New York
November 1975 Issue

Particularly appreciated and recorded by readers were the often heroic efforts their mothers made to adapt to a changing world. As one letter writer explains, in response to a feature in June 1975 on mothers and daughters, "My mother is not famous, but she is special enough to me to deserve being in your magazine."

Two years ago, after almost twenty years of marriage and with seven children, ages eighteen and under, my mother did the only thing possible to save her own sanity—divorced my dad. A year later she used the money she got from the sale of the house to move herself and her children to San Luis Obispo and buy a business, the Kuan Yin Book Store.

Every day I work with her, I am more and more proud of her. She worries about being a good mother, and I wish I could tell her not to worry, tell her how much I love her and how proud I am of her. Although she hadn't worked outside of her home in twenty years and had never worked in the book business, she believed in herself and her ability enough to go ahead and *do* what she wanted to. Today we worked on plans for our "first-birthday party" in the store, a kind of open-house celebration to thank our customers for a successful first year.

Thank you for letting me share my mother with you!

Name Withheld
May 20, 1975

After years of conflict, my mother and I finally got together. Last fall we both entered law school, and we now view each other with pride, respect, and love.

Lorrie Willey
Knoxville, Tennessee
October 1975 Issue

My mom was a child bride of sixteen. This marriage produced two children. She was divorced and remarried and had two more children. Things were not a fairy tale existence for us. The man my mother married was sent to jail for sexual abuse of a minor child. This caused all kinds of trouble for all of us. Other children were cruel to us. Parents did not let their kids play with us. My mother could not get a job that paid enough to support us, so she applied for welfare. Mother was crushed by all that happened, but she never gave up.

My brother was in an auto accident and in intensive care for four days. Then our apartment burned with all our belongings. Welfare was no help at all. Mom had no insurance, but she did have good friends who helped us get together enough clothes and furniture to start over. All during this time she worked for a program geared to helping low-income people.

Mom enrolled in a community college and graduated with high honors in 1974. She got scholarships and grants and graduated [with a higher degree] in 1976 at thirty-eight years of age. She is now in charge of a nutrition program for the elderly.

Mom has given up all chances of a happy personal life because of us kids. We have been into drugs, got caught shoplifting, been runaways and almost anything else you can think of. Through it all she is always there. She must love us a lot to keep on taking us back and loving us.

Name Withheld
February 1980

Adrienne Rich, in an excerpt from Of Woman Born *we published in October 1976, expressed an ambiguity in regard to her mother that many readers recognized. She wrote, "I struggle to describe what it felt like to be her daughter, but I find myself divided, slipping under her skin; a part of me identifies too much with her. I know deep reservoirs of anger toward her still exist."*

I remember my mother and me taking a nap together each day before the years came between us, making our inhibitions dictate our actions. The closeness of our bodies, the warmth, the nonverbal love expressed, and the security I felt were overwhelming. This woman, with her calming abilities, gave me strength that no person can take from me. It is the wonderful recognition of myself as a person—who is by gender a woman—that my mother taught me.

Donna L. Johnson
San Diego, California
February 1977 Issue

My reactions to Adrienne Rich's article included a strong wave of nostalgia for being a little girl again. I have a unique relationship with my mother, and while we live far apart, sometimes I feel as close to her as I did twenty years ago when I would sit on her lap in a rocking chair. I long to create a similar link with a child of my own.

I have transferred this bond to other women, and some of my most rewarding relationships are with them. I have always been encouraged to share with, trust, and love females. It pays off, both with my mother and other women.

Carol Fulkerson
St. Louis, Missouri
February 1977 Issue

Many of the Ms. *readers who seemed to feel closest to their mothers credit their mothers with imparting a critical lesson: how to turn to other women for intimacy and support. As Adrienne Rich wrote, "Before sisterhood, there was the knowledge—transitory, fragmented, perhaps, but original and crucial—of motherhood and daughterhood."*

My mother, Billie Loulan, died on February 2, 1975, after a long battle with breast cancer. During the last three years of her life, she and I discovered each other on many levels.

While I was growing up, she taught me the importance of my life and the lives of other women. She taught me the beauty of women loving women. She had many close women friends with whom she spent years building a beautiful, supportive network. I, too, have many close women friends; one of them owns a business with me.

Mother and I switched roles a lot during her last years. She mothered me through my divorce—I mothered her through her pain. As a result, we became dear friends. I'm grateful I had the time with her that I did. I'm glad I was able to let go of some of my "daughter-to-mother anger." I gained a special person.

Jo Ann Loulan
Menlo Park, California
October 1975 Issue

Another wonderful women's-friendship letter came in response to a memoir by Rolaine Hochstein of her mother's mah-jongg games in the January 1977 issue, "Mah-Jongg Returns."

Although my mother's mah-jongg games began later than Hochstein's mother's— around 1960—the scents, the sounds, the memories are the same. Underlying the ritual of the Thursday night game was a deeper, stronger bond than any of the five women realized. How often did any of them visit their mothers or sisters without the encumbrances of husbands and children, in order to talk about their fears and joys? Indeed, how often did they even see each other on a woman-to-woman basis? The Thursday-night game formed a bond outlasting widowhood, divorce, or the return to work.

What the bond could not endure were the real or imagined slights which were never satisfactorily discussed or resolved. The game would then undergo a sea change, shakily proceed with a new awareness (or even a new player, who never lasted long)—then gather strength once again.

Even the children of the players became involved. We attended the same school; we dutifully invited each other to our birthday parties; we were polite. At first, one mother would say, "Tina, that Janie Civins is such a sweet girl. Why don't you give her a call some day?" Tina would call me, and grudgingly, we would find we could talk to each other for hours. My mother would echo Tina's mother and suggest I call Nancy. Under similar urgings, Nancy would call Tina.

I have not spoken to Tina in ten years, and now I need to find her. I do have Nancy's address, and I think I'll mail her a copy of the article and a letter. My mother's game has endured for seventeen years. Only Tina's family moved away, thus permanently removing one of the original women. Although I have not yet convinced my mother to stop calling them the "mah-jongg girls," maybe she'll let me put the cherries on the pineapple slices the next time she's hostess for the game.

Jane Civins-Mills
Newton Centre, Massachusetts
May 1977 Issue

Sometimes, sharing the experience of feminist events, or even reading Ms. *together, created a strong bond between mothers and daughters of all ages. One pair contributed to an August 1974 Letters "forum" on reactions to a National Black Feminist Organization conference. The mother, Ashaki Habiba Taha, wrote of her daughter Halima, "I was amazed at our ability to communicate on an entirely different level once we rid ourselves of the mother-daughter labels. I found myself thinking how different my own mother's life might have been had she had the opportunity to see herself through feminist eyes." And Halima was equally enthusiastic.*

When my mother asked me to go with her to the first Eastern Regional Conference on Black Feminism, I thought it would be a good chance for us to be together without my two brothers and my father.

My mother and I are probably the only black feminists in town. None of the young black women at my school are interested in really contributing to the liberation of black people. Their idea of being black is just hating everything white, but they don't think or do anything positive about being black. All they're into is boys, music, dancing, makeup, clothes, smoking, getting high, and insulting each other. They tell me feminism is dumb and stupid. It was a wonderful feeling to find so many together black women who think feminism is important. I felt warm and alive and part of something important and good.

When the conference began, and I realized I was really taking part in it, I felt so excited, I could hardly keep myself together. I found that it didn't make any difference to any of the women that I was twelve years old. Even in the two workshops I attended, all the sisters made me feel that I was wanted and that my ideas and thoughts counted. The Female Sexuality workshop was terrific. I learned about my clitoris and cervix, where they are located, how to take care of them and other sexual parts of my body. I felt I was surrounded by people who really cared for me, Halima Malika, black woman (almost).

I have heard about black men talking about being the heads of their households and about women contributing to the black nation only by having babies and keeping the house clean. Now I know that black women have talents and ideas that are needed in order to free all black people.

I am a Sunni Muslim, and I know that Allah wants all human beings to be the best they can be and to do good things for other people. To me, being a Muslim woman is not about covering up my body or giving up the right to make decisions about my life or my uterus. It is about loving and caring about other people, being the best I can be and working with other sisters and brothers to build a strong black nation.

Halima Malika Taha
Ossining, New York
August 1974 Issue

I started my *Ms.* subscription during my senior year in high school, some five years ago. The magazine fitted my radical image. I usually kept it hidden in my room, afraid of the reaction of Mom and Dad.

When I left for college, *Ms.* still came to my parents' home, and I picked it up during visits. A delightful thing happened because I wasn't there to intercept the magazine directly: Mom paged through it and began reading the articles. She'd ask me questions; we'd discuss a specific story or disagree over the tone of a letter.

Last year, Mom went back to school to pick up the required credits as a nurse's aide. Now, after raising eight children—ranging in age from nine to twenty-three—Mom has a new job: a career that is making her very happy.

One day my father and I were talking, and he told me that he believed that I was the cause of Mom wanting to work. All my extreme ideas, all those "liberated magazines" I had sent to the house, he said, had influenced Mom to the point of rebellion. I was glad to be held responsible.

Diane M. Wilke
St. Francis, Wisconsin
February 1979 Issue

Upon the death of her grandmother, one reader, with her mother's help, shared an intimate moment with her father.

When I was sixteen, my paternal grandmother died after a long, lingering illness. Fishnet stockings were the rage in 1967, and as I dressed for the funeral, I put on a pair of blue fishnet stockings to match my somber blue suit.

When I came out to the car, my father became enraged, ordering me back into the house to remove what he called "hooker stockings." We had a big fight, until my mother pulled me aside and explained that he wasn't angry with me, rather he was holding all his grief inside and refused to cry. I changed into a pair of nude nylon stockings and rode to the funeral home in defiant silence.

When we got there, I cautiously approached my grandmother's coffin. We hadn't been close; she was an Italian immigrant who never learned to speak English well, and we were more often frustrated and confused by one another because of our inability to communicate. But when I saw her, I suddenly realized how totally vulnerable one must feel to see a parent laid out in a coffin.

I went to my father, and we stood over her coffin, crying together. I have never seen him cry since.

Nancy Lucarelli Johnson
Garfield Heights, Ohio
October 1980 Issue

One unfinished letter to Ms. *was found by Anne Dallette in going through her mother's papers after her death. She sent it in on October 1984, from Fayetteville, Arkansas, with a note: "Did my mother ever send you this? She liked to type in the dark." Her mother responds in the letter to a very funny piece in May 1981, by Jane O'Reilly, who imagines Carol Rosenthal's biography of Phyllis Schlafly,* Sweetheart of the Silent Majority, *made into a major motion picture.*

There are a jillion things to be done and to see to here, but the new *Ms.* arrived and, as always, I glanced at the cover and the table of contents to see what was in store for me when there would be time. But there was the entry about Phyllis you know who. She was here at the U. of A. this spring; since then, I have had so much bottled-up dismay, amazement, disbelief, and even anger and disgust that I have waited for time to lessen the pressure of all this. Now comes *Ms.* with the lovely Jane O'Reilly, and that smashing piece about P. S. in a movie. Such a relief to have somebody do so well what I would have liked to do.

You may have heard that her appearance and talk at the visit on the campus here went over like two lead balloons. I was so proud to be in that audience (which we had half-feared would be packed with P. S. enthusiasts . . . and not so), so proud and exicted by my own clapping, that I came home and had a heart attack. So much for the old ones who would like to help but can only sit at a typewriter and try to help in that way.

My daughter, now forty-five and living in Ottawa, Canada, bought for me a charter subscription to *Ms.* and kept it going for years until I saw that it was time for me to do a little something and pay for it myself. What a bargain.

Long may you wave. It is so wonderful to read the letters from all over, to know there are so many

No Closing
Spring 1983

I have one child, a daughter, Mary, who turned fourteen Saturday. We're a team.

All of her life we've gone every place together. I've worked since she was two weeks old. Our times together have been very exclusive.

She always liked plays. Sometimes she fell asleep. Opera is her favorite. When my Italian mother laughed at the lyrics, Mary did, too. Today the teacher asked the class to name the seven deadly sins. Mary knew, because she saw *Dr. Faustus* last summer.

When she could hardly walk, she sat on the altar at Mass very quietly, because that's where she wanted to be. The priest agreed.

I'm a firm believer in sharing experiences with your child. Mary is rather indepen-dent now, but she is extremely patient with the first-grade readers she tutors.

She certainly is a feminist.

Rosemary Eismann
Modesto, California
February 26, 1980

Native Americans (one set of my ancestors) and other minority women have always listened to their mothers and grandmothers and learned their stories and songs. Just as important, they listened to everyday words about practical things and saw in those words a kind of poetry that rivals any academic literature in strength and beauty.

My eighty-nine-year-old mother, for example, delighted with the first wild greens of spring that I gathered and cooked for her, began to recite a litany of the wild greens that she and her mother picked each spring. Her reedy voice, retelling the story of the "greens-gathering jaunt" with her own mother eighty years earlier, is poetry.

And I remember my grandmother taking me into her bedroom and opening her son's trunk (the son who died at an young age) and showing me his possessions. The image of that strong woman—who raised seven children alone—sitting there in her long, gray skirts, taking round rocks (his gaming stones, or marbles) out of a leather bag and rolling them between her fingers as she looked far away and spoke of this dead child, that image is a poem she gave to me, her six-year-old granddaughter. I now know enough of life to see the significance of that moment and write of it.

But first I will tell it to my daughter.

Joan Shaddox Isom
Tahlequah, Oklahoma
October 1981 Issue

Daughters all grown up and ready to leave home and mothers watching their daughters go both reported their bittersweet experiences of separation, often at the moment when a daughter went off to college. Relating to one another as adults brought an entirely new set of responses.

I scoffed at turning points until I experienced one. The scene is etched sharply in my mind, like a photograph: my bedroom in the house I shared with three other women. On a winter afternoon in my sophomore year in college, there I sat, in agony over my most recent breakup with my boyfriend.

I called up Mom (long distance, perhaps the tenth time that week) and rambled on incoherently about my rotten life. But most importantly, Mom, what should I do? Poor Mom, for weeks she'd been trying to help—comforting, consoling, listening to me. It wasn't doing any good, and her patience was (understandably) wearing thin. Finally, she said, "Shelly, I love you, but *there's nothing I can do.*"

What? What do you mean, there's nothing you can do? You're my mom! Then, oh, my God, she's right. And if she can't do anything, chances are, neither can anyone else: not my dad, or my friends, or even my all-important boyfriend. My life is my own. What a terrifying, yet exciting, discovery to make.

Michelle Andrews
Madison, Wisconsin
August 1982 Issue

Two months after my daughter left for college, she called me very late and blurted out that she was no longer a virgin. A million questions raced through my mind, but I said nothing—not wanting to invade her privacy. Finally, I just said, "Maybe we should wait to talk in person," and hung up; but feeling that I had failed her, I couldn't fall asleep.

Ten minutes later she called back, crying, explaining that she needed to talk *now*—and we did, for more than an hour. I told her about my first experience, realizing that she had always assumed that her father was the only one. There was no anger, because Mother was not judgmental. Instead, Mother became a person.

I've been thinking about how lucky we both are—my daughter because she has someone to talk to; myself for having done something right all those years to create and nurture that trust.

Name Withheld
October 1982 Issue

Last August, I graduated from college with a B.S. after having paid for my entire education. Yet I didn't bother to attend my graduation ceremony. Similarly, every failure I've experienced has been accompanied by a feeling of relief and an immediate phone call to my mother, who is at her most supportive, loving, encouraging, and attentive when I am feeling my worst, when my goals have been thwarted.

Now I realize that it will be impossible for me to achieve the career goals that I desire *and* feel good about myself, my family, and love relationships until I can resolve the ambivalent feelings that I have. Also, I feel that it will be necessary for my mother to gain self-esteem and feelings of self-worth that are not challenged by her daughters' successes.

Name Withheld
March 1983 Issue

In March 1979, Bonnie Ghazarbekian wrote about a particularly wrenching separation at the end of her mother's life in a prize-winning article, "How My Mother Helped Me Put Her in a Nursing Home." Many readers wrote about how the piece moved them.

My own mother, hearty and spunky in her early fifties, is nothing like the mother that Ghazarbekian describes. Nonetheless, I finished the story and cried.

I saw in an instant a vision from a recent event: my mother had had minor surgery and asked me to pick her up at the hospital. When I got there, I was led to the door of the recovery room. As the door was opened, I saw my mother sitting in a wheelchair. She sat upright and prim, her purse held on her lap, her clothing very orderly, her scarf tied just-so around her neck. She had a far-off expression in her eyes. I kissed her hello, and suddenly a nurse came up and said, "You're not supposed to be here!" As I was escorted from the room, I looked back to see my mother looking familiar and small and very lonely . . . and the big door swung shut with menacing finality.

What will happen when my mother gets old? The things that Bonnie Ghazarbekian says tug at my heart and conscience and remind me that hard choices and decisions may have to be faced in my family some day.

Nani Paape
Seattle, Washington
July 1979 Issue

When it came to mothering, many Ms. *contributors and readers seemed to feel more conflicted about their sons than their daughters. One Lindsy Van Gelder article in October 1975, "But What About Our Sons?," was full of troubled quotes from mothers trying to raise feminist sons in a not-yet-feminist world. The author of a July 1981 piece, "Discovering the Man in My Son," writing under the pseudonym Amanda Ross, talked eloquently about the even more confusing time of a son's adolescence. The first letter is a confident response to the Van Gelder article.*

Oh, did I enjoy your article; it made me feel good. My son and I can get it on and those big-shot feminists can't. Then I decided to write an encouraging word.

If you're having a problem relating to your boy, don't get that mother-guilt-trip jive; try to realize that you're the first generation to even want a real relationship with a son. Most mommies wait on them, spoil them, and turn them into the emotional cripples you have been dating. Love him, and keep on trucking; it might help the next generation.

Dolores T. Whitelaw
Union, New Jersey
September 23, 1975

I had grabbed up Amanda Ross's article and read it only minutes after the last shots had been fired and the door slammed by my eldest, my hope, my love, my handsome, affectionate, witty, and wickedly charming nineteen-year-old son. There have been times when things were much sweeter between us, but for now my charmer has been replaced by a macho, karate-kicking, professional blamer, who is happy to keep me informed of how I have distorted his life by my feminist harping and "cutting down men all the time." He seems to take pleasure in his sexism and bad taste.

Although I feel sure that my son is going through a perfectly normal adolescent rebellion and will eventually emerge as a fine adult, my belief in this fluctuates from time to time. The man my son is revealing these days is the antithesis of everything I value intellectually, politically, and emotionally. If this is not in fact a transient period, a reaction to the intensity of our early years, then the burden of my failure will have to be borne most heavily, of course, by some young woman who, although perfectly capable of taking care of herself and happy to do so, cannot find a man who values that strength and is now faced with exactly the same choice I had twenty years ago: learn how to flatter male egos, or learn to live alone. I had hoped for so much more.

Name Withheld
October 17, 1981

In September 1983, we published a very personal story by Gloria Steinem, "Ruth's Song: Because She Could Not Sing It." Gloria told of mothering her mother as Ruth, responding to the stifling of her own life and dreams, moved in and out of institutions and in and out of "reality." The response to Gloria's identifying the "secret club of children who had 'crazy mothers'" was overwhelming. We devoted the entire February 1984 column to letters in response to "Ruth's Song."

After I read "Ruth's Song" and wiped away the tears of recognition, I carefully cut the pages out of *Ms.* and sent them to my sister.

All our lives my sister and I have tried to make some sort of sense out of our mother's life. I know from photographs and stories that she was once a spirited and fun-loving young schoolteacher. My own memories, however, are of her sinking abysmally into periodic bouts of severe depression. She was eventually unable to function, spent months at a time in a mental hospital undergoing shock treatments, and would return to us a little more beaten down each time.

Since the age of eight, I have gradually become my mother's mother. My sister and I have carried our mother's burdens, have longed for a mother like everyone else's, have felt anger over our loss, protected her, and made her the center of our despair—around which all else revolves.

I have spent so many years trying to distance myself from her craziness that one of the hardest things I have ever admitted is how much I love her.

I thank Gloria for singing Ruth's song. I suspect that there are a lot of us out here trying desperately to make something good come out of our mother's suffering.

Name Withheld
February 1984 Issue

I consciously swore early on that my life would be different from my mother's in that I would not get trapped as she did. When I had my first child, I worked diligently to retain a sense of identity. Just last year I became pregnant again, and had such ambivalent feelings about it that I almost considered terminating the pregnancy—not because I didn't want another child, but because I was afraid of becoming like my mother. For the first time I began to truly empathize with my mother's situation. Then we discovered twins were on the way. Feeling that I was bankrupt in the area of mothering anyway, the prospect of double mothering was totally overwhelming. Gabriel and Rachel are now six months old, and after the past year of confronting so many hidden-away fears, I stand in awe of the growth and courage I have found within myself.

My mother's experiences and mine differ in that I have a supportive mate, a support system of women, an identity to keep and nurture aside from wife and mother, and a society that is more (but not yet enough) accepting of a wide range of options for women. For these things, I am thankful.

Mary LeLoo
Seattle, Washington
February 1984 Issue

I, too, am the daughter of a "crazy mother," who got drugs instead of household help, who was told that my father physically and sexually abused us kids because she was not a good enough wife, who, during a financial crisis after divorcing my father, was put in an institution by the welfare department when all she needed was an adequate income.

I am a grown woman now and have worked through my problems and am happy. But somehow I have never been able to forgive my mother for her life. Feminist that I am, I could forgive every woman in the world *but* my mother.

Gloria's article broke down the wall for me. Yes, I wept. I also sent a copy to my mother—my mother who has been divorced now as long as she was married, who went back to school and is now a nurse, who owns her own home, and who is finally happy.

Name Withheld
February 1984 Issue

Small and Momentous Changes in Everyday Life

———————— 🍎 ————————

Correspondents generally addressed their letters to "the Editor," but they sometimes seemed to do so only as a courtesy: we editors were intermediaries for messages directed to other readers. And, indeed, a primary function of the Ms. *Letters column has been to allow readers to pass on information on how they are making change—or failing to do so. They wanted to share the turning points of their lives as well as tactics for dealing with everyday hassles. Readers would find it especially satisfying to report successful experiments to all their unknown friends—the readers of* Ms.

————————————————

Thanks to *Ms.* magazine's reporting women's accomplishments, I decided to try a man's task myself. I and two friends broke up twelve feet of sidewalk to make room for a thirty-foot-by-eighteen-foot above-ground swimming pool we are assembling. A contractor had quoted $150 to $200 for his labor. I rented the cement chipper for $13.

> Pat Luiz
> Oakland, California
> Spring 1974 Issue

Ms. correspondents knew other readers would appreciate the unending struggle to revolutionize family life. A favorite thing to share was tactics to induce family members to cooperate.

The day our twelve-year-old son stomped up the stairs—leaving behind the mud that had collected on his sneakers—took a shower, came back downstairs barefoot, and complained about the dirt on the stairs was the day Mom and Dad decided we were going to raise the consciousness of our nine- ten-, and twelve-year-olds.

A family conference resulted in a vote to have family cleaning night on Friday. Our ten-year-old son chose to clean the upstairs bathroom and went about it diligently. At bedtime, when the usual teeth-cleaning routine was about to begin, the ten-year-old realized what was soon to happen and yelled at his older brother, "You're not cleaning your teeth in *my* clean sink!" Click!

Jane Wright
Dover, Delaware
July 1974 Issue

I am part of a liberated household—Mother works and actually earns *more* than Dad. With three teenagers in the family, *all* insisting that if they clean their rooms they have done all that might be expected, I am getting sick and tired of the miscellaneous *shit work!*

It all does mount up. All three—and Dad, too—down immense glasses of sweet sodas. They all wait for Mom to spill the ice cubes from the trays into the ice-cube holder. Or they fingernail pry up whatever they need from the frozen trays, leaving the holder empty until Mom comes to the rescue by filling.

Well, no more. I posted today the following note on the refrigerator door:

> *Mother has resigned permanently from the ice-cube detail.* I know you are all capable of filling the ice-cube trays, as well as spilling them into the ice-cube trays.
>
> Regrettably, I expect you will once more follow this with the textbook response: (1) You will leave the freezer door open fully to help rot the food inside and put up the bill—that always gets a conscientious mother. If the phone rings, leave it open while you talk. (2) You will make sure also to spill loads of water over the freezer and onto the floor and will carefully refrain from wiping it up. That may kill your aged grandmother, but *what the hell?* That will really teach *Mom* something. Right? (3) You will also carefully make sure the water will run full blast at the sink—*that* will get her if nothing else.
>
> It is also expected that all of this activity will take place when you carefully have Mom trapped in the kitchen—cooking meals or eating them. Well, think again, because none of the above tactics will work.
>
> You drink the ice-cubed drinks—*you* make the ice cubes.
> *Love* (and I really mean it),
> MOM

Name Withheld
February 5, 1976

Because I was brought up in a traditional Mexican-American family, where the men were served first, I made up my mind, early on during my own children's formative years (and my husband's formative years as a husband), that I would never favor my three sons or my husband by feeding them the biggest, best portions of dinner while my daughter and I would eat or be served last. No way!

When we eat tortillas (which is often), I heat them up, wrap them in foil, and set them on the table so that I may sit down and eat with my family. Never have I stood warming tortillas while my family eats.

My daughter and I get the drumsticks as often as the others. Many times I serve *her* first. Other times my sons serve us, as does their father. My sons will either grow up to hate the kitchen or to learn to shift for themselves. But best of all, my daughter will grow up with a feeling of self-worth, which in itself is worth the effort.

Merrihelen Ponce-Adame
Tujunga, California
June 1980 Issue

Another all too common annoyance that readers dealt with every day was street harassment. As one reader wrote in the midseventies, the first step was to realize it wasn't her fault. Since she was not yet clear about what to do next, she asked Ms. *readers for their ideas.*

Why do some men bother women they don't know, and what can women do about it? By *bother,* I mean all those things a man can do to a woman without violating the law: staring, whistling, smacking the lips, making comments—from almost complimentary to downright crude—approaching her and trying to start a conversation against her will, feeling a woman in a crowd while walking swiftly in the other direction, and following her to her home, car, or place of business.

My methods of coping with these situations are unsatisfactory, but they are the best I've come up with. I ignore the starers, whistlers, smackers, feelers, and rude comment makers. At first (and isn't this typical?), I thought maybe all this was my fault—something *I* was doing was causing these men to annoy me. But I've found that many other women share my experience, including my mother.

I enjoy the company of men—but not the variety that tries to pick up a woman on the street. I come home after one of these experiences and sit down and list all the nice men I've known in my life to prove to myself that not all men are bad. This may seem a small problem at first, but it is basic to men's attitudes toward women and affects the quality of a woman's life.

Joyce Williams
Chicago, Illinois
April 1975 Issue

Last year I was terrorized and raped, and Philadelphia's Center for Rape Concern conducted several interviews with me to see how my personality, attitudes, sex life, and relationships had changed. The major change was in my response to street insults. I, too, had ignored them, "like a good girl," but I found myself seething at them. I started to hurl my own choice comments and give the insulter the finger in retaliation. The topper came the day when a straight-looking man in a business suit and attaché case walked up next to me while I was going to work and asked me if I wanted to fuck. I was carrying a hardback copy of *The Gulag Archipelago* in my handbag at the time, and I belted him with it. The look of fear and surprise on his face was delicious. I felt wonderful.

Name Withheld
March 20, 1975

Women could share responses to harassment that they found effective. But there was a menace that made street hassling more than a nuisance, as one reader expressed in answer to a question posed by Letty Cottin Pogrebin in a November 1974 cover story on male violence.

Women *do* make men violent. The hatred (fear?) that many men feel toward women comes out in the form of violence: insults, rape, or allowing another man to beat up a woman.

I used to live in a town full of churches, of bars, and of trucks too big for the streets. Spring tried to come even there, so I went to the town's one green spot—an industrial park divided by a polluted creek. I sat down to read a copy of *Ms.* while my dog sniffed at the garbage.

Within ten minutes, three boys appeared across the creek. The *instant* they spotted me, they started in, shouting obscenities at me. The more I ignored them, the more enraged they became.

Suddenly, *I* was too angry to ignore them anymore. What gave them the right to harass me, a person reading in a public park? I lost my temper and screamed at them to quit bugging me; *they started to throw rocks at me!* I was amazed to see the violence I had inspired by just being there. I still can't understand hatred like this in people so young. But violence only begets violence, and if I had a gun . . .

Click?

Ildi Holdstock
Burnaby, British Columbia
March 1975 Issue

I am in sixth grade and am scared stiff to walk on the streets in town. Two high-school boys have tried to rape me. Luckily, I can kick and run. My brother taught me some karate. I have to wear loose skirts to be safe.

One day at school a boy pulled me down and tried to feel me up. I am so used to it, my reflexes work fast. I punched him in the mouth, and his tooth went through his lip. I was sent to the principal. He said it wasn't ladylike and next time I will get punished. When I told him what the kid did, he said he'll have a talk with him, but all he said was "never do it again."

I'm sick of having to be scared of every boy I see. They give those stares like "What can I do to her?" Even men twenty or older look at me like that. I think they're all sick!

Lois Hagemaier
Dover, New Jersey
July 1973

I went on vacation the last two weeks in September alone on a motorcycle to various places in New Mexico. In Cloudcroft, I stopped in the last afternoon at a restaurant and a grocery. I had seen a young man come out of the bar next to the restaurant, walk up and down the boardwalk acting as though he were looking for something across the street, then go back into the bar (he was very drunk and/or stoned). When I went out to pack things onto my bike, he came out and looked around again, then stepped over to my bike and said, "Uh—where's the old man?" The old man?! I said, "He's back at the campsite." I wanted to say—I don't know what I wanted to say. I wanted to tell the truth, but then I thought, (1) What's it to him, and (2) He'll give me "trouble" if he finds out I'm alone.

It occurred to me that the entire time I was on vacation, I definitely had an undercurrent of fear. I spent the night camping out in Cloudcroft, and I think there might have been four families in the whole campsite, but there I was, terrified of that (male) pervert that had to be lurking close about. Also, *every* woman who talked to me and found that I was traveling alone, and alone on a motorcycle, asked me if I wasn't afraid. I can't tell you how I resent that fear we all live under and apparently accept and even help to instigate. I had *no* bad experiences on that vacation: I had a lovely vacation. This one I just related was the worst that happened. But I was afraid.

Name Withheld
November 13, 1980

Responses to street harassment were easier with a friend nearby—as in this case of subway sisterhood.

Today a woman defended me from a man who thought he was going to get his jollies standing behind me (*right* behind me; I literally could not move in any direction to keep from being so close) on a very crowded subway car. She saw what was happening, said something to him in another language, and glared at him until the next stop (which was nearly five minutes away, since it was an express train). We both got off at the same stop and talked for a few minutes about what had happened and that sort of indignity in general.

Sisterhood *is* powerful—it bridges the gap of cultural differences and diverse backgrounds. I don't know that young woman's name, and I probably will never see her again, but I feel a bond with her that is hard to put into words, and her actions nearly made up for the unpleasantness of the incident, because they meant so much to me.

Name Withheld
July 31, 1973

When I was with my two sisters in a public park a few months ago, we were bothered several times by males who apparently couldn't stand to see women "alone" and having a good time. We discussed the problem, and when the next male hassled us, we began madly picking our noses and licking our fingers. He sure left in a hurry!

Name Withheld
September 1981

I am seventeen years old and a high-school senior. Last year I spent a semester studying in Greece. Whenever I went out on the street alone, I was usually approached and harassed by the Greek men and boys. (I was an especially easy target, for not only was I away from the protection of my family, but I was a foreigner whose morals were suspect.)

One day I agreed to take a friend's baby out for a stroll. The very same teenage boys who had made catcalls at me before now smiled warmly at me and showered the baby and me with compliments. The men at the *kefeneions* glanced up briefly, then returned to their backgammon games without one comment or disapproving stare.

Imagine that! All that sudden respect, just for chaperoning (or being chaperoned by?) a human being not even a third my size or age!

Kimberly Cox
Round Rock, Texas
May 1983 Issue

One reader offered a solution to another common intruder, the obscene phone caller, and asked advice about a problem she hadn't yet solved.

Thought I'd share my solutions to an unfortunately everyday problem common to the female experience—obscene phone calls.

When simply hanging up or leaving the phone off the hook fails to discourage him, pretend to be the operator intercepting the call. If possible, try to disguise your voice and sound rather bored. "Operator. What number are you calling?" He may hang up, thinking you've alerted the phone company. If he gives you the number, continue: "One moment, please." Pause. "Still checking." Pause. "I'm sorry, that number is no longer in service. Please check your directory or call directory assistance. Thank you." If the fool calls back, simply repeat the above. This always works for me.

Sometimes, however, in the middle of the night, one is not in the mood to play these games.

I finally decided to buy an answering machine. Fortunately, talking to a recording does not turn these crank callers on, and they never call back.

Now can anyone help me? Is there a way to discourage people from calling you "honey," "sweetie," "dearie," and so on when you *don't* want them to know your name?

Pam Palmer
Los Angeles, California
January 1981 Issue

In response to Pam Palmer (assuming that is her real neame): my friend Gloria has what she calls her "bar name" for just such occasions. She introduces herself as "Ruby Foo." And "Grenelda Thurber" does all my typing. Use your imagination and have a little fun with it.

Name Withheld
January 12, 1981

By the eighties, there was evidence that at least some men were catching on to the fact that women didn't find street harassment a compliment.

A few weeks ago I was waiting for a bus alone at night after working an evening shift. I was wearing strictly nonsexy clothes, holding a book in front of my face, carrying a briefcase, and standing under a bus-stop sign—in short, obviously not looking to be picked up. A group of young men lounging about across the street spotted me and began to shout, "Hey, baby! Come on over here! Want a drink? Aw, come on." I was too weary and fed up to take it. I shouted back, "No! Leave me alone and let me wait for my bus in peace. How would you like to be standing out here alone in the middle of the night and have a bunch of strange people start yelling at you?" Not another word was heard from the group until one of the men came across the street toward me—to apologize.

I'm not sure what to call my new approach to verbal assault. Assertiveness? Aggressiveness? Articulated anger? Whatever it is, I think it's working.

Sandra L. Friedlander
Pittsburgh, Pennsylvania
November 1980 Issue

The other day I was talking with a casual friend who is interested in doing some carpentry work for me. As we went into the barn where the work will be done, he said, "Ah, we're alone at last. Now I can molest you."

I looked at him quickly. He had a big grin on his face to let me know that he was just joking. So I put my hand on his arm, and I said very seriously, "I know you were joking, but that joke is not funny. I don't know any woman who would think it was funny. It's frightening. I mean, I trust you, and I know you wouldn't really hurt me. . . ."

He started to grin and then a truly pained expression crossed his face. "Oh, wow," he said, "I'm so far into that game, do you know what I almost said? I almost said, 'You *think* you know.' "

Helen Park
Jasper, Oregon
January 1983 Issue

A male reader responded to letters complaining about street hassling with his own analysis of the problem—and the solution that worked for him.

Even as a child, I knew that making comments and wisecracking at women on the street was wrong and sexist. But I did it anyway when I was with groups of other adolescent boys because I somehow felt I had to. I felt pressured to demonstrate sexual interest and prove my heterosexuality. Somewhere along the line I recognized that the implicit assumption in all that stuff is this: if you show us a slender thigh or reveal a bit of breast, not only do we salivate, we jump through hoops and instantly abandon our brains.

I resent that idea. I resent the notion that I can be manipulated that easily.

So now when I'm with other men and the commenting starts—"Will you look at the legs on that one!"—I try to respond with some version of "So what?" that will be heavier than a ton of bricks. It may be encouraging to your readers to know that most of the time this puts a stop to any further escalations of the commenting, either within the group or to the women. Everyone just goes back to doing what he was doing, and the moment passes.

Name Withheld
January 1982 Issue

When a reader looked for suggestions about how to deal with a more subtle kind of hassling, other readers—including Ms. *author Naomi Weisstein—had dozens of suggestions.*

I'm exasperated because of a particular problem I've encountered both at home and away: men who are not satisfied unless a woman is smiling, preferably at them. On countless occasions, I've had to respond (or not respond) to a persistent plea for "just a little smile, baby."

My insides churn whenever I'm chided for not putting on airs of carefree bliss and charm for someone I don't care about or even notice. During a recent trip, for example, I was having a drink alone at a table in the hotel bar. It was late in the evening; I was relaxing and enjoying the feeling of being detached yet among people. A man left his drinking companions and approached me with the line "I hate to see a lady so serious." I might have said, "Then life must be very difficult for you." But I didn't feel the need to explain my state of mind to this stranger. So I said, "You're bothering me. Please go away." He went back to his friends, but I was angry at him for disrupting my mood.

Why do some men find unsmiling women so threatening? Does anyone have a suggestion for an appropriate response?

Karen D. Sawitz
New York, New York
June 1981 Issue

Men find unsmiling women threatening because we don't fit their image of the subordinate, placating, feminine female. They are compelled to bully us into that role because it makes them feel more secure and powerful. No doubt, to the individual man, he thinks he is being friendly and that we should appreciate his attention. It's time he learned otherwise. The next time a man says, "I hate to see a lady so serious," tell him, "That's your problem."

Mary Louise Ho
York, England
July 5, 1981

Karen Sawitz's letter asks for suggestions for an appropriate response to the request from male anybodies that we smile. How about (preferably snarling), "Say something funny."

Naomi Weisstein
New York, New York
May 22, 1981

A reader recognized that another bit of typical male street behavior was really about power.

I just dashed out onto the busy streets of Boston to run an errand and was struck by an observation. Well-dressed businessmen traveling in twos and threes crowding the sidewalk expect "lessers" (read *women, racial* or *ethnic* minorities, less professionally dressed) to step aside and defer to them in using the crowded sidewalk space. I decided to practice being more aggressive (hard for me) and did not defer. These groups were irritated, surprised, and probably a few other things in realizing it was they who had to step aside. After all, who runs the world, controls the sidewalks, and isn't their ongoing conversation of great importance, et cêtera? Of course, common courtesy is that we all defer at times and share the space, but my tiny experiment was a real click.

Gail D. Hinand
Boston, Massachusetts
April 13, 1984

When, far from hassling, men showed real support, then there was something to cheer about.

How's this for progress? The route of the Boston Bonne Bell ten-kilometer road race—one of the largest women-only races in the world—passes the Massachusetts Institute of Technology. This year a group of fraternity men all wearing identical Greek-lettered T-shirts were out cheering and yelling encouragement, even to us slowpokes in the back of the pack. I can't tell you how it warmed my heart to see *frat men* on the sidelines cheering for female athletes. There is indeed hope!

Sharon Machlis Gartenberg
Marlborough, Massachusetts
January 1984 Issue

I had just finished signing up for jury duty and was going down the courthouse steps, attempting to avoid several leering construction workers. One worker mockingly shouted, "Hello. Good morning. Can't you even say, 'Good morning'?" Before I could yell a harsh reply, I heard another man saying to the worker, "Why don't you leave her alone?"

It made my day.

Donna Englund
Bronx, New York
December 1984 Issue

One of the more momentous changes that readers made in their lives came to be known as reentry—when a homemaker well along in her job of raising a family decides to reenter the paid work force, often first completing her education. The older, returning woman student became such a widespread pattern that the average age of the college student changed dramatically—37 percent of college students in 1983 were over the age of twenty-five, compared with 29 percent in 1973, according to the Census Bureau; and women, who were 40 percent of the older students in 1973, represented 55 percent ten years later. The world seemed surprisingly full of possibilities as more and more colleges and universities, preparing for the end of their baby-boom-induced prosperity, began to welcome these mature students.

I am a thirty-one-year-old mother with three children. I was married at sixteen and have been supporting these children for fourteen years as a waitress. Two years ago, when my youngest entered kindergarten, I enrolled in a junior college to obtain a long-desired college education. At that time, I was working full-time and going to school and trying to be a mother. Scholarships were unavailable to me because of my age.

When I was ready to transfer to a four-year college, I was referred to the Office of Continuing Education at Claremont Colleges in California. Through the efforts of that office I was considered for admittance to Harvey Mudd College, Claremont. I fully expected to get turned down. Surprise of my life! I was admitted, and the school granted me a three-thousand dollar scholarship. The first reaction of the other 424 students was "Are you really a student?" but they have accepted me and are most receptive.

I can only advise women in my situation to keep on trying. I knocked on a lot of doors before one opened for me.

Peggy Anschutz
Azusa, California
January 1974 Issue

Some women pursued life changes via less traditional routes.

Last winter I lived in a women's collective in a Brooklyn loft. Eight of us had journeyed from the Northwest to New York to participate in a loosely structured independent study program called Art Options in New York City. Each had her own interest: one worked on the genesis of an off-off-Broadway company; one painted; one wrote; one took daily voice lessons in her pursuit of an opera career; one's goal was architecture; one was a volunteer at the Brooklyn Museum. We ranged in age from twenty to seventy. All in all, our experiences were as diverse as they were meaningful and life changing. Woman's creative energy *is* one of the only goddamn energies around.

Vicky J. Frankfourth
Eagle River, Alaska
April 1978 Issue

Support of other women, whether through an organized collective or a more casual network, was critical to the success of many women reentering college or the workforce. Even with such support, the effort was heroic, particularly for single mothers.

I'm a thirty-year-old single parent with two children and in college with one quarter to a bachelor's and planning on two more years of college for a master's in social work. I'm being pulled apart by role conflict that is steadily increasing, and I'm not alone here—most of my women friends have similar problems. We're the result of all those glorious articles on "how I went back to college and found myself" that cropped up in every other magazine for several years. Well, let me tell you what it's like in the real world.

I decided to take a few courses at the local junior college. My marriage was going bad, and as a housewife, I needed some indication of my ability to make it outside the home. I quit college when I got a divorce, because I, my kids and I, needed to eat, so I took a ridiculously low paying job only to find that jobs and eating don't necessarily equate. I quit the job and went back to school, figuring that a few years of starving would pay off. Well, so much for naiveté. Community or junior colleges talk about continuing adult education, but that translates to adapting to veterans (almost exclusively male and with all that lovely government funding).

Fortunately, I have been able to seek out a small circle of women who are in a similar position to myself. We support one another by discussing our common problems, such as why children inevitably have a crisis at exam time. How do you relate to a professor that's younger than you are? How do you handle being a social misfit (being neither a housewife, career woman, young student, male, graduate student—they at least tend to be your age or close to it—swinging single, et cêtera). Why the dearth of role models, such as women professors, college administrators, et cêtera. How does one juggle a part-time job, child care, household responsibilities, financial worries, and studying, and still compete with students who don't have those problems? Why are the classes you *have* to take scheduled for 3:30 when your kids get home from school? Why does welfare (a lot of us are on it) deduct financial aid from your already pitifully small grant and treat you like a welfare fraud because you want a college degree rather than their trade-school offerings? Why don't professors catch on that you *cannot* leave a small child home alone when she's sick just because he's giving a mid-term? How will I pass this damn math course when my last math course was ten years ago and I've forgotten my multiplication tables?

How do you explain to the college clinic doctor at your required physical that you're not on a diet and not suffering from anorexia nervosa but that you figure that growing children need at least two meals a day and that means there is only enough food left for one meal for you? How do you handle being thirty and still asking yourself, "What do I want to be when I grow up?" Where do you get child care that you can afford? How do you explain to your kindergartner that you can't go to his class play because you have to retype the term paper he colored to make your teacher like it better? How will you pay off the eight thousand dollars in student loans you've accumulated when your starting salary will probably be only eight thousand to twelve thousand dollars a year anyway? Do you really think that it will be worth it?

Bloodied but unbowed, I'm already lining up *my* admiring throng for graduation; and thank you for reading my "true life" experience.

Name Withheld
February 18, 1978

I can see the problems with career, then marriage and family. Many of us, however, have tried it in reverse. I married at seventeen. My husband wanted to farm (cattle), and I wanted to be a homemaker. We had three children and worked very hard to build our farm business, which is successful. Now, at forty years of age, with no college training and little job experience, I realize my children are nearly grown. I also realize the farm business is my husband's life dream, not mine.

I now have a three-dollar-an-hour job running the service desk in a nearby discount store. I'd love to get a more meaningful job that paid more; this one seems a little ridiculous for a full partner in a 540-acre livestock operation, but it's a start. At least, when I go to work, I'm not "helping" someone else—*I'm doing it!* It's pride we need perhaps more than what others may consider success.

Mary Alice Jett
Liking, Missouri
February 16, 1978

I've been going solo for nine years now. I have five children. I started college when I was thirty-nine and have been going full time, including summers, almost continuously for the last eleven years. (I am now fifty.)

I am currently trying to work on my dissertation on the effects of chronic illness on children. And therein lies the problem.

I cannot be gainfully employed, because the dissertation is so time-consuming. I have no income other than the small amount of child support for the two teenagers I still have responsibility for. My father, who for the last two years has helped me financially, very reluctantly has said he no longer wants to, "because it's not right." A male friend, who makes about $125,000 a year, told me that what I'm doing is "stupid," because I can't afford it.

I find myself so *angry* now. It has been so *hard.* I've been on welfare and food stamps; I've run up twenty-eight thousand dollars in student loans and cannot borrow any more because I'm over the limit, and I have no idea where I can get the money to support myself and my family while I finish my work on my Ph.D.

I am so stressed by my financial situation that the academic stress seems almost insignificant. It must be so goddamn *easy* to do what I'm doing if one has the money with which to pay the mortgage and to buy the food for the family. Or to have a mate that takes care of these things.

I'm not sure how much better I feel since writing this letter.

Name Withheld
November 10, 1980

A reader wrote about what she thought might seem a small step to others but one that transformed her life. Another found inspiration simply from a chance encounter on the street.

You asked for other women's experiences of traveling alone. Here is mine. It wasn't much, I guess. But to me, it was the beginning of everything.

After graduating from college, I went By Myself to Strasbourg, France, to travel a little, study a little, and decide whether or not I could make it On My Own. I had recently received my first serious marriage proposal from a man I only Liked but who I knew would Take Care of Me. (Yes, I know better than to write in capitals, but Some Things in my life are just that important.)

I knew no one in Europe. I was not already enrolled in school there. No one was expecting me. I had no place to live. I had a limited budget (saved from my summer job and borrowed from my surprisingly understanding mother). I had never traveled alone before except on the three-hour train trip to Chicago. I had never been more than a half day's drive from my family and friends. I had never flown in a plane. I didn't know if my college French would be understood by Real Frenchmen.

Okay, so I only made three short, safe side trips during my three and a half months in Strasbourg. So most of the people I made friends with were other American students. So I was not Adventurous. But I went. I communicated. I negotiated hotel bills, claimed replacements for damaged luggage, translated train schedules, bought my own food. And quite simply, the trip Changed My Life. It was the scariest, most assertive thing I have ever done.

And in the nine years since, I have faced every difficult or demanding situation (moving far from my family, getting dumped by my first real love, changing careers, recovering from an operation I couldn't Tell My Parents About, taking my Ph.D. orals, fighting the first stages of alcoholism) by telling myself that if I could go to Europe, Alone under those conditions, I can do anything. And I can.

Name Withheld
July 10, 1980

After a fatiguing but exciting week with friends in upstate New York, I found myself carting an impossible suitcase, sleeping bag, duffel bag, and coat along a dark, cheerless tunnel from the subway to Penn Station in New York City. My main concerns were that my arms not fall out of their sockets before I got to my train and that I not tarry long to rest because the atmosphere down there is not the most congenial.

Many men passed me hurriedly. Finally, as I was about to sink into the pavement, I heard a voice saying, "Let me help you with that load!"

The man I expected to see turned out to be a pert, young workingwoman who jauntily took part of my load as she and I continued in the 9:00 A.M. rush to work.

We *are* strong, in more ways than just the physical.

Julie Rogers
Washington, D.C.
August 1975 Issue

Women finding their physical strength—and with it, both camaraderie and independence—was often the occasion of a letter to Ms.

In March of this year, six women met on a field in Austin, Texas, to learn to play soccer. Because of the enthusiasm of those women and the perseverance of Sally James, our instigator, the group grew from six to one hundred in only a few months. Now we are preparing for our first league season. This fall we will field six teams.

We are not professionals, nor are we highly trained young amateurs who have spent their whole lives working at a sport. Most of us had never played soccer before this year. We represent no particular group, such as a certain age group or school. We range in age from about eighteen to thirty-five and in profession from secretaries to law students to poets to landscape architects to ballerinas. And we are free to experiment with different types of organization and philosophies about sport. For example, we have decided that everyone who wants to play can play. Virtually everyone who plays with us returns, perhaps because of the camaraderie or perhaps because of the nature of soccer, which is very much a team sport, requiring agility and thinking, rather than strength or size.

Linda Cangelosi
Austin, Texas
August 29, 1974

Of course, some letters recorded plans or situations where change seemed impossible.

There are times when I feel that the only interest the women's movement has in women on welfare is the Hyde amendment [a legislative maneuver in Congress used by Representative Henry Hyde of Illinois and others to deny federal funding for abortion]. Our problem is one of very basic survival in a society that cares little about whether or not our children eat.

In the city of New York, the benefits for a family of two on welfare are as follows: housing allotment, $183 per month; food and clothing allotment, $150 per month; food stamps, $65 per month.

Recently, I was forced to move from my previous apartment ($195 per month in rent) because of co-opting. Welfare provides no allotment for moving expenses and no aid in finding another dwelling.

I managed to find, after much hysteria and accosting of strangers on the streets, an apartment a block and a half from where I was living. A one-bedroom apartment for $285.68 per month, quite a coup according to most people. Welfare, however, was not as impressed. They told me that the rent was far too high and that I would have to find another apartment, or they would have to punish me by taking away my housing allotment. So I had to get friends to say that they are paying the difference of $102.68 a month so that I wouldn't be ultimately thrown off welfare. If that weren't enough, food stamps slapped me on the wrists for paying such an outrageous amount of rent and cut my supply from $65 per month to $34 a month.

So between paying approximately $30 a month to Con Edison and $285.68 in rent to the landlord, I freeload every month on $34 in food stamps and $17.32 in cash, to use as recklessly and wantonly as I choose. Just to show that desperation is the mother of ingenuity, I wrote to several pro life groups, but as of yet I haven't received a check in the mail for this child they were so anxious for me to have.

I am quite sure that I don't have to go into the problems of "adequate" child care and low wages for women. If I work, I can't get Medicaid coverage—my son has a heart condition and needs continual medical care. I am thirty-two years old, white, and from an upper-middle-class background. I am at a crossroads in my life, and I'm only one of the many welfare mothers who feel left out and forgotten.

Name Withheld
April 1981 Issue

Much correspondence in the Letters column had to do with living with the choices women were making. Being single, for example, was becoming a viable option, and many readers responded to an evocative article of October 1982 by Mary Helen Washington, "Working at 'Single Bliss.'" But most readers agreed with Amanda Spake in her November 1984 cover story, "Going Solo," the choice was not without its costs.

I am thirty-seven years old, I earn about twenty-five thousand dollars a year. I am joyful, powerful, strong and *privileged* to be single. People love me, and I love them. I graduated from college on the dean's list when I was in my early thirties.

I can still recall thinking about marriage as a child and getting a blank picture.

Later, of course, I expected to get married, because that was expected of me and that was all there was. But I have only really wanted to be married twice in my life. The first time was when I was broke, had no job, no car, and life looked dim indeed. The next time was when I was recovering from a rape and injuries from the rape. I needed "a man" to take care of me.

The cost of being single is that there is more loneliness. But when facing the costs, the price tends to diminish over time. As I have lived single I become less lonely, less dissatisfied. I love silences and stillness; I also love festivity and friendship. When I was growing up in my family I was even lonelier. Nothing is more lonely than being alone among people.

Name Withheld
November 10, 1984

As much as women continued to depend on the sustaining force of female friendship, many readers appreciated honesty about the limits of such a relationship. One reader found that an August 1983 article by Bebe Moore Cambell, "Friendship in Black and White," "eased a longtime hurt."

I met Janet during my freshman year in college, and after much looking each other over, we became friends. Despite our diverse backgrounds—me, middle-class black raised in Harlem; she, an upper-middle-class jew raised in Shaker Heights—we had a lot of common ground. I recall a roast-beef dinner when I was in a financial depression, seafood crepes on my birthday, and terse advice but a safe place to stay when I was emotionally torn apart after my first real relationship ended. I always knew I could get an objective opinion if I asked for one and only an "Oh, Kathy" when I did something she thought dumb. Janet showed me a different world through books she gave me (which came complete with her critique of each), through her friends, and glimpses of her life in her conversations.

Janet decided to go home and attend law school. I visited her there once, met her parents, and visited her friends. She commented on how at ease I made her parents feel, as I was the first black person they had ever entertained at home, and how proud she was of all of us. Then I never heard from Janet again—no card, no call, no letters, and mine to her were never returned.

After reading the article, I think I understand why it all ended. I was literally the only black person in her whole social circle, and maybe there was no place for me in her new life. I just wished we could have discussed it openly. It wouldn't have made the hurt any less, only bearable.

Name Withheld
November 1983 Issue

Readers who wondered whether things were really changing had often only to recall their own past experiences.

In 1966, one week of our freshman general physical-education class was spent teaching us *how to walk*. There I was, eighteen years old, being taught "to walk like a lady." As I crossed the gym, feeling ridiculous and decidedly unladylike due to my rather athletic, natural gait, I fell and sprained my ankle. As far as I know, I'm the only one to have failed the walking test at the University of Tennessee.

Anne Griffith
Freeport, Illinois
June 1984 Issue

When I was a young housewife and mother, I told someone who inquired that I kept my hair set in curlers all day long because "how I look only matters when my husband comes home at night"—thus disregarding my own self-image and how my children or anyone else perceived me.

I blush to think of it still—twenty-five years later.

Joan Benedix
Rhinebeck, New York
November 12, 1984

One reader, inspired by an August 1983 essay by Caroline Bird, "Growing Up to Be a 'Salty Old Woman,' " looks ahead confidently to her own future.

On my wall, I have a hand-lettered saying, "I want to be an outrageous old woman who is never accused of being an Old Lady. I want to get leaner and meaner, sharp edged, color of the earth, 'til I discorporate from sheer *joy!*"

I copied it from a woman who cop. ed it from a woman who copied it . . . there are a lot of us out there preparing to keep Caroline Bird company.

Roberta Parry
Teaneck, New Jersey
November 1983 Issue

II

The Workplace Revolution

❧

When Ms. began publishing in 1972, some thirty-three-and-a-half million women were working outside their homes—enough, certainly, so that the work force and what it was like to be out there in it was of primary concern to Ms. writers and readers. But by the end of 1984, fifty million women were employed: a 47 percent increase since Ms. began. Of all women in the United States, 54 percent now work outside the home. And younger women, those in their twenties and thirties, are in the work force in numbers nearly as great as are men of comparable age. (Rosemary L. Bray, "The New Economy of Women Wage Earners"; John Naisbitt and Patricia Aburdene in an interview by Gloria Steinem, "Here Come the New Megatrends," Ms. July 1985.) While opponents of the Equal Rights Amendment worried noisily that feminists were plotting to force women out of their homes and into paying jobs, the women's work force revolution was occurring rapidly—and our needs and expectations were changing as quickly as our lives.

First, however, we had to understand what exactly we meant by work. Women who chose to be homemakers and raise children full time began to assert the obvious: what they did was work, even though it didn't show up in the gross national product. An early seventies demand of the National Organization for Women and other groups was that a woman's work as a housewife be recognized as having economic value. But as one reader explained, it wasn't that simple.

Rather than hire a housekeeper and baby sitter for our three preschool children, my husband and I decided to "hire" me—to pay me a salary and contribute social security. The Internal Revenue Service said nay; this can only be done for someone not a family member. We tried to contract for disability insurance for me—in the event of my not being able to perform my housekeeping and child-care duties—but we have not yet found a carrier. I am not adding to the family income—and he cannot be compensated for a loss that does not exist.

The implication is clear—the establishment is making it more attractive to leave the home and let others raise their families. So I went job hunting. Results: very few jobs open in my field; higher salaries for men of the same background; hesitation to hire a woman with three "little ones" because I might not be dependable (miss work). Let's find out why men with families are considered good, stable, desirable employees and women are not.

Mary Fortuna
Philadelphia, Pennsylvania
February 1973 Issue

Whatever the difficulties, readers felt free to experiment with what had been accepted as traditional work roles for women—and for men—even if their communities weren't quite ready for these changes.

Two years ago my husband had a very lucrative job, and I brought in a little extra money working part time. Our combined income was great, but there was a problem—my husband was burning himself out. Beset with deadlines and frustration, he was nervous and ill-tempered. All our income wasn't worth a damn, because we couldn't enjoy it. So after much talk and some ego deflating, we switched. Now he is working part time in a low-pressure job, and I have taken a high-pressure job, which I really like. We have been at this for about two years, and we are both very pleased with the arrangement.

Rachel Whitefield Evans
Corpus Christi, Texas
August 1974 Issue

I work part time at a gas station in Oakland. I pump gas, wash windows, put air in tires, check and charge batteries, check transmissions, change oil, hub jobs, and other basic things. I don't claim to be a mechanic; I'm not. But I'm getting a little tired of *women* asking me to get "one of the men" to check their tires, water, and oil. I have been trained on the job to do these things. Men seem to trust and accept my service much more willingly than the women. One woman asked me to check her transmission. I did and found that she was completely empty and suggested she add a quart of transmission fluid. She didn't believe me and asked that I get "one of the men" to check it out. So I did, and he told her the same thing. This happens every day. I wish there was something that could be done. It is hard enough for women to seek positions in fields that are dominated by men without having to deal with mistrust and lack of support from other women.

Name Withheld
September 1973

Good news! The status of women employed by the United States government in Grand Teton National Park has improved. This year, for the first time, the park has employed a woman truck driver, an all-female back-country trail crew, a female rock-climbing ranger, and a woman campground ranger; women also hold positions as general laborers, rangers, park aides, and naturalists. This group of women is the largest ever employed by the park.

I understand that several other parks are watching our back-country trail crew to view its success. So far, I am pleased to say, *everyone* is rather surprised and extremely happy with our work. We have changed many doubtful minds.

Janet Ellis
Moose, Wyoming
December 1974 Issue

Women, many of whom were moving in greater and greater numbers into corporate jobs, had the protection of civil-rights laws passed in the sixties and expanded in the early seventies. Though wage discrimination was illegal—and equal pay for equal work was a widely accepted principle— women still earned an average of fifty-nine cents on the dollar earned by men, a statistic that would hold steadily enough throughout the seventies to be emblazoned on its own protest button. (A green and white button, which simply read 59¢, was put out by the National Commission on Working Women to galvanize support in the struggle against wage discrimination.) In a December 1972 article ("Is Money the Root of All Freedom?"), Carolyn Bird compared actual salaries in a wide variety of jobs where men still earned more than women. But one of her case histories wrote to argue that the issue was more complicated than direct job discrimination.

I am the woman, Wharton M. B. A., placed at thirteen thousand dollars into the personnel department of a commercial bank in New York while my fellow graduate student (male) became a loan officer at fourteen thousand dollars. Ms. Bird implies that it was the bank that made this sex-biased decision. In fact, it was I—coming of age in a work environment that taught me that women belonged in "people-oriented" jobs—who chose personnel as my field; I interviewed for personnel jobs and deserved what I got—a lower salary and a bad job.

Certainly, hiring and salary discrimination do exist, but so do socialization and learned roles. The situation will change only when we women are ready to accept partial responsibility for it.

Incidentally, I have left the commercial bank, and personnel, probably, for Wall Street. The fourteen thousand dollar loan officer, if I have identified him correctly, was fired.

Kate Grimes
New York, New York
March 1973 Issue

It occurred to me the other day to wonder at the discrepancy in wages that I pay to those high-school students who baby sit and those who do lawn cutting and gardening for me. Most of the "lawn and garden" people, who happen to be boys, ask for a dollar an hour. Most of the baby sitters, who usually happen to be girls, ask seventy-five cents an hour.

Now I ask myself, is caring for my children less important, less valuable, less a responsibility? Or is lawn cutting and gardening considered harder and more taxing physical work? (Two active children under five can be pretty hard, taxing, physical work, too.) Or is it that boys just ask for and receive high wages from the beginning? And is it that child care is, anyway, considered to be "women's work" and not deserving of pay? Click!

Marge Mitchell
Baltimore, Maryland
September 1974 Issue

Job division by gender started early, as Ms. *readers reported, and had a long history.*

In Hawthorne, Nevada (population 5,995), Halloween pumpkins were given to each student in the third-grade class of the Hawthorne Primary School.

All the girls in the class got to clean out the pumpkins, and all the boys got to make the faces on the pumpkins.

"Clicklet"?

Faith Greaves
Reno, Nevada
March 1973 Issue

Recently, I was visiting my eighty-two- and eighty-six--year-old parents. My father was in the process of sorting through an old box of letters. My father's aunt Emma received a letter from an individual named Eunice on September 2, 1883. We were unable to come up with a last name; however, I do know that Eunice was a Baptist and that she was much into saving "souls." We were able to surmise that Eunice was not married and approximately in her early thirties:

> I don't know as they would hire a woman teacher in the winter, yet I think if one would teach cheaper, she would stand a chance of getting the school. I won't teach cheaper just because I'm a woman, so I should probably be considered as very wicked & mercenary if I wanted $1.25 a day & my board, the same as they would pay some inferior sort of creature, who has the good fortune to be of the masculine gender, & just education enough to know that there is such a gender.

It is so unfortunate that we will never be able to talk to this woman nor to her friend my great-aunt Emma.

Marjorie Wagner Chodack
Ravena, New York
November 28, 1979

While many women pursued M. B. A. degrees and corporate careers, and others braved the nontraditional world as mechanics, craftspeople, factory workers, and laborers, the world of paid work as a whole remained remarkably segregated. Named the "pink collar workforce" in a book by Louise Kapp Howe excerpted in the March 1977 Ms., 80 percent of women worked at what was traditionally "women's work"—as secretaries, nurses, waitresses, sales clerks, phone operators, flight attendants, and other jobs generally low in pay and status. As a result, pay equity was to become what many would call the job issue of the eighties for women and a priority for unionized women. But first, like homemakers, the 80 percenters began to fight the stereotypes that plagued them. One reader, Pamela Meyer, a nurse from Mount Carmel, Illinois, showed how long such attitudes had existed by sending this quote from Florence Nightingale: "No man, not even a doctor, ever gives any other definition of what a nurse should be than this: 'devoted and obedient.' This definition would do just as well for a porter. It might even do for a horse." Another reader, thanking us for two August 1973 features on nursing by Trucia D. Kushner and Bonnie Johnson, reported the resilience of that attitude.

Thanks so much for finally helping me with my conflict between feminism and nursing. Until I read your articles, I was almost embarrassed to tell my "liberated" sisters that I was "just a nurse."

At the diploma school I attended for three years, the almost medieval practice of instilling a feeling of servitude remains. We were taught never to interpret doctors' "orders," to realize our "limited ability," to accept being scapegoats for the doctors' anger and incompetence, and even how to blush coyly at the lewd jokes and pinches. (After all, you've heard about student nurses, haven't you?) My parents, relying on old stereotypes, talked proudly about the "noble profession," "job insurance in case anything happened to your husband," becoming a "better homemaker," and of course, "marrying well—preferably a doctor."

I've finally gotten out of the subservient, empty-headed, physically exhausting role of the gentle, sacrificing, sexy but dumb nurse. The support and encouragement you've given me have helped me to be comfortable in my profession as well as in my womanhood.

Barbara Hurwitz, R.N.
Bethel, Alaska
November 1973 Issue

I have been working for six years in a suburban law office in New Jersey, where the staff consists of seven secretaries (female) and four lawyers (male). It has always been the custom in this office for each "girl" to have her turn at "kitchen duty." She is expected to set the table in the library with dainty place mats, napkins, spoons, and eatables (such as crackers, which the firm finances) and to make coffee. At twelve o'clock everyone in the office, including the lawyers (if they are so inclined), comes into the library, and we all have lunch. Afterward, the woman who has kitchen duty for the day wipes up the table and washes the dishes, including the lunch containers that each person brings in.

I participated unwillingly in this program for six years. Three weeks ago I decided that I had had it and announced that I was no longer to be given kitchen duty; that I would go out for lunch some of the time and when I had lunch in, I'd do my own dishes.

To say that my announcement caused a sensation is to put it mildly. At present, none of the women is speaking to me except when absolutely necessary in the course of work. I have been told by one of the lawyers that no one can understand my attitude and that the women (and, I assume, he) have completely lost respect for me.

I have taken a stand. How it will turn out, I have no idea.

Name Withheld
March 1978 Issue

The other day I was on the phone with National Car Rental making a reservation. The woman said, "May I have your first name?" And I said, "My last name is Welsh."

And she said, "I can't accept that; I need your first name." And I said, "Why?" And she said, *"So I'll know who to ask for when I call back."* She actually said that! And I said, as calmly as possible, "You can ask for Ms. Welsh."

When she called back, she did ask for Ms. Welsh. How many of these little battles do all secretaries fight each day? Maybe in a hundred years we'll recondition the business world, but not if we don't keep fighting the little daily battles.

Cheryl Welsh
New York, New York
August 31, 1978

As one reader pointed out, it wasn't only the pink collar worker with whom all assumed a first-name relationship.

San Francisco's mayors have been well known. Mayor Shelley, Mayor Alioto; Mayor Moscone, now everyone's favorite city is run by Dianne. Just like Kathy in Houston succeeding Mayor Hofheintz, and Jane fills the office of Chicago's Mayor Daley.*

It's another manifestation of "keeping women in their place."

Name Withheld
January 15, 1983

This secretary found a terrific way to claim her own identity.

Ms. readers who are secretaries may be interested in my daily assertiveness practice, which never fails to give me a boost. I type my initials in upper case next to the upper-case initials of those of the originator's at the bottom of whatever correspondence it might be. Small, but daily.

Kay Kavanagh
Oak Park, Illinois
April 1982 Issue

*Referring, of course, to Dianne Feinstein, Kathy Whitmire, and Jane Byrne.

It got harder and harder throughout the seventies to assume anything about all women in an office setting. And as one reader pointed out in 1981, the same held true for hospitals.

In the middle of an operation today, I looked around the room—to my first assistant, my scrub nurse, and circulating nurse, the anesthesia doctor, nurse anesthetist, and the patient—and suddenly realized that we were performing major surgery, and there was not a man in the room!

Martha L. Hurley, M.D.
Kansas City, Missouri
February 1981 Issue

Stereotypes were not the only thing that pink collar women organized to fight. "Bread and Roses" was a time-honored rallying cry, and women office workers organized first into lobbying and support groups and then into a national union, 9 to 5: National Organization of Working Women, where wages and issues such as sexual harassment and job safety could be addressed. Nurses, too, demanded that they be treated as the highly trained health professionals that they were.

As a nurse working in the operating room, I can't remember the number of times that I have cleaned the furniture in the operating suite, prepared the operating table for the next case, carried heavy equipment to the operating rooms, and rolled recovery-room beds through the corridors when I should have been interviewing and giving emotional support to the next apprehensive patient awaiting her or his operation. This *is*, after all, the real purpose of my being there.

I believe that hospitals should be in the hands of physicians and nurses, not businessmen.

Leigh Wilson Miles, R.N.
Bronx, New York
August 1983 Issue

I finally got up the courage to challenge an old established male tradition in my office. I do telephone sales. Our working area in the office has always been covered with "girlie" pictures and photographs of devastating (and devastated) maidens. This made us few women in the office feel terribly uncomfortable.

When the majority of the male staff was out to lunch, we proceeded to rape the latest issue of *Playgirl* of its best. Over my desk now hangs one gorgeous specimen of the male species, the centerfold. Everywhere there was a girlie picture there are now beautiful stud photographs.

I think the reactions of the men in the office could best be summarized in terms of shock. Although everyone tried to be good humored about it, jokingly or otherwise, they all compared themselves in some way to the models. It was a marvelous experience to see super-duper macho stud types go all to pieces when confronted with the same thing we have had to face for years—images of ourselves as we could never hope to be, images of ourselves as seen only in the minds of men.

Name Withheld
October 13, 1975

The cartoon images of the lecherous patient and the sexy nurse or the boss chasing the secretary around the desk were depressingly familiar, but sexual harassment was a form of job discrimination that few women in the work force escaped altogether. Groups organized "speak-outs," a protest and consciousness-raising technique long used in the women's movement to allow women to share experiences, and the tactic worked to call attention to sexual harassment as it had before with issues such as rape and wife abuse.

Eight years ago I had just graduated from high school and was working as a maid in a motel for the summer. My closest friend also worked at the motel, which was managed by his cousin. I spent the summer trying to do my job as I fought off the sexual advances of the manager, who wanted me to engage in oral sex and inter-course. I was seventeen, naive, and scared. I wondered if I had done anything to entice him. I felt totally alone. I had no idea that other women had similar experiences. I felt powerless. If I quit my job, I might not have found another, and then I would not have the money I needed for college. I worked all summer, hoping that he would not overpower me, and I kept my secret to myself. I was relieved beyond words when the summer ended.

Name Withheld
October 30, 1977

Support groups, speak-outs, working-women networks, and union orga-
nizing were all ways that women found to reinforce each other in the
workplace. Sometimes casual street encounters were encouraging enough
for Ms. *readers to want to share them.*

One day last week I pulled up to a four-way stop in my taxi. At one of the other stop signs sat a police officer in a chase cruiser, and at the third, a telephone installer in a Bell Canada van. What made the occasion memorable was the fact that all three of us were women. We celebrated with much joyful laughter and raised thumbs.

Jill Wood
Toronto, Ontario, Canada
November 1980 Issue

A small pickup truck pulled up outside the restaurant where I was recently having lunch. I noticed the words, Todd and Daughters painted on the door of the truck. When the two riders came in, I had to ask whether Daughters was the surname of a partner or whether the partners were really the daughters of Todd. One of the men said Todd had no sons; his three daughters were his business partners, and he listed the company as such.

Hooray!

Josephine Cerasani
New York, New York
May 1976 Issue

I am an independent nineteen-year-old woman. Last year I landed in a backward, transient community in central Washington. Being completely alone and living in my car, I decided the best thing to do in my financially insecure situation was to put in job applications around town.

A month later I got a job at an apple-dehydrating plant. Of course, I wanted to "move up" from cutting rotten spots out of apples. I got as far as cleaning the floor and scraping trays when the factory shut down for that season. The mechanics (as well as everyone else) really laughed at me when they discovered that my bid was in for mechanic trainee. They made jokes about my tits getting caught in the peeling machine. Because I wanted the job badly enough, I got a bra.

This year the factory called me back in the fall. Because of my mechanic trainee bid, I was offered a newly created job as a process maintenance operator at $4.16 per hour! It shocked a lot of people, especially the women who have been there for many seasons, but it has also inspired several of them to "move up." We now have two women forklift drivers. My foreman would always check on me, but I think he respects me now, because my shift usually produces the most.

The factory I work in is operating about five months per season. So I am also struggling to become a seasonal construction laborer. I went to construction school for six weeks. I was the second woman to attend, and it was nondiscriminatory right down to coed roommates. I can operate pick hammers, wall breakers, lay sewer lines, sandblast, do any concrete work, and build forms. I can also operate concrete cutters, acetylene torches, compressors, compactors, chipping guns, chain saws, and more.

I'm not trying to prove anything. I'm only in it for the money. Even as a child, I didn't feel limited mentally or physically. So maybe I'm more fortunate than some of my sisters who were raised on the American dream. Let us throw that dream away, start something healthy, and reach our true potential!

Suzanne Scommodau
Wenatchee, Washington
July 1976 Issue

With more and more women supporting families as single parents, the main attraction of nontraditional work was the pay. One reader wrote at three-thirty in the morning to tell us how she and her family were getting along. She asked us to withhold her name, because "my company is large and well known and I am small, struggling, and very traceable."

I work in a power plant—one of two women among twenty-eight men. Day after day I work with the last of the Neanderthals. I've been schooled, tested, and I've proved myself more than once; still the majority of my fellow "fellows" continue to degrade, ridicule, and put me down. (The rites of passage on the men working their way up is also degrading, but not to near the same extent.) Each day is like going into battle. I work on a rotating shift with lots of overtime, and days off come infrequently. I'm making good pay (for any person—twelve dollars per hour) at a "man's job."

I'm divorced and without any child support to speak of (an occasional fifty dollars every couple of months) for my two children, a thirteen-year-old son and a three-year-old daughter. My dear son has taken on the role of tending his sister, watching the house, making meals, et cêtera with such aplomb that I feel proud to say he's my child. (Each summer he gets a temporary reprieve by going back east to visit my understanding parents. He and his sister are there currently.) There is one week each month when I barely see him, other than to say, "Hi" and have a short summary of the past day's happenings. I pity the men at work who have their little false sense of pity for me. They've never had the kind of relationship with anyone in their families that I've had the pleasure of experiencing with my children.

At times, I do get totally depressed and want to buckle under to their pressure—but with a little help from my friends I always get a second wind and go back. My hands are rough, I smoke way too much, and my love life is virtually nonexistent, but I enjoy my work. My few male supporters are ardent, and hopefully one day my son will be in their ranks in the work force and he'll support his female peers. I may not be making "herstory" yet, but in my own small way I feel I'm changing at least a few men's preconceived notions. I'll keep on plugging (under rapid fire)—thank you for doing the same.

Name Withheld
November 1984 Issue

Most women who stayed home no longer thought of themselves as "just a housewife." And when a Ms. *author inadvertently wrote something that seemed to slight a homemaker, we heard about it. A 1979 article reported a research finding that women who work outside the home are less likely to be sick than women who don't. This reader didn't like the suggestion that women in the work force simply didn't have time to be sick.*

Any woman who has worked both outside and in the home will tell you who it is who doesn't have the time to be sick: there is scarcely a job in the world that won't wait just one day while you get over the flu—except that of being a mother.

For ten hours a week, I teach college English at a state jail; this affords me lots of prestige, because people (correctly) assume that college teaching is a job that demands a high level of ingenuity, commitment, education, and love. For five or six hours a week, whenever I can find the time, I write; this affords me lots of prestige, because people (correctly) assume that writing is a job that demands a high level of ingenuity, commitment, education, and love. For 168 hours a week, I am the mother of a two-and-a-half-year-old child; for this I receive virtually no prestige, despite the fact that parenting is a job that demands a high level of ingenuity, commitment, education, and love.

Come *on*, you guys.

H. Nancy Spector
Juneau, Alaska
September 1979 Issue

Once we got used to the idea that homemaking was a job, some readers began looking at their working conditions in a new way.

I thought that most of my clicks were behind me, but tonight, as I cleared the table, I had a new one. I was complimenting myself (since no one else had) on a meal I'd gone to some trouble to prepare. I began to wonder why so many of us wait trembling for "the verdict" at every meal; why my mother and so many others risk antagonizing their families by having the gall to ask outright if everything is okay.

I decided it's not just neurosis. We really know they're judging even when they don't say so. Housewifing is an occupation in which every single waking act is judged by the person who means the most to you in the world. Is the house clean? Is the food good? Was it too expensive? Are the children well behaved?

A thousand times a day our contracts come up for renewal. No wonder our nerves are shot.

Kathleen Phillips Satz
El Cerrito, California
November 1982 Issue

A working condition that hasn't changed for homemakers is the career's poor job security. Many readers wrote in reaction to a milestone article by Barbara Ehrenreich and Karin Stallard published in the Ms. *Tenth Anniversary Issue, July/August 1982, which analyzed a newly discovered phenomenon, the feminization of poverty—that if current trends continue, by the year 2000, virtually all of the nation's poor will be women and their children. (This finding was in a report by the National Advisory Council on Economic Opportunity, written by Harriette McAdoo and Diana Pearce.)*

"The Nouveau Poor" hit me at a precipitous moment. I read it the day before my mother went to court to involuntarily end a thirty-year marriage. My mother spent twenty years of that marriage at home raising three children; then, just when the college tuition and the other debts were finally paid off, my father decided to share his income (and himself) not with her, but with a woman fifteen years his junior.

Because my parents reside in a "no-fault divorce" state, my mother was entitled to virtually nothing. Every attorney she consulted told her she had no right to my father's considerable assets. He has these assets because for thirty years he had a wife to raise his children, make his meals, clean his house, and provide support so that he could go out and earn a living. In the eyes of the law, however, this "women's work" is worth nothing. My mother, along with many other women, has become one of the nouveau poor.

If we do anything in the next ten years, it must be to fight for the legal guarantee that our work and our daughters' work (whether in or out of the home) will be valued.

Name Withheld
November 1982 Issue

Women in poverty or just above the poverty line were all too dependent on shrinking government programs—a constriction that became truly frightening for many when the Reagan administration took office in the eighties. But one critical need of women workers was barely addressed at all by either Republicans or Democrats in the seventies and eighties: child care. Once Richard Nixon vetoed a comprehensive child-care bill that passed the Senate and the House of Representatives in 1971, women were very nearly on their own. It took until the mid eighties before another major child-care measure—in the form of unpaid leave for parents— began to make headway in Congress.

Several years ago I was working for Los Angeles County in the Department of Public Social Services (welfare) as a supervisor in charge of fifteen to thirty women and men. Although my supervisor (the *big* boss) was a woman, with children, who had "come up through the ranks," she seemed to have no sympathy or understanding for the average working woman. Perhaps she was trying to impress *her* bosses by her strict adherence to rules.

Whatever the reason, I, as the first-line supervisor, was required to dock employees when they were late even fifteen minutes; to "gram" them (give written warnings) when they were absent without a doctor's excuse; to "counsel" them about excessive tardiness and absences; and to include in written evaluations, submitted every six weeks, a summary of every instance of tardiness or absence and what was done about it (never mind that this left the supervisor little time to supervise).

My supervisor always said she preferred working with men. They were more reliable. And it's true that the men who worked with me *did not* have records of excessive tardiness and absences similar to the women's, although they, too, had children. I'll bet you can guess who did stay home.

I finally quit my supervisory job because I could not continue what I felt was unjust harassment of working mothers. Of course, that did not improve the situation. So what is the solution? Child care for sick children is a serious problem.

Cassie Annschild
Portland, Oregon
January 1979 Issue

Some creative solutions were being developed. A reader wrote about one such program in Tucson, Arizona, which addressed not only the child-care problem, but the growing "displaced homemakers" issue, a cause that had been identified by advocates such as Tish Sommers and Laurie Shields of the Older Women's League—unfortunately, the Tucson program depended on federal CETA funding, which was ended shortly afterward.

Jackie Anderson at Tucson Association of Child Care has put together a pilot program where she trains qualified people to care for sick children whose parents are working. After *six weeks of training* under R.N.s and Red Cross, I became a mini–Pedi [pediatric] Nurse to aid parents during working hours—all at a cost of two dollars per *day*. Aides get paid by CETA and other funding.

The job makes up for *so much* for me—keeps me from getting lonesome for my grandchildren, and I can make ends meet. (My husband asked for a divorce to marry a younger woman ten years ago after twenty-three years of married life and working hard to help him get to the top. I was lost—like so many others I read and hear about, I am a "displaced homemaker.")

This pilot program has vast opportunities for a lot of us over forty and fifty years.

Helen Fraser Cree
Tucson, Arizona
April 1981

Reentry into the work force—whether after divorce or after child rearing—was a common experience and one that many Ms. *readers shared. One reader responded to a personal story by Carol Rinzler, "How to Be the Oldest Kid in Your Law School Class," February 1979, with the warning, "Just wait and see how well you like being the oldest kid applying for a job in a law firm as a first-year associate!"*

I'm a forty-three-year-old third-year law student out pounding the streets for a job next year. I was formerly a successful professional administrator, was actively involved in my community, and have successfully raised three children, who are now out of the "nest." I've done well at law school. *And* I've been turned down for jobs by *thirty* law firms.

The "reasons" for my mass rejections are just another variant of the old "You're overqualified for the job, my dear" routine.

1. *You will not be able to fit in with the other first-year associates.* This totally ignores the fact that I have managed to "fit in" with 250 classmates, most of whom are the same age as my eldest child. I go to parties, participate in study groups, play tennis, et cêtera with them just fine.

2. *You will expect a higher salary and faster promotions.* Just because I am the same age as (or older than) most of the partners doesn't mean that I think I can practice law the way they do after twenty-plus years of experience. I am eager and willing to work hard and long hours to learn—if someone would give me the chance.

3. *You are too sophisticated and self-confident.* One of my all time favorites. If that means I should dress dowdy and take off my makeup and speak only when spoken to—well, no thanks, I wouldn't last a week without my mascara. I can't relearn to be scared. It took me twenty years to learn not to be.

4. *You make people think you're going to come in like gangbusters and reorganize the whole place.* In short, a wave maker. Well, what do you say to that?

5. *Why don't you specialize in tax, trusts and wills, or real estate?* Because I want to practice civil litigation and labor work, which just happen to be the strongest bastions of male exclusivity in the profession.

What it comes down to is that you and I don't fit the mold of newly graduated lawyers which has dominated the legal-apprentice system for hundreds of years. We are not quivering in awe and/or groveling in terror. We may know their wives—and know about their mistresses. Our children may go to college with their children.

I'm still job hunting. I was even going to tell them that I am part American Indian—until I remembered that law firms are not equal-opportunity employers.

Name Withheld
March 5, 1979

Among women in academia, fighting job discrimination was a long and difficult battle. Though affirmative-action measures were required on campus—since almost all colleges and universities received some federal funding—such laws were hard to enforce within that elite world of scholarship, where because of declining enrollments competition was particularly stiff. Challenges would take years and years, and victories were few.

In 1972, as full professor, I sued the university for discrimination in salary on the basis of sex. They were simply paying the men more than the women, especially me. It took all these years of stonewalling, avoiding, ignoring, before they finally admitted I was right, and settled out of court. Of course, I had to promise not to tell *anyone* how much they gave me and to be a good girl and not encourage any other woman professor to do the same heinous act of subversion of the rights of administration to set salaries. At age seventy-two (I retired in 1975), my lawyer and I decided to settle.

So how much I got is a deep dark secret, but you will notice this letter is being written on a new word processor. There are other things I have done, too. But the most is to enjoy, heartily, the last laugh.

Good luck to all embattled species.

Name Withheld
August 14, 1982

In the eighties, women who were "making it" as professionals and corporate executives found their own challenges. One reader warned that the workplace wouldn't be transformed overnight by the addition of more women bosses. She responds to an August 1980 article by Ruth E. Messinger, "Bosses I Have Known and Loathed."

Having worked in several offices under female bosses, I can say that working for women is somewhat different but not necessarily any better. To Messinger's list of weird male personality types in the business world, I must add the following female characters:

The Compulsive Nitpicker. Asks you to retype a lengthy report because the date at the top should be two more spaces to the right.

The Mother of Us All. Calls *everyone* "honey," keeps track of employees' children's birthdays (or, rather, has her secretary keep track).

The Incredible Workhorse. Growls at co-workers constantly because she's too overworked to be nice but can't delegate responsibility without sitting on the shoulder of the delegate to make sure it's done *her* way.

The Ladder Climber and Puller Up With Her. Makes her secretary get coffee for her, can't dial her own phone or staple her own papers together, tends to recommend male subordinates for raises and promotions.

I have also worked for a female Lovable Old Curmudgeon.

Name Withheld
December 1980 Issue

Although many cultural signs indicated that the woman executive had arrived—she had her own magazines after all—questions of the worth of women's work were not confined to the pink collar ghetto. One reader wrote in response to a March 1979 article by Gloria Steinem on one "reentry" woman, Jacqueline Onassis.

Although I am one of the 64 percent of women in the labor force who workbecause-wehaveto, I think it's great that Jacqueline Kennedy Onassis works because she wants to. I deeply resent, however, the fact that she sold her unique talents to Viking Press for a paltry ten thousand dollars a year.

Any woman who works for less than she is worth is doing the rest of us a tremendous disservice, because she is helping to hold our salaries down. If publishers know they can get Jackie's talent, education, experience, and taste for ten thousand dollars, they'll certainly expect us ordinary people to work for less than that.

Marsha Gutierrez
Los Angeles, California
July 1979 Issue

Bumper sticker seen pasted on my twelve-year-old's schoolbook bag: When I Grow Up, I Want to Be An Executive Like My Mom.

Steven P. d'Adolf
El Paso, Texas
January 1983 Issue

Two of many concerns that arose for professional women were how to be comfortable while away on business trips and, conversely, how to be taken seriously if you stayed home to work.

Several years ago my previous employer sent me on a fact-finding trip to Newark, Baltimore, Richmond, and Seattle—all to be visited within a time span of one week. Although anxious to make the trip, as a black woman I knew that extra care in planning my travel would be required for my well-being. Unaccompanied black women circulating in hotels are often perceived as being in "the business" (prostitution), and I wanted to avoid that hassle.

My defensive strategy included arranging my flight schedule for daytime arrivals and departures, registering in hotels under my professional title of Dr., and wearing an official-looking brown trench coat and carrying a briefcase. I suspect that my appearance was that of either a policewoman disguised as a hooker or a hooker masquerading as a policewoman.

In Richmond, the atmosphere struck me as distinctly Old South, and the anxieties I had as a child growing up in another Southern city began to return and encroach on my usually steady outlook. By the time I reached my hotel, I was bordering on paranoia.

The hotel was one of Richmond's better hotels and, like the city, refined but frayed at the edges and somewhat dreary. After checking into the hotel, wearing my trench coat of course, I was escorted to my room by an elderly white bellman sporting both a limp and a leer. Upon settling me in the room, he announced in a sinister manner, "Call me if you need me." I firmly resolved to myself that I wouldn't need or call him and left the room to conduct my business.

Around eight that evening I returned (in my trench coat) to my hotel room just in time for a planned treat, a television drama starring Ruby Dee. I turned on the television but got no response. My heart began thumping. I sensed that the leering, limping bellman was outside the room now, waiting for me to seek his aid with the television set.

I sat on a chair facing the door and thought that I could hear him panting on the other side. Finally, I had to use the bathroom. I cautiously got up from my chair and flicked on the bathroom light. The television set came on. I should have guessed!

That night I lectured myself on having a runaway imagination and the next morning I slunk in an embarrassed fashion past the innocent bellman. On this occasion, my trench coat was worn with the collar pulled up. I'm sure I looked like neither a hooker nor a policewoman but more like an idiot, because that's exactly how I felt.

Elaine P. Adams
Houston, Texas
December 1980 Issue

As a professional writer for hire, I've survived all the natural traps of working from home—firmly turning away friends and neighbors who don't think I'm "really working," kissing my daughter goodbye in the living room (on the days she's home from school) before going to work in the next room, conditioning my clients to call during *their* working hours instead of making assumptions about mine, convincing IBM that my office-supply order is just as important as the electric company's, and keeping the cats off the desk.

I'm still there at home after five years and have no desire to go out and work in a "real" office.

Judith Pynchon
West Sayville, New York
December 1981 Issue

A major eighties trend for women was going into business for themselves. Whether motivated out of frustration with slow progress in the corporate world or lured by the sometimes dubious advantages of working from home, women went into business on their own at a rate six times faster than men from 1974 to 1984—though many of these businesses were small. According to the Small Business Administration, 22 percent of all sole proprietorships in 1982 were woman-owned.

Y*oung, gifted, black, educated,* and *qualified* no longer appear to be magical words that suddenly open doors of corporate worlds. After years of struggle to complete my Ph.D., I was asked recently, when I attempted to volunteer for a local task force on mass transportation, the inevitable question: "But do you type?" Yes, but I also can analyze data, write research reports, evaluate programs, write proposals, and train personnel. All irrelevant skills to my listener's ear.

I am now my own boss. Still struggling, but loving every minute of it.

Marion T. Johnson, Ph.D.
Performance Systems Associates
Dallas, Texas
February 1982 Issue

Some men were changing their work habits, too—John Naisbitt and Patricia Aburdene reported in our July 1985 issue that there's a 25 percent refusal rate among all executives asked by their companies to transfer. Other couples chose the radical solution of a commuter marriage.

W*hen* my husband completed his Ph.D. at Ann Arbor, Michigan, and was offered an excellent opportunity at Washington University, in St. Louis, Missouri, it was assumed by everyone—including myself—that I would leave a successful psychotherapy practice, built up over four years, and begin again in St. Louis. After all, we were only in Michigan for my husband to pursue his education; we had always known we would leave someday. And besides, I could probably work anywhere.

As the time grew nearer for us to leave, I began to feel outrage at being expected (even by myself) to give up a job in which I had discovered real self-worth. Then my husband came up with the idea of commuting. My initial reaction was more outrage, but he spent many hours working out the details to show me how it could work. And work it does!

Our situation may be unusual, however, in that I only commute part time. I work intensely, seeing upward of twenty-five clients in two and a half days. But I can work long hours without having to worry about being wife and mother. I am home four full days a week, during which time work is the furthest thing from my mind and I can concentrate on my family and home. While I am gone, my husband is basically a single parent. He now makes decisions and responds to the needs of the kids totally on his own. We never fight any more about who stays home if the kids are sick— Tuesday through Thursday he does, Friday through Monday, I do. The children seem to have adjusted easily.

My commuting has added freshness and new romance to our fourteen-year marriage; and my work has improved. Pulling this off gives me renewed optimism in the ability of couples to work out reasonable living arrangements without one partner always giving in to the other.

Judy Leon
Olivette, Missouri
September 1984 Issue

Corporate America was opening its doors to women—but still on its own terms. When Ms. *suggested in a April 1984 cover story that women didn't have to dress like men for success, a reader wrote to tell us "not so fast."*

The day I showed up at work wearing a blue business suit for the first time, my male bosses were visibly taken aback. One said, without hesitation. "I liked you better before." Another said, "Nice. Very nice. Next you'll be wanting my office."

It's unfortunate that a man (John T. Molloy in *Dress for Success*) had to tell us how to dress, but only a man *could* tell us. Just because we're "in there" in greater numbers does not mean we should stray too far away from the regulation pin stripe of the business world. Businessmen have been wearing those uniforms for centuries, and therefore dress-for-success suits are mandatory under the current dress code in the business army. Let's not kid ourselves: if it's true that those clothes make the man, they make the woman as well, so we should not be rushing to loosen our ties just yet.

Reid Stewart
New York, New York
July 1984 Issue

Another reader, responding to a personal work saga in the March 1984 issue, "Whither Thou Goest?" by Patricia Sweeney, told how she followed tens of thousands of women into M.B.A. programs to get her passport to the corporate world. But like many other women headed for the "fast track," she stopped to reconsider her life choices in the mid-eighties.

I have always wondered if there are others out there like me—graduated from college in 1974 with hopes of being an art teacher at a time when there was such a glut of teachers. I went on to work for the N.Y.P.D. for a couple of years. Then I joined in the rush for the M.B.A. to get a new degree and be welcomed as a professional in a new field. I think I am doomed to having my timing always a little off. My job search was another struggle with too much education, too little business experience, not the Ivy League school diploma. We do persevere. I, in a job that I was overqualified for—no promotion but a corporate merger, and a job is eliminated, my job. I have come to terms with myself and am happier now. I have come full circle back to art as an artist and part-time arts-organization administrator. Thank you for a story about the others who persevere and never quite "make it" . . . there will always be the unfulfilled part of me that is the art teacher.

Mary Prozora
Atlanta, Georgia
March 18, 1984

Woman's Body, Woman's Mind

———————— ❧ ————————

The August 1972 health column, in the second regular issue of Ms., *began with author Donna Handly's question, "Have you ever looked at your cervix?" Those of us who hadn't soon got a chance to do so, as the women's self-help movement distributed speculums along with information about our bodies through consciousness-raising and that movement's unique teaching technique, self-examination. Already available for thirty cents in a small press edition was* Our Bodies, Our Selves, *the health manual "by and for women" that was to become a much-enlarged best seller over the next decade (New England Free Press; later Simon and Schuster in its updated versions). We were determined to learn to be comfortable with our own bodies and to know enough to become demanding medical consumers.*

If a woman felt dissatisfied with her treatment by the medical profession, her gynecologist seemed most often to be the target of her discontent. We at Ms. *knew that one of the main services that we could perform for our readers was to provide up-to-date medical information, to air controversies when they occurred, and to help in changing the patronizing attitudes of some doctors, reported on at length by our readers.*

————————————

Upon suspecting I was pregnant for the second time in one year, I went to a highly recommended male gynecologist nearby. The first pregnancy was a result of being told by another doctor that I could never become pregnant and that I would "have to get used to the idea of adoption"! I was told birth control was not necessary, and so I became pregnant by my fiancé, who is now my husband, after my very first sexual experience. We agreed on an abortion.

After my return from N.Y.C. [Abortions were legal in New York State for three years before the Supreme Court's 1973 Roe *v.* Wade decision], I had some difficulty securing an IUD, because I had never had a child! I insisted and finally received one before our marriage. I cannot take the birth control pill, and I wanted to be sure!

Well, I became pregnant very shortly after our wedding. I went to one of the "best" gyn doctors in town for a thorough checkup. His thorough examinations consisted of getting my charts and medical history mixed up with everyone's in town and a five-minute quickie look. The tests were positive, but he would not certify me as pregnant, because he knew that I was unhappy and that my husband and I would seek another abortion. It was financially and emotionally impossible for us to have a child, but he insisted we "work it out." He even went so far as to tell me that if my husband would not accept this pregnancy that he really didn't love me! He tried to make me feel as guilty as he possibly could, citing my "duties" as a woman and my biological destiny.

I went to Planned Parenthood, where I was certified as indeed pregnant and scolded for waiting so long to find out. I barely made the deadline for the aspiration method of abortion. I was also told that the clinic was more interested in preventing pregnancies than in terminating them and they hoped I would be more careful.

My God! I didn't enjoy the abortions and would have loved to have prevented them. I didn't think I needed to prevent the first pregnancy and did all I could to prevent the second one. I am a college graduate and know all about biology, and yet I was talked to as though I were a junior-high-school girl in trouble, taking up their valuable time. I feel very uncomfortable about going to a male doctor now, and deplore the incredible lack of female gynecologists.

Thank you for allowing me to let off steam!

Name Withheld
April 2, 1973

A November 1972 review of a best-forgotten book called Confessions of a Gynecologist *by Dr. Anonymous, brought this response.*

Lucy Rosenthal's review "Dr. Anonymous Is a Dirty Old Man," reminded me of my visit to a gynecologist. He sprang into the examining room waving my medical history and inquired melodramatically why I was so terrified of pregnancy. Without waiting for a response, he informed me that I have one two-year-old child, a fact which had *not* escaped my notice, and that it was high time I had another, especially in view of the dismal statistics on the incidence of Down's syndrome and other misfortunes in change-of-life babies. I am all of twenty-eight.

Since I didn't then jump off the table and rush home to attempt conception before my time ran out, he coyly reminded me that if I stalled too long, and my one child died, I'd be *(choke)* barren. He darkly hinted at past patients, too numerous to mention, who had suffered nervous breakdowns after being unable to conceive that precious second child. My observation that a woman whose whole self-fulfillment rests on producing children needs a psychiatrist more urgently than a gynecologist fell on deaf ears.

In a last-ditch effort to summon up a satisfactory haul of guilt on my part, he spoke of women with serious physical problems who risk death to bear a child. "And then," he said, "there are people like you. . . ."

Dianne C. Felder
Old Bridge, New Jersey
April 1973 Issue

Though there are certainly supportive men in the medical profession, our readers tended to write in about the women.

During the past summer I worked as an intake interviewer at Planned Parenthood here in New Haven. We were fortunate to be able to hire for three months a young nurse-midwife to work in our clinics. The response to her was wonderful—people asked to make appointments with her, something that rarely happened with our doctors. It was not that she knew more gynecology than the gynecologists. She simply took more time, explained more thoroughly, and often came across as more empathetic. (Male doctors tend to shrug off menstrual cramps, for instance, because they never have them.)

Unfortunately for us, at the end of the summer she moved on to Yale's teaching hospital. Luckily, we have continued to have midwives at the teen clinics, where they are perhaps most valuable in helping to teach young women about their bodies.

Anne S. G. Hartney
New Haven, Connecticut
January 1974 Issue

During a routine pap-smear examination, I requested that my daughter (age thirteen) be present. My female gynecologist not only agreed but showed my daughter female anatomy as she examined me, inside and outside. It was a great experience for my daughter. She learned more about her own body, will be more relaxed when her time comes for examinations, and it made her relate to me more closely. My gynecologist was surprised at the request, but became an excellent and patient teacher immediately.

Name Withheld
May 26, 1976

A number of readers wrote about how a sense of one's own body developed in themselves or in their daughters, some inspired by a very funny essay by Gloria Steinem in the October 1978 issue.

After reading Gloria Steinem's political fantasy "If Men Could Menstruate," I remember how, when I started menstruating, at twelve, I was very proud. Why, I don't know—no one had ever explained to me what it was all about. I was never encouraged to look forward to it. Nevertheless, it seemed so very natural, and I felt womanly.

In spite of the jokes, the ignorance, the cultural taboos, cramps and water retention, I still like my period. I *do* think it's fantastic that I have my own cycle corresponding to the moon's—if that's cosmic, so be it.

Name Withheld
December 12, 1978

The analysis of power-preserving notions of behavior based on biological characteristics in Steinem's article was topical for our family. Only a few weeks ago our three-year-old daughter added to the list of attitudes toward genitalia undocumented in print.

Her behavior occurred in the locker room with her father after a swimming lesson. Observing all the male genitals, she asked if all people grow up to have penises. Her father told her that only men and boys have them. She studied him carefully and consoled him. "Don't worry, Dad, it's only a little one."

Alice Fredericks
Mill Valley, California
September 23, 1978

At twelve years old, I had my first period. On discovery of this, I ran to where my parents were relaxing in the yard, yelling triumphantly, "I got my period!"

That night we toasted my womanhood with champagne. I still have the empty bottle.

Name Withheld
June 16, 1981

I recently had an experience that I suppose falls into the click category. I was sharing the bathroom with my daughter, who is not yet three. She made an observation and the following conversation ensued:

"You don't wipe your bottom when you tinkle."

"No, Kristin, I don't."

Reflective pause, then, "Why?"

"Because my tinkle comes out a different place than yours."

Another reflective pause, then, "Why?"

"Because boys and girls are different."

Another reflective pause, then with certainty, "No, boys are different."

My interpretation of this sample event is that she does not see the society or the world in terms of masculine "norm," with her own status defined only in relation to that "norm." I hope my interpretation is correct. As parents, we must be doing something right.

Robert J. Shaw, Minister
Tabernacle Christian Church
Franklin, Indiana
July 1981 Issue

Painful lessons could come from society's notion of the ideal female body, as one reader told us in 1972.

I doubt any scorn could meet my own for my body, which I've despised. Teenage years flash back . . . a year, maybe less, of gloating over my new-forming orbs. I soon became known for my "boobs," and thus began my shame. I was ashamed, because they far exceeded the accepted "handful" requirement of my male classmates. My breasts were not even rounded and firm like most of the other girls. They were heavy and hung and embarrassed me.

I didn't become obsessed or hysterical about it; I just quietly loathed my "figure." The braless look then came in to mock me, and I gazed with envy at small, tight breasts and nipples protruding everywhere. And I looked upon the big, drooping breasts of other braless women and felt ashamed for them as I did for myself.

Of course, it slowly dawned on me that what I was suffering was useless bullshit, but it took a long time, and I'm by no means there yet (can I ever really *dig* my body?). My disgust has found its rightful place—in the "status quo" of the female body, projected by insane people. The media's message of "body beautiful" must be rejected, and the individual's right to her own body restored.

Name Withheld
December 5, 1972

A few years later Eve Babitz's "My Life in a 36DD Bra; or The All-American Obsession," in the April 1976 issue, brought some laughs of recognition.

How I can identify with Eve Babitz. I detest getting viewed as a sex object, and large breasts only make it worse. If I ever had my bust reduced, I think over half the people I know would not recognize me! I guess that's the worst part—being known by some people just because of my breasts. I hate it!

P.S. Thank you for letting me get this off my chest—see, women with big chests have a sense of humor, too!

Name Withheld
July 20, 1976

In our September 1977 issue, a special section called "Why Women Don't Like Their Bodies," included several memorable articles. Two of them discussed the dangers of breast implantation: "Beauty and the Breast—A 60 Percent Complication Rate for an Operation You Don't Need," by Marjorie Nashner and Mimi White; and "A Shot—or Two or Three—in the Breast," by Deborah Larned. A number of readers took our warnings to heart.

I was scheduled to have breast implant surgery on August 31. I had had mixed feelings about doing it, but the prospect of a new buxom me by September outweighed my doubts.

Then the September *Ms.* arrived.

How fortunate for me that the article on breast implant surgery appeared in this issue! After reading it, I canceled the surgery, and with a sense of tremendous relief I now thank God for what I have.

Although the doctor I had chosen was probably ethical and competent, I realize now that he deemphasized the negative aspects of the operation.

Thank you for saving me from a possible disaster.

Name Withheld
January 1978 Issue

Warnings about doctors and hospital practices also came in a May 1975 article by home-birth advocate Suzanne Arms. Her charge was that doctors and hospitals treated pregnancy and childbirth more as an illness than a natural occurrence.

As a nursing student, I found myself feeling defensive after my first reading of the article "How Hospitals Complicate Childbirth." However, a second and third reading finds me more in agreement.

I agree that many obstetricians tend to pattern their assistance with normal labor and delivery after the management of high-risk patients. But I question Suzanne Arms's contention that most women would not question the use of fetal heart monitors. I feel she underestimates the assertiveness of many women. The rigidity with which such assertiveness is met seems to me to be our biggest problem in obstetrical care. It is up to us as health workers to become more flexible and meet the needs of the individual woman.

Susan Krohmer Freeman
Iowa City, Iowa
September 1975 Issue

A year later, in the December 1976 issue, Barbara Katz Rothman told her own story, "In Which a Sensible Woman Persuades Her Doctor, Her Family, and Her Friends to Help Her Give Birth at Home." She found an unlikely supporter in this reader.

I, too, had a baby (Daniel) this year, but I had complications and had to have a Caesarean. Because of this, I am very much for home deliveries. Why? Because then doctors would have to deal more openly with *all* their patients. My doctor knew of the likelihood of a Caesarean but chose to "protect" me from the possibility. Because of this, I was unprepared for a C-section and felt I had failed. My husband was suddenly excluded when we needed each other most. And my family was devastated by the turn of events. With home deliveries, doctors couldn't play games with their patients, trusting hospitals to bail them out.

Name Withheld
April 1977 Issue

Other readers were more skeptical, and one nurse argued that Rothman's example of treatment, "If you're a very good girl and you show how cooperative you're being, then the nurses probably won't strap your hands down," absolutely couldn't happen. But another reader supplied her own evidence.

It happened to me on January 16, 1975, when in the wee-est hour of the new day I was lying on the delivery room table of a reputable local hospital. I was thirty-three years old, and my husband and I were using Lamaze techniques to help me give birth to our first child.

The nurse poured a warm solution over my thighs and pelvic area. Shortly afterward, I had a ferocious cramp in my left thigh. I reached down and massaged it away, just as I had done many times during my pregnancy. I was less than prepared for what followed.

In a tone of voice mothers use when their partly potty-trained child "forgets," the nurse said, "Shame on you. You've contaminated your sterile leg. Now we'll have to strap your hands down before I can sterilize you again."

I had successfully refused almost every drug the doctor and nurses wanted me to use, but suddenly I was as helpless as a two-year-old. She strapped down my hands, fortunately placed so I could still grip the handholds to help me push. And my husband was there to scratch my nose.

Fortunately the state of being in labor doesn't permit one to focus on indignities. Also fortunately, I didn't have any more leg cramps. Later, however, the same nurse was very supportive. After the birth of our incredible son, my body began to shake. The doctor wanted to give me an injection of Valium to stop the shaking. I knew it would put me to sleep, so I refused. When the doctor was out of earshot, the nurse told me that the shaking was caused by lack of oxygen in my muscles. It had been used up during labor, she said, and the shaking would stop in fifteen or twenty minutes without Valium. It did.

The support she gave me kind of balanced out her "score card."

Beverly S. Miller
Austin, Texas
March 29, 1977

In the mid seventies, of course, Valium was not only used as a muscle relaxer. In an article in the November 1975 Ms.—"Do You Take Valium?"—Deborah Larned reported that about 15 percent of all Americans took the tranquilizer, making it the largest selling drug of any in the world, and that it seemed to be marketed particularly to treat women suffering from anxiety. In a remarkable letter, one reader reconsidered her prescription.

I received the November issue with Deborah Larned's article on the day I had awakened at 3:30 A.M., and could not get back to sleep. I took a third Valium (five milligrams) and wrote myself a reminder to obtain a new supply. Because several points that Larned made seemed sensible to me, I postponed obtaining the Valium in order to review the events of the last six months and consider some alternatives. A summary of my anxiety-producing events follows:

¶Last April my husband moved out. My thirty-eighth birthday fell on the day of a hearing at which I protested my dismissal from my teaching assignment. My car was vandalized that same day.

¶The first of May both children broke out with measles. The hearing officer decided that several of the teachers, I among them, were being terminated illegally and should be reinstated. The school board refused to accept his findings; we were terminated. I began searching for another position. I applied for a graduate-school summer program in my teaching field.

¶In June, I received a letter from a personnel director in response to my job inquiry. I was too experienced, too well educated, and too expensive to be considered for an opening, he said, although none was expected. The teachers' organization filed suit in superior court for a review of the dismissal case. I was accepted into the summer seminar, and I returned to school as a student. I continued to apply for teaching positions for the fall. I registered at the unemployment office.

¶During July, the light switch in the dining room broke, and the soap dish above the tub fell out of the wall while the children were bathing, revealing water damage behind the tile. I took a recess from the therapist with whom I'd worked for two years.

¶Early in August the refrigerator began defrosting continually, and the frozen food thawed; the repairman came. The fan belt in my car broke during an evening trip back from the city. The plumber arrived to attend to three leaky faucets and to fix the hot-water supply in the washing machine. The faucets in the master bath were damaged beyond repair; replacement meant opening the wall. I wrote to my parents about my separation and received a flood of accusations. I concluded my summer session. Responses to my many applications began trickling in, all rejections—most answered with form letters. The superior-court judge issued his ruling supporting the hearing officer's opinion: the group of teachers had been terminated illegally and must be rehired.

¶Early in September the school board voted to accept the judge's decision. I was given a part-time assignment, based on my employment status of two years earlier. The special-education program I had developed required a full-time teacher and was given to another person. I was sent to the substitute pool. The repair work began in the children's bathroom. The removal of the tile revealed dry rot of such severity that a revision of the original estimate was required. The third week of school I was assigned to substitute for the person who'd taken my position. I began a graduate course in the evenings. I was contacted by a real-estate agent, because the mortgage payments on a piece of investment property handled by my husband were delinquent, and the foreclosure was being considered.

¶In October, the early fall rains were accompanied by winds that blew with such velocity that a short, wide ventilation window shattered, and glass was strewn across the room. I was invited to be interviewed for a full-time position for which I had applied in late August. Although I was among the top three candidates, I was not chosen for the job. My husband stated his desire to see neither me nor our children until further notice. I met with an attorney to discuss and file for dissolution of our marriage. My husband declined to work on the property settlement. I closed the window in my son's room, and the handle fell off in my hand. I returned to my therapist; her support and acceptance were as helpful as in the past. The teacher assigned to the full-time special-education program became ill, and I was asked to prepare the accreditation report in his absence.

As I look back over the last six months, I realize I have been in a "stress-filled situation"—a real mess involving every aspect of my life. Outlining the events has given me some perspective. I really have had problems! I have denied myself an awareness of how much anxiety these events were arousing in me. I do want and need relief from the anxiety, but I'm not getting that Valium prescription. Instead, I'm getting more neighborhood help with my children, listing the jobs I have yet to do, and doing them.

Thanks for the impetus to get all this down. I needed writing paper, not a prescription pad.

Name Withheld
March 1976 Issue

While some women were reconsidering taking Valium, others were getting off the Pill. It's a debate that continues today but was more heated in the seventies, partly because the early birth control pill was comparatively high in dosage. A June 1975 article by Barbara Seaman, a women's health activist and author of The Doctor's Case Against the Pill, *reported on new findings on the Pill's side effects in "The New 'Pill' Scare."*

It once seemed a miracle that a small pill every day could take care of all contraception, but as we became suspicious of a daily dose of chemicals, many of us took a second look at this modern wonder. So it is a bit ironic that fifteen years after the Pill was allowed on the market, and a "sexual revolution" later, most women I know have returned to the method our mothers used: the diaphragm. So much for the miracles of modern science.

Name Withheld
May 22, 1975

It was no wonder that women continued to be suspicious of doses of chemicals, particularly when the DES story began to emerge. In March 1977 we ran an article by Jan Worthington, "The Cancer Time Bomb— Did Your Mother Take DES?" Some readers criticized the scary title, but many DES daughters were suffering the consequences of the drug widely prescribed in the fifties to prevent miscarriage; later it was learned that sons were also affected.

As a mother who took DES in 1955 in order to carry my second child to full term, I cannot describe to you the anguish and guilt that has consumed me over the past two years.

I cannot take back what I have brought upon my daughter, which I thought would only ensure her her right to life. I also will never be able to justify my stupidity in never thinking to ask if there were any side effects from the drug I took.

Worthington is right—this generation of women will *never* allow what happened to us to happen to them. For that, I am very grateful.

Audrey Warren
July 1977 Issue

Like Jan Worthington, I am twenty-four years old.

Mainly because of her article, I was concerned enough to ask my mother the same basic questions that she did. It turned out that *my* mother, too, had taken DES.

I have cried and anguished. I am angry, frightened, and confused. How could the FDA let his happen to me?

Barbara O'Neill
Ithaca, New York
July 1977 Issue

In October of 1958, my mother took DES in an effort to save the baby that she was likely to miscarry. Seventeen years later, I was diagnosed as having adenocarcinoma of the cervix, its origins rooted in my prenatal exposure to DES.

I have had a radical hysterectomy and the surrounding pelvic lymph nodes have also been removed. Conservation of my ovaries was predicted as probable but not definite.

Today, though I am damn mad, I am considered cured and have lost little else save my reproductive ability and the adolescent characteristic of taking my health for granted.

Name Withheld
July 1977 Issue

A January 1979 landmark article by Maureen R. Michelson announced, "There Are Alternatives to Mastectomy," and included a note on how to find hospitals and clinics that would consider less invasive treatments for breast cancer. That note produced some fifty inquiries a day for more than a month—from individuals seeking help as well as from health professionals and medical schools. One reader took matters into her own hands.

I don't believe what I did after reading the article by Maureen R. Michelson. Let me explain.

I work in the admitting office of a hospital, and women are admitted all the time suffering from tumors in the breast. If the tumors are diagnosed as malignant, a radical or partial radical mastectomy is performed. These women have decided upon surgery because of their doctor's advice, and he has not told them of other methods of treatment and recovery percentages. Patients have the right to be informed, and so also does the doctor.

What I did after reading the article was to take copies and covertly place one in each of the surgeon's mailboxes. If they were not aware of alternate treatments, they are now!

Name Withheld
May 1979 Issue

The eighties produced new controversies concerning the medical treatment of women. The Dalkon Shield, an intrauterine device used for birth control, was proved to cause infection, infertility, and sometimes death. The device was taken off the market, but the courts held the manufacturers, Robins, responsible for injuries. And a new treatment for what was a newly diagnosed, or at least newly named condition—premenstrual syndrome—was a growing controversy.

The best cure for premenstrual tension is to stop calling it premenstrual tension. Call it PME—premenstrual energy—instead.

Tension implies sickness. *Energy* suggests a gift. I think that tension, virtually any kind, is energy that has not been released.

Tension implies that you're stuck with it. *Energy* suggests it can *be* released, and in creative fashion at that. It may suggest to the woman who has it that she take her emotions out not on the poor innocents around her but rather on a canvas, typewriter, guitar, or Nautilus equipment.

Tension suggests a problem, an error in the design of woman's anatomy. But there are no errors. It's as normal as the phases of the moon, which probably had a big hand in evolution. It may be no coincidence that the cycles of the moon and woman should take the same length of time.

Well, my body's telling me it's that time of the month again; I feel premenstrual energy coming on. It's time to work on my sculpture.

The pen, words themselves, may well be mightier than either the sword or the hormone.

M. Grace Melucci
Orange, New Jersey
October 1982 Issue

M. Grace Melucci suggests that the best cure for premenstrual tension is to call it premenstrual energy. Unfortunately, she is suffering from the same blindness we accuse male doctors of: they never have menstrual cramps, so they conclude that the pain is either nonexistent or insignificant.

As a PMS sufferer, I can assure her that using the tension to "work on my sculpture" sounds lovely, but instead I find myself crying for hours without reason, questioning the use of trying to get anything accomplished.

I do agree that we can profit from stressing the positive in what we thought were weaknesses, but changing the name of PMS will not change its nature. Instead of telling women, once again, that they are not feeling what they do in fact feel, why don't we find a safe, effective treatment for an unnecessary, *real* problem?

Julie F. Cameron
Lawrence, Kansas
December 1982 Issue

In the October 1983 issue was an article by Andrea Eagan, "The Selling of Premenstrual Syndrome—Who Stands To Gain?," which raised questions about the long-term safety of progesterone treatment and warned readers that some of the PMS clinics that were cropping up could be basically a marketing scheme.

As Andrea Eagan tells us herself, she doesn't have severe PMS, and she doesn't fully understand the desperation of women who do, or she would not have written an article denouncing the use of progesterone as treatment.

I had periods of depression ever since I started menstruating regularly. For six years, I was treated for "depression." The connection between these depressions and my menstrual cycle was not made until it was noted that I had been hospitalized thirteen times in a period of two years for attempted suicide. Each hospital admission was one to two days before my period began. The last time this occurred, I was unconscious for several days. When I awoke, I had my period and felt fine. I was taken off all anti depressants and sent to a gynecologist who started me on progesterone therapy. I have never again made an attempt on my life, and I now hold a full-time professional job.

Whenever any medication or treatment is given for any illness, a decision must be made as to whether the seriousness of the illness offsets the risk of the treatment or drug toxicity. Progesterone therapy is worth the risk of any long-term effects—"even cancer." I would rather die in the future of cancer than to have no present.

Name Withheld
January 1984 Issue

Ms. readers participated in the eighties obsession with fitness, but first we had to become comfortable with the idea of muscles—something, among other things, unimaginable to this young reader.

I believe in women's liberation to a certain extent, but I don't share your views on women being drafted. In my opinion, here the movement is going just a little bit too far.

I am thirteen years old, and I certainly don't want to be a woman soldier in five more years.

I also disagree with your idea that exclusive men's clubs should become "coed." Men do more strenuous exercises than women. Do you plan to lift weights? Think of all the money these clubs would have to put into remodeling programs. That's ridiculous!

A woman's place is in the home.

Name Withheld
August 1972 Issue

Of course, that was thirteen years before the documentary Pumping Iron II: The Women *and a July 1985 article by Gloria Steinem called "Coming Up: The Unprecedented Woman," on Bev Francis and other body builders. In between, we had to become much more comfortable with muscles.*

A professor friend suggested, in a class this spring, that a dispute between myself and a bigger, younger, much more muscular male colleague be taken to the floor for actual arm wrestling. I was so stirred up that I was on the floor in a thrice. In the back of my mind, I knew I couldn't win, but as the seconds passed, and I held my own, I changed my mind.

The class was at first hushed, but as time ticked on, the other men there began to egg my opponent on, appealing to his masculinity, his pride, whatever. My arm hurt. I heard a woman friend of mine say, "Hey, I'll bet she can do it!" You know what? I did. I beat him cold. Nobody could believe it. I reached over to pat my opponent, who had buried his face into the floor. And for the rest of that night, for weeks, indeed months now, I have felt a beauty in myself, a vitality and strength I didn't know I had.

I was boasting about the incident some days later to my folks, and my mother requested a match. She's fifty-six years old to my twenty-seven, 135 pounds to my 114. She beat me cold.

To those who say it is mental power rather than physical strength that determined the outcomes, I would like to say from my experience that the two reinforce each other. Let us all develop both!

Janice Rayner
Worcester, Massachusetts
January 1975 Issue

One reader took offense at the no doubt hastily thought-out title of a piece on weight lifting by Signe Hammer in the December 1978 issue.

"Strength Without Muscles," indeed! What is so wrong with a woman looking as if she can climb two flights of stairs without passing out? I have been lifting on and off for the last year or so. I have nearly double the muscular bulk of many of my women friends, and I'm not in the least ashamed of it.

Name Withheld
December 26, 1978

Before becoming pregnant, I was swimming one mile daily approximately five times a week for three years. During my pregnancy, I continued doing so and even signed up for a swim class at the local university which met every day. After class ended, the instructors still allowed me to swim between classes for twenty minutes daily, which by my ninth month was quite enough. I became quite a spectacle, with my huge belly, waddling out to the pool area amid the astonished gazes of the eighteen- to twenty-one-year old students, plopping in the water and swimming laps as usual.

Ten days before I gave birth, the head swimming instructor saw me come out of the locker room at my usual time and asked me not to swim anymore. When I questioned her request, she informed me that the lifeguards (who were males) were feeling uneasy, since they were not trained to deal with any emergencies should I go into labor! I left the pool area, thinking how unfortunately ignorant one is to think that most labors last only ten minutes. (The hospital is not more than ten minutes away from any part of town.)

I labored three-and-a-half days at home before checking into the hospital. My pelvis was too small and my baby too large (almost eight pounds) for a vaginal delivery. I had a Caesarean section. Baby and mother came out fine.

Our son, Rafael, is now seven months old, and I am getting back to swimming. I feel swimming contributed immensely to my excellent state of spiritual, emotional, and physical health, especially during my ninth month. I am down to 117 pounds and have not been this healthy since I graduated from high school ten years ago.

Janice R. Gagerman
Chico, California
June 21, 1978

With the fitness fad, we began to appreciate muscles, but fat was another matter entirely. We had only started to examine women's food obsessions in an August 1976 article by Judith Ramsey, "Dying of Thinness." A reader recognized herself.

Overeating is *repulsive* to me! When I am with others who are gorging themselves, I stop eating. I am obsessed with being bony. During my first two years of college I weighed a normal 130 pounds for my height of five feet six inches. Now, eight years later, I weigh 100 pounds or less.

After my sophomore year in college, I became pregnant. I did not marry. I could not accept abortion then. Throughout my pregnancy, I was extremely self-conscious of my bloated stomach. I fasted. I had gained a mere four pounds during my full-term pregnancy. I gave the child up for adoption. I never wanted to feel "fat" again.

Friends and family are constantly telling me that I am too thin. But my figure in the mirror is distorted: I think I must still lose *more* weight!

Until reading the article on anorexia nervosa, I had never admitted that I may have a psychological-emotional problem. I can now admit that my unplanned pregnancy continues to cause me guilt and makes me deprive myself because I feel I am not deserving. But thanks to the article, I know I am not alone. I have been able to acknowledge my problem—and seek help.

Name Withheld
December 1976 Issue

By the mid-eighties, everyone knew what anorexia and bulimia were, but controlling the conditions was no easier.

Having been a restrictor anorectic for eight years, I prepared a turkey sandwich with mounds of mayonnaise before sitting down to read "Is the Binge-Purge Cycle Catching," [*Ms.* October 1983]. Feeling adequately armed with food, I read the article without triggering my brain into a food elimination thought mode. Any definition of a 25 percent weight loss as evidence of anorexia is translated by my mind as an excuse for restricting food intake: since I am at five feet four inches, 110 pounds, I could always lose a little, for my eyes and mind perceive my body as being large.

My most recent anorectic bout occurred after ten months of stability. I lost twelve pounds in two weeks, and only when I realized that I might someday kill myself with this disease did I resume eating. Staying on track is a struggle, since each period of anorexia is more and more difficult to reverse mentally.

The article was basically accurate in defining root causes such as stress, yet the inference that eating disorders are synonymous with college age women is incorrect. My therapist has suggested that anorexia will remain with me on some level until I reach menopause. That information is terrifying. I am only twenty-six.

Name Withheld
October 20, 1983

For our September 1977 issue, "Why Women Don't Like Their Bodies," Judith Thurman wrote an article exploring, among other puzzling phenomena, how a woman's body image doesn't necessarily correspond to her actual body. Again, a reader saw herself.

I have never before identified as strongly with a magazine article as I did with Judith Thurman's "Never Too Thin to Feel Fat." I, too, was an overweight child. My mother criticized my looks but offered goodies to me at the same time. My husband is one of those whose "self-maintenance" is effortless; who cannot conceive of a food binge; who blames part of our marital problems on my weight. (He insists that I am at least thirty pounds heavier now than I was when we were married, when in fact I weigh about five pounds less!)

I am not "fat" in the true sense of the word; I am, however, very solid, athletic, and strong. Only now am I beginning to appreciate these qualities and develop them.

For reasons both related and unrelated, I recently began my first extramarital affair. My lover has had weight problems in the past and knows what it means to have to watch yourself constantly, but the best thing is that he loves my body exactly the way it is! For the first time in my life, I can be nude in front of a man and not cringe. Can you even imagine how delightful that is?

Name Withheld
January 1978 Issue

A number of letters responding to that special issue on food obsessions began in an obsessively similar way: "With a large chocolate bar, I settled into the pillows to read the latest issue of Ms. *. . . ." And, "After receiving my September issue of* Ms. *in the mail yesterday, I sat down with a glass of iced tea and read all the articles in the special section, 'Why Women Don't Like Their Bodies.' . . ." And, "Sitting on my bed, munching green grapes, I came across Ms. Thurman's article and read it with great reluctance as to what I would find. . . ." And, "I got up this morning, did half an hour of yoga (for my body of course) and ate a very nutritionally balanced diet breakfast. Then I read your article on being fat. . . ."*

A June 1980 article by Mary Peacock, "The Fashion Industry Courts 'The Big Woman,' " brought some readers a little relief.

In polite circles, I am referred to as "big-boned." I am not obese, but my dress size is somewhere between 9 and infinity. In some styles I can wear a size-16 dress, but in others a size-16 looks like Polish-sausage casing on me.

I, too, am tired of pastel checks and stripes that don't match and styles that my mother wouldn't wear to paint in. I diet sporadically—when the fear of having to go to work in a bed sheet becomes near reality.

I am tall (five feet ten inches) and proportioned like a linebacker . . . but healthy and happy. I am encouraged that the clothing industry is starting to open its eyes to the needs of larger women who want stylish clothes. I hope this trend continues and that *Ms.* will encourage these clothiers to advertise in the magazine.

Lee Bird
Yuma, Arizona
October 1980 Issue

Language
The Great "Personhole Cover" Debate

———————— 🍐 ————————

The first bit of copy in the Spring 1972 Preview Issue of Ms. *appeared on page four under the headline "What's a Ms.?" The half column that followed explained that "Ms." had appeared in secretarial handbooks for more than twenty years—recommended as a form of address when a woman's marital status was unknown—and that now "Ms." was being adopted by women who wanted to be recognized as individuals rather than identified by their relationships with a man. The column told how "Ms." was pronounced ("miz": later we explained that the plural was "Mses."), suggested somewhat prematurely that the practice of using titles was going out of style anyway, and ended by saying that the use of "Ms." is meant "only to signify a female human being. It's symbolic, and important. There's a lot in a name."*

In the first article in that Preview Issue, "De-Sexing the English Language," authors Kate Swift and Casey Miller offered a volley in what they called "the present assault on the English language by the forces of Women's Liberation." Noting that enlightened folks were substituting forms such as she and he *and* him/herself *for the generic personal pronouns* he and him, *they also recognized the enduring difficulty of such a practice: it "may be politically smart and morally right, but the result is often awkward." The Miller-Swift solution: a common-gender singular pronoun—*tey *in the nominative,* ter or ters *in the possessive, and* tem *in the objective case. They threw out this challenge: "If anyone objects, it is certainly* ter *right—but in that case let* tem *come up with a better solution."*

It would be hard to imagine a better participatory game for Ms. *readers than the one born of that challenge. All felt in equal possession of the*

English language, and ter *and* tem *were decidedly unintimidating as examples. The nomination of pronouns soon was joined by the coining of new words where readers felt that satisfactory ones didn't exist. And many also enrolled in the lengthy campaign to gain acceptance for the title "Ms."*

———————

According to the assorted mail that comes to our house, everyone has an identity, except perhaps me. I am lost somewhere—in the range of labels identifying the recipient—between *occupant* and *homemaker.*

The early part of my years was spent being somebody's daughter; later I became somebody's wife; after that, I became my children's mother. It is my fervent hope that Congresswoman Bella Abzug sees her Ms. bill passed, and soon.

Nikki Richardson Sheresh
Chula Vista, California
July 1972 Issue

Bella Abzug's bill, which would have forbidden the federal government to use titles that indicate marital status, did not become law, but the initiative did influence federal agencies to begin accepting the title "Ms." It was an important protection of privacy for women, and it also caused the government to treat women as independent individuals in everyday dealings. But governmental acceptance certainly didn't entail universal acceptance of "Ms." So Ms. readers continued their struggle.

Recently I was "called in" by a secondary-school district where I substitute-teach. I was told that I would be dropped from their list of substitute teachers, unless I stopped using "Ms." when writing my name on the board at the beginning of a new assignment—"because 'Ms.' makes students think of sexuality and liberation."

When I asked if there weren't other women on the faculty using "Ms." with their names, I was told, "No, we don't have very many young, unmarried women working for us." Click . . . crash!

Patricia R. Bristowe
La Honda, California
October 1973 Issue

I finally turned eighteen, so I rushed down to the Board of Elections to register to vote. The woman who was to swear me in asked if I was "Miss" or "Mrs." I replied that I was a "Ms.," and she promptly circled "Miss." I asked her why. She laughed and said, "Oh, all the unmarried girls come in and call themselves 'Ms.' because of their embarrassment over not having caught a man." Click. . . .

Jane Yackshaw
East Cleveland, Ohio
November 1974 Issue

Good news! We British women have won our case and we are now entitled to be designated "Ms." on our passports (or any other official document) if we so wish. Another small step forward for womankind!

Julia Percivall
London, England
October 1974 Issue

Nearly a decade later people still had their own idea of what "Ms." indicated.

While revising the phone directory of the law firm that I work for, I noticed that all the women's names were followed by either "Miss," "Mrs," or "Ms." (All of the men, of course, were simply "Mr.") My name was followed by "Mrs.," and I asked a co-worker whom I should notify that I preferred to have my "title" changed to "Ms." The woman looked shocked and said, "Oh, you can't do that! We only use Ms. for women who are divorced!" (My husband suggested that a scarlet *A* would serve the same purpose.)

Dawn Geisler
Mount Orab, Ohio
June 6, 1983

I thought, apropos of the ongoing discussion of titles, that you might be interested in the following item from Ambrose Bierce's *Enlarged Devil's Dictionary* (Penguin, 1971; originally published in bits and pieces in newspapers in the late nineteenth century):

Miss, n. A title with which we brand unmarried women to indicate that they are in the market. Miss, Missis (Mrs.) and Mister (Mr.) are the three most distinctly disagreeable words in the language, in sound and sense. Two are corruptions of Mistress, the other of Master. In the general abolition of social titles in this our country they miraculously escaped to plague us. If we must have them, let us be consistent and give one to the unmarried man. I venture to suggest Mush, abbreviated to Mh.

Carol J. Clover
Berkeley, California
November 1980 Issue

A woman who works for me has been going through very hard times with her man recently. Not wanting to preach to her about self-reliance, independence, and self-preservation, and yet wanting in some way to hold her hand, I bought her a couple of *Ms.* issues to read, saying, "This is by way of moral support."

To which she said, "Oh, is *that* what *Ms.* stands for—moral support?"

Jean C. Sobers
St. Eleanors, Prince Edward Island
July 1983 Issue

One reader's wry comment on what happens when a public figure chooses "Ms." as a form of address showed that the "Ms." debate was alive and well in the mid eighties. The troublesome public figure was Geraldine Ferraro, who was running for vice-president. Not only did she prefer "Ms.," she had retained her birth name when she married John Zacarro.

I haven't heard so many journalists tripping over their tongues since Phnom Penh. Curiously, the troublesome pronunication is over a one-syllable word—"Ms." I keep hearing "Ms . . . iss. Ms . . . iss." Is there an epidemic of lisping?

Although "Mrs." is technically correct, and "Ferraro" is correct, simply adding the two together don't make no sense at all. Like the well-known comic sketch by Mr. R. J. Johnson, "You could call her Gerry, or you could call her Geraldine, or you could call her Ferraro, or you could call her Ms. Ferraro, but you can't *really* call her Mrs. Ferraro."

For all those journalists who can't seem to pronounce "Ms.," here's a tip you may relate to more easily: it rhymes with *his.* Feel better?

Kate Lyn Reiter
New York, New York
July 22, 1984

There was much rejoicing in the Ms. offices and among our readers two years later, on June 19, 1986, when a major holdout, The New York Times, finally accepted "Ms." as a courtesy title.

The word game Ms. readers seemed to like best was finding a universal term applying to humankind to replace man. Person and people and human beings were relatively accepted usages but the problem came in compound forms. Although grammarians told us that statesmen and businessmen were genderless words, we all knew what gender speakers and writers meant to include in those terms. But many didn't like the sound of such words as chairperson or chairpeople. Among those who offered other solutions was folk singer Pete Seeger.

The words *congressperson* and *chairperson* are awkward words, typical of the ugly words created by scholars and scientists. Working people traditionally simplify language. God bless the English peasants who gave us a handy, if irregular slanguage, by combining Anglo-Saxon and Norman French and discarding the formalities of both.

Why not use a vowel like *o: congresso* or *chairo*? And for those who don't want to use the syllable *man*, likewise change *foreman, boilerman, anchorman, newspaperman,* et cêtera.

The language, agreed, needs more neutral words. Now's the time to make the changes more creatively. Incidentally, we might as well face it: we've got to invent some neutral pronouns. Saying "his or her" all the time is awkward unless we want to slur it into "hizar."

As a man, perhaps I have no right to make such suggestions, but as a user of words, I think I do. Building a new and livable world will necessitate thousands of little changes.

P.S. I've been the chairo of *many* committees, and I like the word.

Pete Seeger
Beacon, New York
February 5, 1974

Another male reader had a unique approach, as well as a wonderful sign off.

I would suggest, rather than changing the suffix of so many words, that a prefix be added to one word: *man.* The term *man* could then be retained as the generic term for *Homo sapiens,* while some other term, a form of *man* prefixed, much like *woman* or *human,* refer to those of us with XY chromosomes. I am not a linguist, but the prefix to *woman, wo,* suggests *womb.* Perhaps a prefix should be invented from some portion of the male's anatomy. I suggest *scroman* or *tesman,* possibly *vasman.* Thus we can now have *policeman, policewoman,* and *policescroman.*

Yours in siblinghood,

Name Withheld
April 20, 1975

None of these creative forms caught on—except, for a time, chairone, *which the National Organization for Women used to describe its officers. But that hardly discouraged readers who had fun with—and made fun of—the idea.*

We have all been longing, I am sure, for a single, yet suitably dignified suffix to replace the awkward and tonguersome *person,* as in *chairperson.* I have two legitimate objections to that suffix. In the first place, the word *person* has two syllables. I think semanticists would agree that the addition of another syllable to a much-used suffix goes against all modern trends to simplify our language. Second, the word ends in *son,* every bit as gender-ridden as *man.* Obviously, we must immediately shelve the term. In its place, may I suggest the petite yet compelling, and completely association-free, *peep?*

Try it out on your nouns: *chairpeep, congresspeep, firepeep, policepeep, weatherpeep, Chinapeep,* and *hupeepity.* It's equally adaptable to popular exclamations, such as "Whew, peep, oh, peep!" as well as to well-known mottoes ("The proper study of peepkind is peep") and famous book titles (*Everypeep* and *Peep's fate*).

As a spokespeep for those concerned with both equality and aesthetic excellence in our language, I would urge eager acceptance of this term. To paraphrase the stirring words of the first English speaker on the moon, "One small step for a peep, one giant leap for peepkind."

Shelley Mintier
Napa, California
May 1975 Issue

While I admire Shelley Mintier's suggestion concerning use of the word *peep* in place of *man,* I find the word not completely association free. To me it suggests birds, Toms looking in windows, and other subhuman creatures.

After experimenting with various vowels (*pap, pop, pup, poop*) the obvious solution came to me: '*peop.*' No one will be quite sure how to pronounce it, which gives it both status and authenticity as a truly *English* word. Another possibility is that questionable vowel *y,* giving us *pyp,* which shares the virtues of *peop.*

We must remember that the title "Ms." gave rise to much discussion about how it should be pronounced; surely a word so important to all humankind should be equally difficult to pronounce.

Toni Head
Satellite Beach, Florida
September 1975 Issue

I have been trying to use and explain the word *wam*—which is a humanized contraction of *woman* and *man*. *Wem* is the plural. There would be, for example, a *mailwam, batwam, chairwam,* and so on. There would also then be "Peace on earth, good will to wem."

Paul A. Henningsen
Milwaukee, Wisconsin
September 1975 Issue

It had not escaped the attention of some feminists that the dreaded syllable man *corrupted the name of our own sex. This critic of our December 1977 Arts Issue thought we were definitely too male identified.*

As a womon-identified artist, I am not clear about your priorities in communicating with wimmin. In reading the December issue ["The Arts Explosion"], I waded through male-identified wimmin executives, a mainstream mentality of wimmin in theater, and a general attitude of keeping wimmin plugged into the system throughout. What we need is more coverage of wimmin who are not covered by male media. This means more coverage of lesbian-identified artists, emphasis on groups and group process rather than on individuals as stars, and art as living revolution.

I suggest that your writers do more research to find out what's really happening in wimmin's communities across the country. Good luck in becoming more womon identified.

Dian Hamilton
Philadelphia, Pennsylvania
April 1978 Issue

For use as a neutral pronoun, ahon *was suggested by one reader as a one-word-fits-all replacement for* he, she, her, him *and* one. *Much later, a practical reader offered scholarly grounds for the use of* they *as a singular pronoun covering both genders, and we all breathed a sigh of relief.*

I should like to call to your attention some information on the use of *they* as a singular pronoun. ("Everyone should do as *they* think best.") The word has been used that way since medieval times (see *The Oxford English Dictionary*), and the rule against that usage was only made up in 1746.

Karey Harrison wrote to the *Chronicle of Higher Education* (May 15) that the rule was invented by a grammarian named John Kirkby, who simply asserted that the masculine gender was more comprehensive than the feminine. Only in the nineteenth century did prescriptive grammarians try to enforce the rule, and writers such as Thackeray and Shaw continued to ignore it.

Don't apologize for using *they* as a singular pronoun of common gender. It is entirely proper, and the rule against it is indefensible.

Katharine Rylaarsdam
Baltimore, Maryland
July 21, 1985

In the concept-without-an-appropriate-word department, readers spent a lot of time trying to decide how to refer to their live-in lovers who weren't spouses. The discussion began sensibly enough.

Dianna is not my wife. She is more like my friend. Unossified, she is not my "constant companion." At twenty-six, she is not my "old lady." "The woman with whom I spend my time"? Suggested by a writer, but too verbose. She has the same problem with the words referring to me. We're content with "couple" to describe us. We've grudgingly settled on "my lady" and "my man." Every couple we know has the same problem.

Michael Alexander
San Francisco, California
March 1973 Issue

Editor's Note: An unofficial survey of our staff produced little agreement except on one point: nobody is totally satisfied with present solutions, which included "my lover," "the person I live with," "my roommate," and "my friend."

Soon the suggestions and comments became more bizarre.

I have recently come across a word without a concept, to fit a fairly new concept that does not yet have an adequate word.

The number of people living together in reasonably stable, responsible, loving nonmarriages is growing steadily, and includes, among my acquaintances, not only young people but couples in their forties. Yet there is no word that precisely denotes a member of this group, which can be a problem in introductions. For instance, "This is my lover" leaves out social aspects of the relationship, and connotes to many people an extramarital rather than nonmarital situation. It is also historically loaded with sin and guilt; one couldn't say it to one's grandmother in most families. *Mate* or *spouse* implies marriage, to most people. *Friend* is far too broad, while *boyfriend* and *girlfriend* define more casual relationships, and seem frivolous when applied to older couples. *Roommate* or *cohabitant* is imprecise, since many people share living quarters without any sexual or deep personal involvement. *Concubine* and *mistress* are sexist words, and imply an economic situation that rarely exists in these cases. *Partner* is used by some, but is most often interpreted in a business or dancing sense.

The word I'd like to suggest for males and females in a relationship (hetero- or homosexual) that involves love, sex, and usually shared living space, is *groonblid*. Though *groonblid* may seem strange at first, it does have a few advantages. It is spelled simply. It has no negative connotation that I can see. It is totally devoid of etymology, sexist or otherwise, having been created to compensate for missing letters in a Scrabble set and pasted down as the permanent first word. The newness is a problem, since *groonblid* has to be explained on first hearing, but were *groonblid* to gain acceptance as "Ms." has, it would eventually save effort and explanation.

Lynne Derus
San Jose, California
October 1975 Issue

A word of timely warning before a well-meaning suggestion achieves a too-enthusiastic welcome. For offering casual inspiration, Lynne Derus's Scrabble set, like a Ouija board, obviously has a mind of its own. The word that it offers her—*groonblid*—is not, as she supposes, devoid of etymology and therefore freely available to define a loving nonmarriage.

Had she traveled at all extensively among the sausage-based cultures of Lower Saxony, she would have found the term well known and in common usage. The derivation is from *Grund blitz,* which may be rendered as *ground,* or more accurately *bottom-lightning.* Therefore: **Groonblid.** A diarrhea, a forceful or uncontrollable ejaculation of the bowels. Whilst this, particularly with its connotations of looseness and free running, might have admittedly a certain appositeness, nevertheless it is an unfortunate label to be attached to one's mate!

Lance A. Haward
London, England
May 1976 Issue

Other would-be coiners of brand-new words concentrated on terms they found too male identified. We gave many of them a chance by publishing the letters—but somehow, they suffered the fate of tey *and* tem *and* groonblid.

I protest the use of the word *testimony* when referring to a woman's statements, because its root is *testes*, which has nothing to do with being a female. Why not use *ovarimony*? Think it sounds funny? Think it sounds funnier than *testimony*?

Rachel W. Evans
Premont, Texas
May 1978 Issue

I take sexism in language very seriously; I also enjoy looking up words. When I saw the letter protesting the use of the word *testimony* in reference to a woman's statements, I promptly took down my three heavy friends, *The American Heritage Dictionary, The Oxford English Dictionary,* and Eric Partridge's *Origins.* The word *testimony* comes from the Latin word for *witness,* and so does our English word *testicle* and our word *testes.* The male reproductive organs came to be called, it appears, "the witness to virility," a circumlocution of some interest in itself.

I personally am not about to limit my use of a convenient word like *testimony* in its various forms because it is a sort of cousin to the word for male reproductive organs. Does Rachel Evans realize that *protest* bears about the same relation to *testes* that *testimony* does? It means, in essence, "to testify in public."

There is plenty of real sexism in language, much of it terribly subtle. This we must testify against, protest, detest, and contest the very use of.

Sue Willis
Brooklyn, New York
September 1978 Issue

The other day I was reading *Words and Women* by Casey Miller and Kate Swift. In this book, they state that there is no complimentary word in English for a strong woman. As I am somewhat of a mythology buff I would like to propose *cyrene* (noun) and *cyrenic* (adjective) to designate a woman of exceptional strength. These words are derived from Cyrene, a shepherdess in Greek mythology who was very, very strong *and* beautiful. The god Apollo met her while she was wrestling with a lion. I think it is very important to have a complimentary word for a strong woman. What do you think?

Catherine J. Gittens
Philadelphia, Pennsylvania
August 31, 1981

Please, please let me help you be aware of the wonderful word for all of the wonderful women doing so much for all of us these days.

The word is *shero*. And I would like to see it become common usage in our language today. I have many sheros in my life.

Hero is a man's word. *Heroine* is a diminutive and sounds like *heroin*. *Shero* stands proudly. Let's use it.

Name Withheld
June 1983

Talking to each other in the Ms. *Letters column was one thing. Making change in the real world was definitely another—particularly when it was the ritualized world of business correspondence. One reader laid her job on the line.*

I resigned from my job yesterday as a matter of principle. I was given a letter to type by a senior secretary to the auditing firm that had recently been in our books. A woman headed up the team of accountants at our company for several weeks.

The letter was opened to "Gentlemen." I changed it to "Greetings." I was told that the letter must be redone because it was the policy of the company to use the salutation "Gentlemen." I was told that management determined company policy, not uppity secretaries who didn't know their place. I decided to resign and didn't redo the letter.

I'm looking for another job, but I did raise quite a few eyebrows and, hopefully, someone's consciousness.

Name Withheld
September 12, 1982

Our organization publishes and distributes a manual on jury work. A high percentage of the orders we receive are routinely addressed "Gentlemen" or "Dear Sirs." In return we send out the following memo, which we borrowed almost wholesale from Nancy Schimmel of Sisters' Choice Press:

> Gentlepeople:
> We have received a communication from you with the salutation "Gentlemen" or "Dear Sir."
> While most of the people who give orders in the world of business are men, most of those who fill them are women. And at the National Jury Project, it happens that most of the staff are women.
> We realize it may seem awkward to use new forms of address, yet new forms must be found which acknowledge the presence of women in the world of work.
> Thank you . . .

It's a gentle letter, and one that usually receives favorable responses.

Recently, however, one of our letters was returned with the notation "Sorry, dear." Click. Sigh . . .

> National Jury Project Staff
> Oakland, California
> April 1981 Issue

This may not sound like much, but my boss just asked me a question that made my day and that I am dying to share with someone. He was in a meeting when he called out my name. I thought I was going to have to make copies or do some other chore, but he asked a question: "Dianne, who is the new girl . . . lady . . . *woman* over at Mud Island? Hooray, he's thinking! I felt wonderful. I don't know if he kept correcting himself for my benefit or not, but his *awareness* is all that matters!

> Dee Butler
> Memphis, Tennessee
> September 1983 Issue

Another anecdote from a woman professional came in response to an April 1980 article by Lindsy Van Gelder called "The Great Personhole Cover Debate," and perfectly illustrated her point—that personhole *arguments are red herrings.*

I attended a workshop of professional women, many of whom directed large, not-for-profit corporations, at which a male management consultant was the speaker. He spoke all morning without mentioning a single woman except in sexist jokes, including one about factory "girls" and one about flight attendants.

When I later confronted him about his mistaken idea of how to address professional women, he became very defensive. Immediately, and irrelevantly, he began telling me why nonsexist language was cumbersome and ridiculous. (This from a man whose motto was "What have you done differently lately?") He further interrupted me to tell me that I probably advocated saying "personhole."

At the time, I could think of no adequate response. Later, I found it by applying the same logic one uses to find nonsexist occupational titles: describe the activity (in this case a thing) as accurately as possible. I knew the hole was not in a man, or even in a person. So I sent him my response in the mail: "Why not use the expression *streethole*? What have *you* done differently lately?"

Carol Fitzgerald
Rock Falls, Illinois
March 20, 1980

It wasn't only bosses who called grown women girls. *Readers tried to educate wherever they went, though one thought, with some justification, that we were carrying things a little too far.*

Last week we had lunch in a restaurant. Our waiter said, "Well, girls, have you decided what you would like to eat?" We then explained to him that we were no longer girls. We were women. He laughed and pointed to two older women at another table and said that he had even called them "girls." Later, still infuriated, we called him "boy." He went off in a rage. We tried to explain to him that he was as much a boy as we were girls. He didn't understand.

Lynn Ubell
April Dworetz
Great Neck, New York
April 1973 Issue

I am writing about the column in January entitled "In a Class by Herself" by Paula Span. Ms. Span refers to the subject of the article as a "fifteen-year-old woman." I fully agree that to call an adult female a *girl* is insulting and demeaning. There is, however, a time when males are boys and females are girls. If this keeps up we are going to have "ten-year-old women" and "five-year-old women," and heaven knows where it will stop.

Lisa Smith
Garden City, New York
December 27, 1975

The next letter came in response to an article by Lucille G. Natkins in the February 1983 issue called "Hi, Lucille, This Is Dr. Gold," in which Ms. Natkins imagines Dr. Gold's response if she began calling him Jim.

Some years ago I published a short article about the significance of names in a medical magazine and got two interesting responses from physicians. One was from a member of a group practice who was told that it was the group's custom to use patients' first names but to insist on physicians' last names, because "otherwise the patient-doctor relationship would seem equal." The other was from a black physician who was told by his black professor never to call *black* patients by their first names, since this would be insulting. There's a moral to be extracted here.

Trudy Drucker
River Vale, New Jersey
May 1983 Issue

A high school student told us that language was the easy part of changing things in her school.

Liberation in our school is "fashionable." Everyone is quick to change *mankind* to *personkind, history* to *herstory,* et cêtera. But just try to get those same people to let you carry a few books across the hall!

Our English teacher maintains that lifting heavy things when you're young will give you a miscarriage later. When we proved her wrong, she said that even if the surgeon general *him*self proved her wrong, she would not change her mind.

Liberation is even harder to obtain for a teenager when adults think that it is a passing phase.

Lili Stern
Lexington, Massachusetts
April 1973 Issue

We all know that the word *man* refers to mankind—to human beings of both sexes— but when we hear it or say it, we seldom imagine anything but males. I have used a simple exercise to demonstrate this in my classes. The students are asked to draw their concept of Neanderthal Man. When we look at the pictures, we find that rarely has anyone imagined a Neanderthal female. (In five years, there have never been more than two female Neanderthals per class of fifty students—and some of them were drawn being dragged off by their hair!) Similarly, we find that in recent books using the generic *man,* the intention is to include all human beings, but usually only male examples are considered when specific behavior is being discussed. Clearly, the use of the generic *man* makes it very easy to ignore women.

Elizabeth Nelson
California State University
Fresno, California
August 1980 Issue

With the younger set, nevertheless, feminist usage was making some sort of impression.

I was observing in my daughter's class during sixth-grade open house when the discussion turned to immigration. Why did people immigrate to America? The teacher and the class discussed pestilence, war, persecution and then addressed famine. "What is famine?" the teacher asked one of the boys in the class.
   "Discrimination against women."

Name Withheld
April 1, 1981

In cleaning out my desk at the end of the school year, I ran across this paper. It was written by Cari Shepherd, a delightful third grader, in reaction to a *Weekly Reader* feature on Jane Addams. Enjoy!
   "Jane Adams helped my annsisters have a better place to live, to play, and to have love."

Shirley Copeland
Morristown, Tennessee
June 1983

One reader thought to experiment with nonverbal language. We found it an interesting idea and published the letter—only to learn from those who knew better.

A suggestion for a nonverbal "sisterhood signal" was passed my way: the deaf-mute sign for *sister* is the stroking of your thumb across your cheek. I believe the sign is based on the bonnet strings that tied under the chin. It seems significant to me: our bonnets are off, but we are still struggling for freedom from other confinements. It is also pleasant to stoke another sister's cheek with your thumb as a loving gesture.

Julie Sillaway
Fort Wayne, Indiana
April 1974 Issue

Julie Sillaway suggested we adopt the deaf sign for *sister* as a nonverbal sisterhood signal. As a teacher of the deaf, I feel I must share my insight into this sign and all other signs used to designate the female sex versus the male sex.

The deaf sign language had its origins in the 1700s and is a vehicle for perpetuating the severe sexist attitudes of that era. To this day, all signs for males are made at the forehead, connoting the mind and thought. All female signs (*mother, sister, wife, daughter, aunt, grandmother,* and so on) are made at the mouth, connoting gossip, talk, gab. Need more be said?

I long ago stopped using "Miss" with my name at school and taught my students to call me "Ms. Marley." My name sign is now the finger-spelled letter *M* made on the right and then left shoulder—an area meaning power. The children never questioned the change—only the adults remarked. *Hmm!*

Jo Marley
Philadelphia, Pennsylvania
July 1974 Issue

The deaf are neither "mute" nor "dumb." If deaf people do not speak, it is because they have not received the extensive articulation training necessary to speak confidently and "normally" or because they have been rebuffed too often by the impatience of hearing people.

Twenty-one Students and Faculty Members
National Technical Institute for the Deaf
Rochester Institute of Technology
Rochester, New York
July 1974 Issue

An offhand remark in a piece about language offended another constituency.

I had hoped a linguist would take care to employ more tact ["You Are What You Say," July 1974]. Robin Lakoff's analogy–" 'She thinks like a man' is, at best, a left-handed compliment' "—is yet another slap on the wrist for the left-handed minority who must struggle daily with the tools and inventions of a right-handed, "right-minded" world.

Although the persons whose preference for the left hand are no longer being burned at the stake for their tendency (as they were during the witch hunts), and although few teachers now stalk their classrooms with rulers ready to rap the knuckles of a child who would dare reach for her or his pencil with the "wrong" hand, still the verbal belittling lives on.

Tempest in a teapot? Perhaps. But over the years, I have had my ideas dismissed as logically inferior, not just for their issuing from the mouth of a woman, but for their being the product of "left-handed thinking" as well.

Megan D. Price
Fair Haven, Vermont
November 1974 Issue

Some of the most universal problems involving names and titles came up within families—particularly on the occasion of marriage. And when it came time to name children, parents had to decide whether or not to add to the hyphenated generation.

After twenty years of not even attending a wedding, I was recently asked to be in one. A young woman in the neighborhood said, "I hear that you're to be the maid of honor in the wedding." I chuckled to myself and answered yes. (Can a once-married forty-two year old still qualify as the *maid* of honor?) Then the minister at the rehearsal said, "Oh, and you're the matron of honor?" "No, no," I practically yelled at him, "maybe you could have a Ms. of honor?" When the minister recovered, the wedding party decided that I would be the best woman.

Barbara O'Steen
Seattle, Washington
October 4, 1976

When I married, I decided not to change my name. I was used to it and too lazy to change all my credit cards. My husband has always liked the idea, being eager to explain during introductions that *he* decided to keep *his* own name.

We have no children, but easily decided if we should have any that tradition is best, with the middle name being my surname. In fact, this decision was a snap. Deciding now whether we want children is much harder.

What's wrong with seeing tradition as simply tradition. I have no qualms about having my father's name. . . . I have his nose.

Therese M. Nolan
Columbus, Ohio
November 19, 1983

My husband and I agreed when we were married that any children would have a hyphenated combination of our last names. When I became pregnant, however, the furor began. My father-in-law, who has three sons, said, "But I've spent my whole life trying to make a name for myself." They thought my parents would be happy, but my father sent us a twenty-page letter telling us why it was a bad idea. Until recently he still called my daughter by her first name and my husbands last until she corrected him. She is four and a half years old!

Dayna Deck
Durham, North Carolina
December 14, 1983

In my husband's and my case, we didn't dare hyphenate. It would have come out Frankenstine (Frank-Stine). So we made a pact: if the baby was a girl it would have the last name Frank, and a boy would be Stine.

Janrae Frank
Haltom City, Texas
December 13, 1983

One reader tried to reassure us regarding a word we had just about discarded.

Your readers may be interested in learning the origins of the word *housewife,* which many of us find so demeaning. The *hus* in *husband* has the same origin as the *house* in *housewife.* The words are Old English. *Hus* survives in the modern *house* and *band* in its modern counterpart—"band, that which holds things together." A *hus-band* was a householder. A *hus-wif* (pronounced, as far as we know, "weef") was the gender-appropriate identical term. *Huswife* and *husband* were titles of respect and honor in the community, carrying the connotation "substantial person." *Wif* meant "adult woman" as well as "married woman," much the same way as the modern German *frau* does. The *huswif* was the equal partner in the formation and maintenance of the household, even though she may have been gainfully employed as a weaver, seamstress, farmer, or whatever. The closest translation we can come to in modern English is "householderess."

JoAnne W. Scott
Annandale, Virginia
October 17, 1977

Finally, as readers were quick to tell us, kids knew sexism when they found it.

My four-year-old niece was sharing a snack of cheese and crackers with her grandfather. Halfway through the plate he noticed she was gobbling it up at a pace rivaling his own. He proclaimed, "Boy, Erin you're really a 'cheeseman'!" Amused at his obvious error she replied, "No, Papa! I'm a cheese 'person'!"

This wasn't a statement of the influence of feminism; it was an innocent recognition of an obvious mistake in word usage. At four years old, Erin was aware of someone's casual denial of her womanhood. Before long she may no longer notice it and begin to accept it . . . not if I can prevent it.

Name Withheld
June 24, 1981

I thought you might enjoy hearing a discussion I heard between my son and his neighbor friend. They were playing together and the little boy got the giggles. "Hee-hee-hee-hee," he giggled, whereupon my son replied in a very condescending tone, "What are you, Danny, some kind of chauvinist? In *this* house we say 'Her-her-her-her!' "

Her who laughs last,

Name Withheld
August 7, 1975

Would you like to hear a nonsexist chuckle?
s/he/s/he

Name Withheld
September 1975

Up Against the Institution

———————— ❦ ————————

When Gloria Steinem is asked about the future of the women's movement, she often responds that for the last fifteen years or so, we've been engaged in the naming of problems—in consciousness-raising. And the difficult task of making institutional change is just beginning. While some institutions seem stubbornly resistant to change, others—out of self-interest if nothing else—seem at least slightly more amenable. Where women are perceived as a potential market, as in the credit industry and the advertising community, change has been accomplished and the Ms. *readers provide a record of it.*

Progress was often two steps forward and one step back, of course. In banking and credit, it took the stick of federal legislation—the Equal Credit Opportunity Act of 1974—to reinforce the carrot of a growing market that came from the increased earnings of some women. During the first couple of years of publication, readers wrote constantly of their battles with credit institutions as they struggled to insist that women were independent earners, spenders, and borrowers. But well before the enforcement provisions of the equal-credit act were fully operative in 1977, some companies were going after women's dollars in an enterprising way—sometimes before their own corporations were quite prepared to deal with the new policies.

————————————

I was delighted when my December 1972 issue arrived and, right there, in front of God and All the People, American Express had an ad for "Women Only" with some beautiful rhetoric about wanting to "start evening things up."

Since I earned a good deal more than the eighty-five hundred dollars per year needed to apply, I jumped to the conclusion that here at last, thanks to *Ms.* and

158

American Express's sudden enlightenment, there was *money* to be made off us professional women. Here was a chance for me to obtain a credit card without giving information about my husband's employment, salary, credit record, and so forth. I joyously filled out the application.

Some weeks later someone called me to check out my husband's employment as associate director of the ACLU of Northern California. I informed the poor soul that she was mixed up, that I was the associate director here and that my husband was a professor at San Francisco State. I was told that my husband was being checked out by a credit bureau. Since I knew of no credit application made by my husband, I asked what this was all about. She answered that Eason Monroe had applied for an American Express card a few weeks earlier. The intriguing part was that although I had filled out the application for Laura B. Monroe, she did not even have my name. She did have my husband's, which mystified me, since I had not given his name. She informed me that American Express had asked the bureau to do a computer credit check on my husband and that was the usual procedure.

Still clinging to my innocent joy about finally being a credit grown-up, I said, "You must be mistaken. I applied on an application provided in my beloved *Ms.* magazine, entitled 'Women Only.' No one would pull a shabby trick like using our very own magazine to exploit the women's movement and just plain rip us off."

She answered, "Well, this is the way we handle the credit check."

I guess it was pushy of me to think I was grown-up. I'm only forty-five. Perhaps in a few years?

Laura B. Monroe
San Francisco, California
July 1973 Issue

We reported in an editor's note that Laura Monroe did finally get her American Express card: it was made out to Mr. Laura B. Monroe, who was also invited to apply for an associate's card for his wife!

Another reader used a different kind of pressure to get her coveted American Express card.

I read with interest and sympathy Laura Monroe's account of her experience with American Express. I, too, after seeing their ad in *Ms.*, thought I would have no problems.

My initial application was turned down. I rewrote, explaining in great detail my financial holdings, which I knew to be equal to or more than some men who hold the American Express card. Again a polite turndown.

I then had my attorney (male) write for me, and all he actually wrote was a reiteration of what I had already told them with the added message that he knew all that I had said was true.

Within a few weeks I received my card in the mail. Click!

And, Laura, a few more years won't do it. I'm forty-nine.

P.S. Congrats to my attorney for wondering out loud whether I would have received the card had my attorney been female.

Name Withheld
July 7, 1973

At least American Express saw the potential of women's dollar power—and the company continues to set standards in marketing to women today. As another reader reported in response to Laura Monroe's letter, other companies were slower to treat women as credit grown-ups.

Several times I (a husband) made applications for American Express cards for my wife and myself. Each time I applied, a rejection notice was sent stating that I didn't make enough and/or that I was a student. (I am a grad student on an assistantship.) When my wife, a registered nurse, applied for a card using the *Ms.* application form, she received a card, and I was able to get one as a dependent. So the system *does* work.

Local credit cards, however, are another matter. In applying by phone for a Central Charge card here in the Washington, D.C., metropolitan area, I was assured that cards would be issued in the names of Dennis D. McDonald and Carol S. McDonald. Instead, we received Mr. Dennis . . . and Mrs. Dennis . . . cards. (This upsets me more than it does my wife; "McDonald" is not exclusively mine, any more than it is exclusively the property of my father. But Dennis is mine, and I am sorely offended when we receive mail to Mr. and Mrs. Dennis. They even give her my middle initial, which I'm *really* attached to!) One card was mailed back with a note explaining my feelings about the matter; no answer for two months. Another letter prompted their mailing another card to "Mrs. Dennis D. . . ." Needless to say, we don't use these cards very often.

Dennis D. McDonald
Washington, D.C.
July 1973

Beneath this issue of names, of course, was the critical need for a wife to establish her own credit history independent of her husband. This need was particularly acute in the case of divorce or separation, but it was important to any couple that depended on two incomes.

Computing my husband's and my credit status, our bank wouldn't count a penny of *my* salary. My husband and I both work part time and both do the housekeeping. I work five hours a day, teaching nursery school, and then have time to myself. My husband works six hours as a custodian and then works on his art. Our salaries together make us a comfortable living.

The bank's credit representative said the bank couldn't count my salary because I'm female—because I am of child-bearing age, because I might get pregnant, and because we might not be able to make payments if I were pregnant.

The laws need to be changed to give all women's incomes equal credit status, especially for women whose income is not just supplementary but a necessary, integral part of the total family income.

Name Withheld
July 31, 1973

I am still seeing red over an incident with a prominent Washington, D.C., bank. Tempted by its advertisements of a checking account that is backed by an approved credit limit, I applied. I was promptly rejected, because "the breadwinner is a student."

Puzzled, I then spoke with the bank official from whom I received the letter and explained that my husband, from whom I have been separated for six months, is indeed a student and has been for the seven years of our marriage. I emphasized to her that during those years I had always worked and provided the sole income for the family. When I completed the application, it was for my own use, not my husband's, and my own annual income was well within the bank's requirements.

Frustrated, the bank officer snapped, "Well, I'm sorry, honey, but as long as you're legally married, you can't be the breadwinner—you're a woman!" Case closed.

Susan P. Roberson
Alexandria, Virginia
October 1973 Issue

The annoyance of being viewed as not in control of your own assets was such a universal frustration for women in the early seventies that a successful encounter with the banking and credit industry was definitely something to write home to Ms. *about.*

As two women who have been inspired and emboldened by *Ms.* magazine, we would like to share our recent success in buying a house. Tired of pouring our money down the rent drain, we found a reasonably priced house—reasonable for the Washington, D.C., area. Our initial offer, considerably lower than the asking price, was accepted.

The real-estate firm then put us in touch with a mortgage banker, who had a commitment for a federally insured loan at an unbelievably good rate of interest. We are now living in the house. We consider ourselves fortunate in that we dealt with women in both the real estate and mortgage-banking firms, and they never conveyed to us any feelings of pessimism. They were true sisters in our endeavor. If we women automatically accept without challenge the prevailing horror stories about women and credit, we will be beaten before we begin. We can do it!

Names Withheld
December 7, 1973

I am beginning to feel my oats and want so badly to share that feeling with you. I recently applied for credit at a large local bank and was turned down cold after having used their services for nine years. After some soliloquy, I decided I'd been royally screwed.

I am enclosing the letter of rejection from the bank and my retort. I just want you to know that the letter reached the bank president this morning by mail, and by 10:00 A.M. he had already begun tracking me down.

I feel so good. Of course I got the line of credit, which had ceased even to be the issue by the time the letter hit the poor bastard; but doubly great is the fact that my letter is now in the hands of my congressman, four newspapers, and my mother.

Margie Horowitz
Maplewood, New Jersey
July 26, 1973

With skillful lobbying by the Women's Equity Action League, the Women's Lobby, and other women's organizations, the Equal Credit Opportunity Act passed first in the Senate in a version introduced by Senator Bill Brock and then, in 1974, in the House, taking effect in 1977. It was the first major piece of legislation in an effort still going on today to guarantee women's economic equity through pension and tax reform, adding to, so far, less successful efforts in areas such as childcare, poverty, and pay equity.

One place where Ms. *readers regularly confronted American business and financial institutions was in the magazine itself—the advertising pages. As we constantly told potential advertisers,* Ms. *readers took their messages seriously, and certainly not passively. When we asked for comments on the advertisements in our first regular issue, July 1972, readers were articulate about the images they preferred. Usually, they didn't wait to be asked, and the Ms. sales staff used readers' critiques to try to educate the advertising community on how to appeal to our audience of feminist consumers.*

You asked for our comments about the ads in *Ms.*, so here goes:

Most of them are gratifying, at least in approach to us. The Lelani Rum and Panasonic TV treated us as human beings. Coppertone and Chantilly were not offensive, but for a brief moment I thought I had regressed to *Mademoiselle*.

More important, however, are the ads that *could* be in *Ms.* . . . . Let's face it. Most of the *Ms.* readers will continue to use cosmetics, brush their teeth, wear clothing, and keep their homes reasonably clean. Couldn't we *just once* see a cosmetic or hair-care ad that would portray a woman who wants to look well groomed because she has to make a presentation or pitch an account? Couldn't a woman want to look nice because she is meeting a woman friend for lunch? Couldn't a woman be portrayed looking for blueprints with other women or a group of men and women? Is it true that we never comb our hair unless it will guarantee us a romantic involvement with a man?

Win Ann Winkler
New York, New York
September 1972 Issue

Madison Avenue had changed enough by 1981 that we ran a One Step Forward column in the September issue, full of ads that celebrated women's friendship. But the first thing we needed to do was convince the business community that women did indeed buy such things as stereos, financial services, and even automobiles—products that, when we began publishing in 1972, were not marketed in traditional women's magazines. It was an enormous advance when this kind of advertiser decided to go after the women who read Ms. It was even nicer when the ad copywriters got the message right.

Well, those Honda folks put an ad in *Ms.* that talked about rack-and-pinion steering, and it sold me their car. The car is terrific, and the steering is even better, and I think you should know that I wrote them and told them to keep advertising in *Ms.*

When I went down to look the Honda Civic over, I took the issue of *Ms.* in which the ad appeared with me, and the salesperson took me on a tour of the engine before he started going over the advantages of color schemes. I don't know whether he took me seriously because his consciousness had been raised or because Honda tells their salespeople to watch out for grim women clutching *Ms.* magazine and marching stoically along mumbling things about disc brakes. But he *did* take me seriously. It was a great change for the better, and they should all be told it works.

> Mallory Kirk-Marshall
> Yarmouth, Maine
> June 1975 Issue

Unfortunately, a car dealer who took women seriously as consumers still seemed the exception rather than the rule in the mid seventies.

I set out one day recently to price new cars, to make a choice, and to finance and insure the choice I made. At the end of the day, I was exhausted and bitter. To say that the men I talked to treated me in a patronizing way would be an understatement. I am not used to this, for most of the men at the high school where I work regard me as an equal, and I am married to a liberated man. Car dealers, on the other hand, referred to me as "the little woman" (I am five feet nine inches tall), "the Mrs.," or "dear." Initially, I asked the salesman *not* to talk to me in this way, but by the end of the day, all I could do was laugh at their bizarre comments.

When my husband returned home and accompanied me to the car dealer I had chosen, he could not believe what he heard. For instance, at one point the salesman told him that he *should* put his own sound system in the car because he was a musician, but that if he *did* take the standard stereo system, "the Mrs. will love it." (I also am a musician.) And before I signed the papers (for the car was to be in my name), the saleman stopped me, handed the papers to my husband, and suggested that he look them over first. My husband said it wasn't necessary, for I had checked everything earlier. That salesman looked at him as if he were crazy—as if he were breaking some sacred rule.

I hope that my daughter will benefit from all these "little" battles I fight, but how long *will* women have to wait for equality?

> Rosalie A. Allen
> Mount Clemens, Michigan
> September 1976 Issue

Activists that they are, Ms. readers would often use whatever power they had to change things.

We wish to remain anonymous, but that's nothing new—we are usually referred to as "the girl" or "some stupid secretary." We operate from Pasadena to Toronto. When any of us reads an ad such as "Fly me," or "We wiggle our tails for you," or "Pinch our maids, not our towels," or "Like our waitresses, our pancakes are stacked," we promptly inform our secretary friends, who inform their secretary friends (and anyone who will listen), and as we are responsible for making accommodations and transportation reservations for employees in our companies, we make it a point *not* to book at the hotel, motel, restaurant, or transportation outfit with the offensive, demeaning ad. We hope that this letter prompts others to join our crusade and that our collective actions will hit the offenders where it will do the most good—in their pocketbooks.

> Working Quietly for Sisterhood
> January 1976

One campaign by Ms. *readers started with submissions to our No Comment column—a collection of retrograde images of women confronted in the media or in the everyday world of business memos, junk mail, and cocktail napkins—and took off from there. The offender was a manufacturer called Skan-a-matic, who advertised their electronic scanner in trade publications with a visual of a model with the scanner pointing to her cleavage—the ad copy read, "Sexy Skanners to detect small stuff." Our readers didn't like it.*

I had already written a letter to Skan-a-matic to protest the use of a partially clad woman in their advertising brochures when I saw that the same ad had been submitted by twenty-eight readers to No Comment [October 1978]. When Skan-a-matic officials replied to my letter, they informed me that they intended to continue the ad and that no ad could please everyone. They mentioned that very few people had written to criticize the ad—the tone of the letter implied that I was clearly someone on the lunatic fringe, whose opinion could not be taken seriously.

I would like to suggest to *Ms.* magazine readers that they express their opinions directly to Skan-a-matic.

> Dr. Susan Dahlberg
> Murray Hill, New Jersey
> February 1979 Issue

Of course, readers followed Dr. Dahlberg's suggestion, and eventually Skan-a-matic capitulated and pulled the ad campaign, though they

*claimed it had nothing to do with any feminist complaints. A more
satisfying resolution happened when an unintentionally offensive ad did
slip through our somewhat haphazard screening process. We quickly ran
an apology in our July 1980 Letters to the Editor column, being as
respectful as we possibly could be to the advertiser in question.*

Editors' Note: As we completed our June 1980 issue, we noticed the
double entendre of a line in an advertisement on page 36. It shows the
smiling and triumphant face of a middle-aged woman (in fact, the kind of
real and vital woman we are always urging advertisers to use instead of
impossibly beautiful models), with a bottle of The Club Pina Colada and
the line, "Hit Me With a Club." Even though the same ad had been done
elsewhere picturing a man—and though this woman, in the context of
Ms., was being directed at women readers—we realized that we should
have let the advertiser know that the copy could be taken seriously as
referring to violence against women. But it was too late: the page was
already off the press.

We would like our readers to know that this is one of a series of ads
created by an agency team that included women as both copywriter and
art director, and that are intended by them to be humorous—certainly not
to refer to real violence. Nonetheless, we should have anticipated the
possibility.

*We should have indeed. An avalanche of outraged letters came to us as
well as to the Heublein/Spirits Group, which produced the product.
Finally, a letter from the Heublein vice-president for marketing, J. E.
Corr, Jr., announced that the company was moved by the conviction of
Ms. readers and others to withdraw the national campaign. We published
the letter—addressed to Ms. publisher Patricia Carbine—in which Corr
said graciously, "Indeed, you, your staff and the Ms. readership were
instrumental in our reaching the decision, which was not an easy one.
However, we have come to understand and are now in full agreement with
your position on this important issue."*

*A happy ending. Often, however, we continued to displease our most
rigorous readers, particularly when they found an ad sexually exploit-
ative or the product dangerous.*

Please explain to me the difference between the view of this woman's crotch and rear and legs and what *Playboy* uses to tantalize their readers. This ad belongs in your No Comment section. It's clear to me that your commitment to the women's movement stops where the buck starts.

Susan Murray-Friend
Ann Arbor, Michigan
June 1979 Issue

That particular ad was for a shaver, and our explanation was that it seemed reasonable to show body parts or skin in an ad if relevant to the product—but I'm not sure how many readers bought the rationale or the product.

Perhaps the most constant complaints came in response to cigarette advertisements. Here a reader makes fun of a reference in an article to the salutary effect of trees on an environment.

I read your article "Hug a Tree Today" by Cynthia Cooke, M.D. and Susan Dworkin [June 1981], while sitting under my favorite tree and smoking my favorite brand of cigarettes. I looked up at the leaves of the towering oak above me and took a puff on my cigarette. I breathed deeply of the oxygen emanating from the tree and took another drag on my cigarette. My anger rose. How dare they cut down trees? How dare they assault my health by depriving me of oxygen? I took two more puffs on my cigarette. Trees are a natural phenomenon, essential for life on earth. I lit up another cigarette. Thank God for *Ms.* At least you have my health in mind. Thank you for such an enlightening article, and most important of all, thank you for your cigarette ads. It's just me and my tree and my cigarette and my (pardon me while I cough) health (?).

Name Withheld
May 26, 1981

All in all, it was much more satisfying when readers criticized the ads in somebody else's publication instead of our own, and they continued to find plenty of material. One reader sent in a help-wanted ad from her local newspaper. Another sent in an ad for little girls' makeup featuring the line "Dressing up for Daddy."

I thought you might be interested in this classified ad, which I ran across this week. It is not the usual promotion of T. and A. [tits and ass], but it is every bit as stereotypical:

Envelope Stuffing. Persons with finger dexterity needed to work for a temporary help service. Must have phone & reliable transportation. Tedious work/minimum wage. Ideal for homemakers.

You'll excuse me if I cut this letter short. I must rush to line up that job. It's not every day that a good position, suited to my skills, comes along.

Name Withheld
February 15, 1983

My God! The Total Woman begins her training at age five! I wonder what Avon will be pushing next year for the six-year-olds—black garter belts?

I think the "Dressing up for Daddy" is such a sick way of preparing girls for this lunatic idea of "pleasing the men in your life!" And to begin a girl in this odalisque mentality should prompt us to ban this product forthwith.

Sorry for the underlining. But this kind of crap is what I've been batting my head against for years. I'm fifty-two years old, attractive, and sexual. And thank God for *Ms.* I finally realized that I have not really been a crazy lady all these years!

Name Withheld
May 21, 1981

I read your note on the reemergence of cosmetics for little girls. No need to worry—if our daughters are taught that makeup is solely for fun; a uniquely female, creative and artistic tradition—with us since Egyptian queens put kohl on their eyes. Makeup is often called a mask—only true if the woman wearing it believes it. A woman's true soul shines through squeaky-clean skin or a pound of pancake stick.

Let little girls play with makeup. Emphasize the play.

A few weeks ago I was going to a party and being in the party mood decided to party up my face. Closeted in the bathroom, I had the greatest time painting and coloring. I emerged feeling (and thinking I looked) glamorous. My boyfriend's reaction? "Gee, you look pretty. I love the way your eyes twinkle when you smile."

Name Withheld
June 17, 1981

Generally, advertisers got more sophisticated in the eighties. At least they realized they were marketing products to women who led busy lives. But the "superwoman" image wasn't what readers were after either. Meanwhile, the old favorite "ring around the collar" Wisk campaign persisted well past the time men should have learned to wash their necks.

Why do advertisers persist in selling the image of the beautiful, shapely woman executive who keeps the same perfectly made-up face and styled hair, even after a hard day of earning a six-figure salary, dining in expensive restaurants, having a brisk game of tennis at the club, and a late night of discothèque hopping? It's no surprise that real women are tempted to wonder what they're doing wrong.

Deborah K. Smith
Brookline, Massachusetts
July 1980 Issue

Will "ring around the collar" commercials go on year after year *forever*? Am I the only one who feels insulted when the camera zooms in on the face of the *wife* looking guilty and ashamed? For heaven's sake, it's *his* shirt! I'm ashamed that American women continue to buy the product.

Name Withheld
December 3, 1980

Being sold to in an insulting way was distressing enough, but some marketers didn't seem to think women were responsible purchasers.

I am fifteen years old, and when Mother's Day came close, I called a local flower shop and ordered a very nice arrangement with a card to be signed with my name, my four-year-old sister's name, and my two-year-old brother's name. Of course, they had no way of knowing how old any of us were, but they had *my* name on the order. The flowers were sent, and a week later we received a bill, addressed to my *brother!* Perhaps I should have left the bill for him to pay with his pennies. Click!

Name Withheld
July 11, 1973

The name of the selling game may have been narrowly targeting one's market, buy many Ms. *readers thought stereotypes got in the way of sales.*

One evening this week I answered the phone and began talking to a very friendly woman who was working on a market-research survey. The survey was on the most popular brand names of beer in the Washington, D.C., area.

I was all set to discuss the merits of various beers—sitting there on the phone, a Pabst can in hand, when the woman apologetically told me that she could only take replies from men. My boyfriend (who loathes beer) was present, and I asked her for the reasoning behind this. She said, "You know, I continually get this situation in my calls. I think it's grossly unfair to deny women the right to express their opinion on something. I don't know how long I'm going to keep this job, and I think I'm going to write a letter to *Ms.* about this situation."

Name Withheld
April 19, 1974

I recently received a phone call from a survey company inquiring about whether I owned or rented my home. I said that I owned the home. The surveyor then asked if there was a yard, as the client was a snow blower and lawn mower manufacturer. I stated that there was a yard. He asked to speak to the man of the house. I told him that there was no "man of the house." He paused and said that he had to terminate the survey—on the manufacturer's orders.

I have no other comments to make!

Sue Simler
Trafford, Pennsylvania
November 1981 Issue

Ms. Simler had no further comments, but other readers did.

Noting Sue Simler's recent letter on sexism in telephone surveys, I write to report a similar incident. A surveyor phoned me yesterday and asked whether she could speak with the woman who buys the groceries for the household. When I replied that I (a male) buy my own groceries, the surveyor abruptly hung up without explanation.

Name Withheld
October 20, 1981

We were happy to let syndicated columnist Liz Smith have the last word on the Simler story.

I was interested in the letter from Sue Simler.

This caused me to reflect on what my own "no man of the house" household had purchased for two separate homes in the past three years. Are you ready?

A Cadillac Seville, a Ford station wagon, a three thousand dollar John Deere tractor, a snow blower, a chain saw, an electric drill, a rotating TV aerial, hydraulic hedge clippers, two ban saws, an L.L. Bean sawbuck, a rolling log carrier, two videotape recorders, many tapes, a color TV set, two tape recorders, an IBM Selectric typewriter, a Sony Walkman, cross-country skis, lawn furniture, lots of camera equipment and film, hundreds of yards of garden hose, a new chimney, a new roof, other repairs, hundreds of dollars worth of assorted manure, seeds, bulbs, pots, hardware, and flashlights.

Of course, I also bought makeup, soap, toiletries, shampoo, perfume, clothes, booze, and groceries. But then, so did the men in my life, who are not necessarily "the men of the house."

Liz Smith
New York, New York
March 1982 Issue

The press as an institution seemed surprisingly resistant to change, given the amount of news that we saw women making—and given the fact that by the mid eighties the field of journalism was some 40 percent female. But before male editors would see women's news as "hard" news, women journalists were making change from within, and sometimes not getting the proper credit even in our pages. One reporter responds to a January 1973 article on Shirley Chisholm's campaign the year before for the Democratic presidential nomination.

Elizabeth Frappollo remarks in "The Ticket That Might Have Been" that a press conference was attended by "thirty male reporters and two women, one of whom was a society-page editor." The inference is that she didn't count as a "real" reporter since she just writes for the women's section. News about women is described as "being buried between recipes" on the women's pages—obviously a fate worse than death.

I write for a women's news section. It's not a society section and hasn't been for many years. But still the women's section remains a joke to most women and men. On my paper, we are referred to as "soc broads" and our copy as "just more women's crap." Well, that "women's crap" has included stories on the new Family Code for Texas and on the new tax deductions on child care—the only stories on these subjects in the paper, and a story on the importance of women having their own wills, and the efforts of Texas women to pass the Equal Legal Rights Amendment to the Texas constitution, and stories on consciousness-raising groups and on how textbooks perpetuate sex-role stereotyping.

Our section is the only place in this paper where you will read about the women's movement. And we have made some progress. Now women's names are mentioned in obituaries of men, instead of being listed simply as "survivors include his wife." This year the women's section reporters were included in the lectures given to our summer interns. Prior to this, every department but ours was invited to speak to these young journalists.

We hope, someday, to do away with our section. Having a special section for women is as ridiculous as having a black section, a Chicano section, a WASP section. Women are human beings, but the only place this is acknowledged is by women in the women's news section.

Don't put us down, sisters—we are working very hard for you.

Katie Brown
Fort Worth, Texas
April 1973 Issue

Ms. Katie Brown of Fort Worth, Texas, outlined some of the problems faced by the "women's department" of a daily paper. I would like to offer some further comments based on my experiences over the past five years as head copy boy for a major Montreal daily newspaper.

As copy boys, we are responsible for primary distribution of wire copy. We divide copy into four categories: finance and business, sports, city (local news), and news. The last category covers everything that does not fit directly into the first three. Unofficially, we also relay copy directly to other departments. A story on women's fashion, for example, is obviously going to the women's section.

I have discovered, however, that giving a news item about women to the news desk usually means the end of the line for that story. If the slot person on the news desk does not want it for a news page, it may or may not be offered to the women's section. More often than not, it is simply "spiked" (stuck on a metal spike with all other unused copy).

Recently, United Press International sent a story, with an East Coast dateline, about the well-known advocate of birth control, William B. Baird, Jr. I asked the news-desk slot person—who is also the night news editor—what he wanted to do with the story. He answered by tearing the item in a number of pieces and scattering them on the floor.

Name Withheld
August 1973 Issue

"Ms." readers are close media watchers—alert in particular to coverage of the women's movement and changes in women's lives.

This past week my husband and I bought several old issues of *Time* magazine at our public library. We thought it would be interesting to compare the social climate of 1956 to that of 1981. We were amused by the old advertisements that depicted women as the ever-efficient housewife, teacher, nurse, or secretary. In several articles, women were referred to as "girls." The ideas and opinions of women and minorities, even when printed, were often treated unseriously and condescendingly. All contributing editors but one were men, but all editorial researchers listed were women. Things certainly have changed.

We were greatly encouraged by all the advances that have been made by women in the last twenty-five years. That is until I happened to read an article in the September 21, 1981, issue of *Time* magazine discussing the debate of to fight or not to fight when confronted by a rapist. The man who wrote the article actually stated that the safety of women is being gambled with by feminists, who are "angry at the prevalence of rape" and wish to "rouse female pride and punish rapists." That a woman fights back not so much to save her life but because she's angry at men seemed to be the message of the writer. It sure put a damper on our assumption of progress. It was more of a clack than a click.

Karen A. Geary
Kansas City, Missouri
October 7, 1981

An enormous institutional adjustment to women in the seventies was their admission to previously all-male colleges and programs, and to the military academies.

On May 2, and 3, I attended graduation exercises at Texas A&M University. My best friend's eldest son was receiving a degree and was also being commissioned a second lieutenant in the air force.

All the graduates received their diplomas and a congratulatory handshake from President Jarvis E. Miller. All, that is, but one; the "odd man out" was a young woman by the name of Melanie Suzanne Zentgraf. After presenting the diploma, President Miller turned his back on her.

My friend's son explained that Zentgraf, who was also a member of the Corps of Cadets, had earned the displeasure of her classmates and the establishment by taking the university into court (case still pending). According to his account, Zentgraf had applied to join the Corps of Cadets band but had been refused on the basis that it was an all-male group that dormed and traveled together, and that there were no proper facilities to accommodate a female. Zentgraf apparently felt that her rejection as a band member was discriminatory, and she instituted legal action.

According to my friend's son, President Miller's studied insult to this graduate was very popular, since she was a "troublemaker." Even the other female cadets didn't like her, he said.

It was with great interest, therefore, that I witnessed the air force commissioning ceremony the next day. Zentgraf was the last in this contingent to go up and receive her commission, since it went in alphabetical order.

As each of the cadets went up, they received a sort of hoot from their fellow corps members in the gallery. When it became Zentgraf's turn, you could hear the cadets ssh-ing one another—a reminder that Zentgraf was beyond the pale.

But, to their eternal credit, six or seven female corps members in the balcony not only gave the hoot but also rose to their feet and applauded, leading me to believe that at least a portion of my friend's son's information was less than accurate.

I was very impressed with Zentgraf's dignified bearing and evident courage. She must have had a tough row to hoe.

Name Withheld
September 1980 Issue

I am a graduate of the first class with women from the formerly all-male bastion of ego and "macho-ism" the United States Naval Academy. For four years, every time one of the women turned around, there were photographers and newspaper persons recording our "firsts." It was not, however, so much the media that harped on us, it was the male midshipmen. They all seemed so concerned about everything we did— whom we dated; our grades; our physical prowess or lack thereof; our appearance, whether we gained or lost weight; how we got along with our roommates. The list is endless. The majority of the women in my class put up with this for the four years, more because we didn't want to make waves than because we got used to it. I'm confident that the women at the other academies went through the same problems. I'm also confident, however, that these attitudes will change in time—I hope.

Name Withheld
July 1980

The above woman graduate needed to be confident to have survived that "all-male bastion of ego," as she called it. Not only women in the armed forces but military wives as well had to deal with the sometimes archaic sexism in the services.

Because my husband is in the army, I've begun fighting the vicious sexism so prevalent in a military family's life.

One Saturday I happened to be in the office where my husband works. While there, I saw a map with what was obviously reference lines and points for a field exercise, marked on it. I was shocked into mute numbness when I read the words used for the coordinating points. The words were: *breast, murder, plunder, pillage, burn, kill, rape* and *incest*. The anger went so deep, it was two days before I could make a calm, comprehensive phone call. Fifteen minutes after I'd spoken to the post commander's office, the post chaplain, and the company chaplain, I had results. They had all been shocked and helpful and had dealt with the problem quickly. My husband's operations officer called and asked if "a woman had been in the office Saturday and seen anything that could be called lewd and lascivious." While I chuckled over the Victorian euphemisms, I was happy to have gotten such fast action.

My joy was short-lived. When he came home that evening, my husband told me that while the map has been removed (it was the creative work of one man), a new rule had been made. Dependents, that ridiculous army term, were now barred from the office.

The captain whose warped mind has used these deadly words in such a charming manner, was heard to comment, "What is your wife, one of those libbers?"

Oh, indeed I am, sir.

Arlene Ritner Sherian
Oak Grove, Kentucky
April 1981 Issue

Often readers took time out, as this correspondent puts it, to "bitch" about things that got to them recently. But also they wrote to celebrate.

I am writing to you with this "bitch," as my friends and relatives deem it, because I want to share it with someone who cares; even more so since I was widowed last year.

I have been the nurturer of three young sons; I have also been the sports critic, the softball coach, the fishing instructor, the knot tier, the arbitrator, the camper, the sex counselor, the laugher, joker, friend. In short, I do damn well at raising healthy people. When my oldest son, age ten, was a Cub Scout, I was active in that group and helped my son with his various projects and work toward his merit badges. I was no different from lots of other busy parents, male and female, who took some time out to work with the young boys. We all had a lot of fun.

This year, when my son turned ten, he was no longer considered a Cub Scout but had graduated because of his age into a higher branch of scouts, called Webelos. Here a problem developed. Under no circumstances is it permitted that a woman can lead a Webelos or Boy Scout troop. In Fond du Lac Bay Lakes Council, we had a real shortage of men who wanted to participate as leaders, thus we had a number of boys who were unable to participate in scouting at all, my son among them.

The BSA National Council's thinking goes something like this. When the boys are eight to ten they are still really mere children (babies) and have a more "home centered" program with a den *mother* (baby sitter). When they pass ten, however, they will begin to explore the world through the achievement of the following badges: Aquanaut, Artist, Athlete, Citizen, Craftsman, Engineer, Forester, Geologist, Naturalist, Outdoorsman, Scholar, Scientist, Showman, Sportsman, and Traveler. (There is not a single "domestic" activity badge to earn.) The den mother must then be replaced by a man, the more capable and worldly den *leader,* not the den father. It is thought to be better to have an overcrowded den led by a man or no den at all than to have one led by a woman.

Now one more short paragraph about this sexually bigoted world we live in. My fiancé is a radio announcer and, since I have known him, has worked for three different stations: one rock, one country, and one country and polka station. He graduated from Brown Institute in Minneapolis, one of the country's leading accredited schools of radio and television broadcasting. On a few occasions, I have helped him out on his show by selecting the music. He informed me that he was taught at Brown and instructed by the stations' program directors never to play two records back to back that were by female artists. It is, however, quite acceptable to play the records of male artists back to back or even to play many of them in succession. Isn't that stupid? I don't know why it even occurs to anyone to make up these rules. Are men that fearful of us?

Name Withheld
February 8, 1982

Last night I attended a college sporting event at Western Michigan University. The match was exciting and aggressive, and the audience was loud, involved, and on the edge of their seats. The crowd also set an NCAA record with 8,543 attending. The sport? Women's volleyball.

Valerie Salestri
Kalamazoo, Michigan
July 1984 Issue

The story of institutional support for women athletes began much earlier and with players who were much younger. Athletic girls faced a bleak picture when we began publishing, before equity in sports programs began to be insured by Title IX of the Education Amendments of 1972 (with regulations that took effect in July 1975).

I am in the ninth grade and on the girls' varsity basketball team at our school. I'm captain of the team and lead it in scoring, steals, and assists. I love basketball.

During our whole season this year, we had only five games: we had to furnish rides to the games ourselves; we had to play in our gym suits, because we had no uniforms in which to play; we were able to use the gym only when the boys were through with it; and we had a grand total of about thirty spectators at all our games combined. Our principal did not announce any of our games and did not provide a late bus, so that kids could stay and watch. One time I asked if it would be possible to get uniforms for our team. I was told to earn the money through car washes, dances, and bake sales. Yet each of the boys received thirty dollar brand-new uniforms this year.

Everyone seems to think that girls playing basketball is a big joke, but I am dead serious. If we are good enough to be called varsity, aren't we good enough to be respected?

Jane Lundquist
Bangor, Maine
June 1973 Issue

By the late seventies, the effects of Title IX were evident. The athletic programs in high schools and colleges were producing world-class women athletes, who in the eighties would win Olympic medals for the United States as individuals and in team sports such as basketball and volleyball. Some girls even took the difficult route of playing on boys' teams.

Watching team sports was never especially interesting to me. Lately, however, I have become a really avid basketball fan. The Warriors or the Celtics still bore me, but suddenly the Squires, the seventh-grade team at Newcastle Elementary School in Newcastle, California, has a real fascination. As the father of the only girl on the team—the only girl ever on the team—I never miss a game.

When Jennifer first said that she was going out for the team, I was sure she would have second thoughts after a few practice sessions. After all, her friends were making plans for cheerleader tryouts.

"Why not go out for the girls' volleyball team?" her grandmother suggested.

"Basketball's my game," she responded in the matter-of-fact way she has.

Jennifer went out for the team and she made it—not the first string but the team nonetheless. I should have expected what would come next, but I was naive enough to think that women's liberation had made real strides. Anyway, I thought, this is my daughter; no one could possibly be upset by her being on the team. How wrong I was.

Since only the boys' locker rooms are open for the games, Jennifer must wear her uniform under her clothes and change in the stands. She cannot shower after the games until we return home. All this she has accepted with equanimity. The hard part to take, to endure, is the rank bigotry and discrimination on the part of some of her teammates.

"On the court," Jennifer says, "they treat me okay, but in class and outside, some of the boys try to get me to drop out."

Once at a practice where no teacher was present, she was hit on the head with the ball, and two or three boys threw rocks at her to keep her off the court.

Jennifer refused to give up. Slowly, she has become more accepted and, slowly, the whole idea of having a daughter on the basketball team has begun to seem commonplace. Now when Grandmother asks about her future plans, Jennifer says that she wants to be a professional basketball player.

Richard Guches
Newcastle, California
October 1979 Issue

Another major institution that women were busy shaping to our own needs was religion. Some feminists worked within the major religions, while some looked elsewhere for their spiritual homes. This writer, taking issue with a historical article in the April 1974 issue by Andrea Dworkin on witchcraft, shows just how far outside the flock women were straying.

I am a witch. I was initiated into my first coven in 1967 and have been a student and active practitioner of the craft ever since. I am a charter member of the Council of American Witches—having nothing except spiritual connections with the Women's International Terrorist Conspiracy from Hell [referring to the "W. I. T. C. H. Manifesto," a sixties tract written by, or attributed to Valerie Salanis, whose later claim to fame was wounding artist Andy Warhol]. So, having stated my credentials, I have a bone to pick with Andrea Dworkin about her article "What Were Those Witches Really Brewing?"

She writes of our rites and practices, using Pennethorne Hughes and Jules Michelet as her only sources, who are not only *men* but *Christians* as well, which is enough to ruffle any wiccan's feathers! There was not *one* mention of the goddess: the Great Earth Mother, the Maiden Flora of the Plant Kingdom, Diana-Hecate, Queen of Sorcery and Night. The primary deity of the craft was and is the goddess. The Horned God, Faunus, her consort, is Lord of Animals, the Sun, and the Underworld. None of this has anything to do with the Christian devil, in whom only Christians believe. Witchcraft is a religion with a primarily matriarchal orientation. The Great Triple Goddess was the Primal Deity for most of the world at one time. The practice of witchcraft and numerous other pagan and neo-pagan fertility religions is based on her worship.

Witchcraft and the other matriarchal neo-pagan earth religions exist today and are constantly growing. They are a viable spiritual alternative to the dogmatic, patriarchal, and authoritarian systems such as Christianity, Islam, Hinduism, and Judaism. Witchcraft is also the only religion which has a female avatar: Aradia.

In the midst of the current male-aggression-generated ego catastrophe, what could be more beautifully logical than a return to our Holy Mother Nature? Thou art goddess! Blessed be.

Name Withheld
July 1974

Readers who remained within the religions traditional to their families adapted rites and rituals and celebrated women ministers and the new phenomenon of women rabbis and Episcopal priests.

I grew up a member of Monmouth Reform Temple, where Rabbi Sally Priesand is now the full-time rabbi. [Sally Priesand was ordained as the first woman rabbi in 1972 and as the first woman full-time rabbi nearly a decade later.] I am proud that my father was on the committee that offered the position to Rabbi Sally.

As I listened to our new rabbi read and speak during the High Holy Days, I was impressed with her and with our congregation for hearing her. I beamed (and almost cheered) when my father (the father of three daughters) stood on our bimah and, unlike the previous readers, followed the rabbi's example by also changing his reading to nonsexist wording. I overheard his friend whisper to his wife, "I guess even Milt is getting into the act!"

Mazel tov to Rabbi Sally!

Beth Klein
East Windsor, New Jersey
June 1982 Issue

Bette Howland's story "The Minister's Wife [December 1980] was of special interest to me, since I not only am the wife of a minister, but a minister as well.

For more than thirty years, my husband and I have juggled two careers in professional church work, along with a home life with three children. I still share some of the ceremonial roles as the minister's spouse, as does my husband for special occasions within my parish. Fortunately, both our congregations have fairly reasonable expectations in this regard.

But the point Bette Howland makes about "positions in life which actually require a wife" is well taken. While the minister as a professional person may not have a wife, most ministers, of either gender, must perform wifely and motherly functions professionally!

Relatively few churches are large enough to have multiple staffs, and most churches have small and increasingly elderly congregations, frequently with large and also elderly edifices to maintain. The church may be the Bride of Christ, and the building the House of God, but the minister is truly the housewife!

Rev. Mary Alice Geier
Los Angeles, California
April 1981 Issue

My daughter married recently, and I gave her away. The minister had a terrible time trying to handle that! He said it was not "proper." When he realized that that was the way it was going to be, he said I could just stand up where I was sitting when he asked who gives the bride away.

My daughter said, "No, she has been my mother for twenty-five years, and she is walking down the aisle with me!"

My other daughter, who is quite a feminist, beamed proudly as she snapped one picture after another.

Pat Moss
Atlanta, Georgia
September 1982 Issue

Where the strength of religious hierarchies was pitted against feminist goals, women became rebels within their own churches. This was particularly dramatic in the case of the Mormon Church's opposition to the Equal Rights Amendment, when Mormons for the ERA leader Sonia Johnson was excommunicated, and in the Roman Catholic Church's refusal to consider the idea of women priests, not to mention its attitude toward birth control and abortion.

I have just finished reading Sonia Johnson's article "The Woman Who Talked Back to God—and Didn't Get Zapped!" [November, 1981]. All I can say is *bravo*. It's time that the world knew the reason the Mormon Church and other "religious" organizations are opposing the Equal Rights Amendment. I'm glad she didn't get zapped. In fact, I think that God (whatever sex) views all of this squabbling over equality with sadness. It must be tough to watch beings with such potential waste themselves. Don't give up the fight. We will win in the end.

Robin Lee Cacy
Anchorage, Alaska
March 1982 Issue

Several years ago I was asked to teach one of the first women's studies courses at a religious institution that awarded M. A. and Ph. D. degrees to nuns and priests. I prepared for this course partly by meeting with religious women and attending several meetings and conventions, including one on the ordination of women into the priesthood. The culmination of my encounters with radical activist nuns was an invitation to attend a secret Mass to be celebrated by a nun. We met in the basement of an obscure building. We had to use a special knock to be admitted, and we were carefully scrutinized through a peephole before we were allowed to enter. "It's like the early Christians meeting in the catacombs," one nun explained. "Only now it's the pope and the hierarchy of the priesthood who play the part of the emperor and the Roman soldiers."

Name Withheld
December 1983 Issue

A short feature in the April 1984 issue on a twelve-year-old girl's unsuccessful struggle to become an altar girl brought a historical perspective from a reader. It was a surprisingly timely warning from suffrage leader Elizabeth Cady Stanton.

As a female rejected by my church, I sympathize with Julie Ann Smith. In light of the Catholic Church's current policy and Pope John Paul's recent ruling on women priests ("Never!"), it may be time for women in traditional religions to seriously consider the following quote from Elizabeth Cady Stanton:

> It is not commendable for women to get up fairs and donation parties for churches in which the gifted of their sex may neither pray, preach, share in the offices and honors, nor have a voice in the business affairs, creeds and discipline, and from whose altars come forth Biblical interpretations in favor of women's subjection.

Name Withheld
July 1984 Issue

III

You Can't Win Them All; Or, Critics (and Crackpots) Take On Ms.

———— ❦ ————

At the Schlesinger Library of Radcliffe College, where the collection of Ms. Letters to the Editors is housed, there are a couple of files labeled Crackpots. The staff at the Schlesinger Library has carefully noted in the description of the collection that the designation of some of our correspondents as crackpots was the decision of Ms. editors and not the library's.

While there were many zealous anti-feminists who wrote to Ms., the bulk of criticism, it can safely be said, came from sister feminists who would wonder sometimes at our credentials to that title. They would provoke many lively debates in the Letters Column.

Some more or less friendly critics wrote often. One J. M. Hopper, for instance, of Hendersonville, North Carolina, was a regular correspondent from the mid-seventies through the early eighties. Former Ms. editor Valerie Monroe would always tell the rest of us what was on Brother Hopper's mind with an entry at the bottom of her monthly in-house Letters Report. Another correspondent, Jo Anne Winter, of Riverside, California, would write about once a week in the mid-seventies, apologizing that her letters often became essays. She finally confessed that her letters "were a little sneaky. I was trying to win you over to my side, that is, the side of Christ." Brother Hopper and Ms. Winter—who sometimes signed her name Michelle De Santis—were clearly regular readers of Ms. as well as letter writers. Other correspondents seemed to have blundered into Ms. readership, such as one man who didn't quite get the point of our No Comment column, where we regularly published samples of offensive and sexist advertisements.

————

I was leafing through my wife's copy of the January 1973 issue of your magazine, and I noticed on page 126 the ad for the Italian Fanny Pincher. I was preparing to send away for one when I realized that you had omitted the manufacturer's address. Could you send it to me, or can I order this item through you?

Name Withheld
March 1973 Issue

Editors' Note: No Comment.

If we were at all in doubt that there were anti-feminists out in the world beyond Ms., *one sympathetic reader set us straight.*

Perhaps you are unaware of a national organization founded in Richfield, Utah, called HOTDOG, standing for Humanitarians Opposed to Degrading Our Girls. The organization states: "The name was chosen because the government has been telling women that they are getting a beef steak in the Equal Rights Bill when in effect all they are getting is a hotdog, and a spoiled one at that. This organization will be doing its part in the future to stop R- and X-[rated] movies from appearing on TV and anything else that is degrading and demoralizing to our girls." The information I am quoting comes from a solicitation request for membership support and active participation in passing around a petition to stop the Equal Rights Amendment: "As women, we cannot see how we can maintain our homes and teach our children moral principles under such conditions" as would be imposed by the ERA. "*As men,* we feel it our duty and privilege to protect our mothers, wives, sons, and daughters against such evil designs."

I thought *Ms.* might find this material as appalling and amusing as I and my friends do.

Anne S. Courtney
Peoria, Illinois
November 1973 Issue

If HOTDOG were alive today, the members would certainly change the first word of their name—the radical right has since discovered the evils of "secular humanism." But we didn't have to depend on our readers for the views of ultra-right critics. They would write to us directly.

Please remove my name from your subscription list. Someone other than myself entered my name as a subscriber.

I get to read enough in the local Houston papers about niggers, kikes, and communist lesbians without having to look at your trash.

> Imperial Wizard
> Texas Fiery Knights of the Ku Klux Klan
> Houston, Texas
> October 1975 Issue

You have given me the supreme insult of my life by offering to let me subscribe to *Ms.* I hate the sound of it. It sounds like the hiss of a snake.

Are you proud of what you have helped do to our world? The family is almost destroyed; children by the millions have no parents or homes; divorces, crimes, dehumanization, are the norm now. Has it been worth all this just to get some women in the military academies?

> Mrs. H. Sims
> Mount Olivet, Kentucky
> January 1977 Issue

Out of curiosity I purchased the April issue of *Ms.* It appears to have one dominant message—the goal of castrating all males.

I originally believed that the women's movement was only interested in equal rights, wages, and job opportunities. Now I fully understand your philosophy. Your articles are filled with incest and sick attitudes, and they express a general hatred of most males. I have one feeling for your group: pity.

> William D. Nueske
> Phoenix, Arizona
> August 1977 Issue

After seeing a copy of your rag recently, I don't know who are sillier—*Ms.*'s editors or the emotionally retarded women who follow them.

> June Wright
> Sheffield, Massachusetts
> December 1977 Issue

Anti-feminists were capable of such colorful vituperation that it was inevitable someone would eventually turn ultra-right rhetoric into satire.

No one does it better than a group called Ladies Against Women—an offshoot of the Plutonium Players in San Francisco—who would grace the Ms. Letters Column with their humor as they would conferences and other feminist events.

I was so very pleased to see the very nice write-ups of Ladies Against Women in your April and August issues. LAW has been working very hard to bring back the good old days, whenever they were. Our current focus is on the right to life . . . the right to the right *style* of life, mandated for us girls by the men in power.

We are most concerned now with the sperm's rights. Are you aware that *billions* of unconceived and totally innocent Americans are massacred by the male sin of self-abuse? And that by avoiding your duty of perpetual pregnancy, you ladies are also ruthlessly squandering the souls of little unconceived citizens? Please join us in our crusade to protect the unconceived. Write to Ladies Against Women for your petition for a constitutional amendment against menstruation, masturbation, and other forms of mass murder.

> Virginia (Mrs. Chester) Cholesterol
> Ladies Against Women
> Berkeley, California
> February 1983 Issue

Our own satire, an eight-page magazine called "Mrs.: The Magazine for the Post-Feminist Woman," written by Barbara Ehrenreich and Jane O'Reilly and bound into our April 1983 issue, inspired this response.

We cannot begin to tell you how thrilled the Long Beach Chapter of Ladies Against Women was to see the première issue of *Mrs.* magazine. For quite some time now we have sponsored the National Institute to Train Women in Tastefulness (NITWIT), dedicated to retraining former feminists to adapt to their new roles as right-thinking ladies. We will certainly make *Mrs.* required reading for all students.

We were surprised to read in your editorial that you had heard of our other auxiliary organizations: THEN (Total Housewives Expect Nothing) and THEN (Their Husbands for Equality Never). These are two separate and certainly not equal organizations dedicated to keeping women in their place. We look forward to seeing more of *Mrs.* and hope that it will inspire others to turn their old ERA T-shirts into dust rags and join the ranks of Ladies Against Women.

(P.S. Susanne Gilmore subscribes to *Ms.* magazine. I just accidentally read her copy.)

Mrs. Kirby (Eureka) Kenmore Hoover III
Long Beach, California
July 1983 Issue

It would be hard even for the most skillful satirist to top one 1976 correspondent: the great Gerald Robert Wildermuth. His letter inspired Ms. *readers to an unprecedented crescendo of response.*

I thought I would take a few minutes out of my busy schedule to write this letter. Then perhaps you can get a better picture of what you're really up against and what other people really think about your opinions.

First, I would like to state that I am a father of three girls, ages six, four, and two. Also, my wife shares my thoughts and ideals. You feminists all seem to think that you are hurting men's feelings or insulting them by calling them male chauvinist pigs. I would like to state that the greatest honor anyone can give me is to call me a male chauvinist pig. I'd consider it a great honor. I teach all my girls that all feminist women are "lesbians." I drill this into their heads so that the schools, churches, and their friends cannot set their futures on the wrong path. You always talk of what women can do to help women's lib. I would like to tell you what I and my family do to *stop* women's lib. Now I know that one family cannot change women's lib, but we feel better for doing our part.

¶When we pull into a gas station and a broad is working there, we tell her that we don't believe in women working in service stations and that she can't put gas in our car. If the *man* in the station wants to fill the tank, he can. If not, we go to the next station. I would like to give you 95 percent of the responses we get: "Sir, it is against the law to discriminate." Then I tell them that if the law says that the station has to hire her, I am the public, and I can do as I please. Then we drive off, and the woman stands there looking stupid.

¶If our car breaks down and we call a cab and a woman cabdriver shows up at our house, we *refuse* the cab, but we always tell the feminists why. Their reaction is always the same as the station operator's.

¶My girl is taken to school by myself because we have a woman bus driver. I have told the school my reasons! Their reaction is the same as the others.

¶We screen all television shows. If any woman is playing a man's role, we don't watch those programs (*Police Woman* or *Christie Love* or any of the news programs with women as reporters). My point is no matter how much you do, you'll never change me or my family, because the law is on my side. If you're on television, we simply turn you off. If you're in a magazine, we simply throw it away.

¶We also screen all our friends. My wife doesn't hang around with any feminists.

¶I also wish to say that I support my own family. I am an over-the-road driver. My wife *does not work*. When my girls look for their mother, they know where they can find her.

I could sit here and write you all night long, but my time is valuable to me, and you are nothing to me but another bunch of feminists.

You can print any or all of this letter if you wish. My only desire is to show you that your time is wasted. You can't change me or my friends, no matter what you or television do.

> Gerald Robert Wildermuth
> Address Withheld
> May 1976 Issue

Regarding Gerald Robert Wildermuth—*is he for real?*

> Sharon K. Chapman
> Detroit, Michigan
> September 1976 Issue

Editors' Note: Yes, Sharon, there *is* a G. R. Wildermuth. Here are some of the many responses to his letter.

I think Gerald Robert Wildermuth is suffering from acute testosterone poisoning, complicated by severe close-mindedness and bigotry.

> Martha Root
> Buffalo, New York
> September 1976 Issue

Gerald Wildermuth was so right! He sounds just like my husband Harry.

We had three daughters, ages one, two, and three. If the next one isn't a boy, Harry says he'll beat me till I can't stand up, but it's only his way of kidding—I think. He works hard all day and then has to come home and drive me around because I'm not allowed to drive. Harry says women drivers cause all the accidents, and he's trying to protect me. We also don't receive *any* services from *any* workingwomen because they're all lesbians. It'll be hard when we send the kids to school, because all those women teachers will try to give the girls "ideas." We'll have to teach our girls never to stay alone with the teachers after school, "just in case."

We don't watch much TV these days, because even the daytime shows have women playing the parts of doctors and lawyers and unmarried mothers. These shows used to be okay, because they showed women how to act properly, but now they have a lot of women writers, who let even the loose girls get away unpunished. It scares me about what's happening in this country, but Harry says we just have to do what we can to stop what he calls "woman's lip."

Anyway, Harry is all I need to be happy. He says that all you women at the magazine need is "a good one," whatever that is, but I bet he means a "male chauvinist pig" like Mr. Wildermuth and him. They could make you happy, and you wouldn't need "woman's lip" anymore.

> Mrs. Harry R. Stillwaggon*
> September 1976 Issue

I'm fourteen years old, and I'm trying (successfully) to steer every child I know in the right direction. They're learning that *everyone* is to be treated as a person and *everyone* has a chance to make it. My little brother heard me read the Wildermuth letter, and he thought it was very stupid. I know more and more boys like my brother, and it makes me happy.

Also, Mr. Wildermuth says his wife doesn't work. What does he call cooking, cleaning, and taking care of the kids? A vacation?

> Grace N. Luppino
> South Norwalk, Connecticut
> September 1976 Issue

When my wife and I finally stopped laughing, we, too, thought we should waste a little of our "valuable" time to point out a few contradictions to G. R. Wildermuth:

¶ If your wife had to seek employment because something happened to you, would she fall into your "lesbian" category because she had to work?

¶ It is apparent that not much news of any kind is viewed in your household, with or without women reporters. Times have changed, friend, and if you watched the news, you'd realize this.

¶ We support our family also. I am a sportswriter and political-science student; my wife is a counterperson at a drive-in. We share domestic duties and the enjoyment that two paychecks offer.

¶ If you ever have a few free minutes of your "valuable" time on hand again, pick up a copy of our Constitution at the local library (that place where the city and mostly women keep all those books). I direct your attention to the third word in the preamble.

A word to the wise should suffice.

> Steve and Glenda Steinbrecher
> Lodi, California
> September 1976 Issue

---

*No doubt a member of Ladies Against Women.

I honestly believe *Ms.* ought to inform anthropologists Mary and Richard Leakey about Wildermuth; it seems we've very probably uncovered the missing link between humans and apes!

M. Constance Jenkins
Ogdensburg, New York
September 1976 Issue

Mr. Wildermuth: I hope the next female gas-station attendant or cabdriver you turn down gives you the finger and spits in your eye!

By the way, I am not a disgruntled female; I am thirteen years old and as male as you are.

Andrew L. Eddinger
Boyertown, Pennsylvania
September 1976 Issue

I've worked my way through school, Gerald Robert Wildermuth. You know what I do? I'm in law enforcement. That is something I love. Every day I meet with Gerald Robert Wildermuths, who say, "I want to talk to a *man!*" What am I, a snake?

You should remember me. I am the police officer who might cradle your wife, you, or your children in her arms after a stabbing, rape, or accident. I am the police officer who stops a burglar from entering your home.

And I still want to do that for you.

Linda Wollum
Madison, Wisconsin
September 1976 Issue

I have never considered myself a feminist, although I support the ERA and believe that a woman has the right to decide if and when she will have children. My husband, a truck driver, shares my views. We would like to say that Mr. Wildermuth is giving husbands and truck drivers a bad name. Such bigoted, narrow-minded men are going to find they cannot stop the women of this country—including their wives and daughters—from attaining their goals of equality. The women's movement is like a tidal wave, and anyone standing in the way will be washed away.

I have been a wife and mother since I was sixteen, and with the help and support of my husband and son I will be entering a community college this fall. Real men are able to stand by our sides and share our bright futures.

Linda Cozad
El Paso, Texas
September 1976 Issue

The Traiger family would like to express their deepest sympathy for the tragic loss of G. R. Wildermuth's mind.

Robin
Terrie
Sy
Marilyn Traiger
Bellmore, New York
September 1976 Issue

It is probably best to ignore people like Gerald Robert Wildermuth (which is German for "wild mouth"). But I can't resist responding, because if there's anything I dislike more than chauvinism, it's *illiterate* chauvinism.

Fortunately, his species of mammal is fast becoming extinct.

Diane K. Mitchell
Los Angeles, California
September 1976 Issue

Imagine the shock and dismay of Gerald Robert Wildermuth (which translates to "savage spirit") when he gets to that Last Great Gas Station in the Sky and finds that all the attendants, as well as the owner, are feminists. Just think, he won't even be able to warn his unsuspecting wife and daughters of their impending doom!

Since I do not welcome the sight of this savage-spirited truck driver cruising my neighborhood, please delete my address.

Robert K. Pring
Address Withheld
September 1976 Issue

Thanks for writing, Mr. Wildermuth—even *you* know that you can't ignore us now.

Jeri S. Darling
Ann Arbor, Michigan
September 1976 Issue

Thank God for my daddy!

Barbara Joyce Smith
Oklahoma City, Oklahoma
September 1976 Issue

If any of us ever hoped that Gerald Robert Wildermuth was, perhaps, just fooling, another accidental reader wrote in to reassure us that his point of view was real enough.

I leafed through my wife's September *Ms.* and saw the hysterical response to Mr. Wildermuth's letter. What a shrill shrieking. I note that *all* the mail was anti Wildermuth. Nobody was *for* him? Not one solitary soul? Well, girls, here's my vote—a vote of thanks to him for having the balls to say it like it is. I'm proud of my MCP status, too!

1. Equal pay—sure why not? That's really a woman's issue—women are materialistic. That's all they really care about anyway. Security is *the* woman's hang-up.

2. Equal opportunity—great, but only if standards are not lowered. If women can get into the service academies by meeting *all* standards, I have no objections. What happened was that they couldn't—so physical standards were lowered. Even hazing is out for women—not able to take it. So women appear physically weak and emotionally weak—but politically strong!

3. Personally, I like my women to cook good, smell good, and feel good—but if she wants to pump gas, it's her privilege. We all know women are masochists.

4. One thing I will never accept—women police. I don't think they can do the job. More important, I happen to feel that it's a man's job to protect women, so don't humiliate me by inferring that you can handle an aggressor better than I can.

It may be difficult for women to comprehend, but death before dishonor. To me, a picture of a woman with a gun or any weapon in the police or military has the same effect as I imagine *Deep Throat* has on the editors of *Ms.* It's no wonder that the rise of women's lib has coincided with three other phenomena—impotence is becoming prevalent (I know, that's their problem, right), rape (but that's yours, baby), and the obsession with pornography. It's no accident that the only societies that have survived are male dominated. Women can rant all they like, but cream will always rise to the top.

5. I don't think all, or even most feminists, are lesbian—feminism is just an illustration of the old adage that imitation is the sincerest form of flattery. But policewomen, female prison guards, and women military careerists—well, I question their sexual identity. To my way of thinking, "lady cop" is another way of saying "dyke."

Incidentally, my wife is a professional, and I could care less. But—if my wife chooses to labor in the salt mines rather than spend her day reading Dante, attending the symphony, or at the museum—the more fool she. It's her hang-up.

I don't mind women working, and I don't mind them making all the money their greedy, grasping little souls could want—but as a great philosopher put it, "Man is the

Warrior, woman the warrior's plaything—all else is folly!" Put that in your—uh, pipe—and smoke it.

Now let's see if you have the manhood to publish this.

Name Withheld
August 16, 1976

We didn't take this man up on his dare. Of more concern were the critics who were also loyal readers. We could never get the balance of coverage right for some—Ms. was turning into a parenting magazine, or we were against mothers. Ms. didn't have enough for the career woman, or we neglected the homemaker. Ms. was anti men and anti marriage, or we wasted too much space on men. This last debate was brought to the forefront when we published our first Special Issue on Men, in October 1975.

A few days ago my back issues of *Ms.* magazine went into the fireplace, and I'll tell you it's been a long time since your rag has provided me with any warmth. With that Special Issue on Men you have become as irrelevant to me as prophylactics.

When you regain your senses and have a little news concerning lesbians, or maybe even feminism (remember that word from way back when?), then you may just be worth my while again.

Joan Regensburger
Cambridge, Massachusetts
February 1976 Issue

Another reader saw an "emphasis on" lesbianism. We knew that Ms. *couldn't please everyone, but sometimes it seemed as if we couldn't please anyone.*

I don't know what's happened to *Ms.*, but I feel that I can no longer bring it to the office because of the emphasis on sex-sex-sex and lesbianism that makes my cause for feminism look a little suspicious. A man could only believe that it's another horny female publication and that women are preoccupied by their bodies and each other's bodies. I don't see *Ms.*'s value any more. It looks as though it's become the official publication for women with sex-identity problems. Please cancel my subscription.

Name Withheld
March 1977

Well, six days into the new year, I've made my resolution. To stop buying *Ms.* magazine. One of the biggest laughs is "Now That It's Reagan . . ." by Gloria (Apocalypse Now) Steinem [January 1981 Issue]. In all your liberal paranoia and your rabid, distorted, leftist posturing, you've lost all sense of responsibility and reality. Goodbye.

Name Withheld
January 6, 1981

In 1977, one reader analyzed our problem for us.

I am repeatedly struck by the "I am a feminist, but . . ." genre of critical letters *Ms.* receives. Recent categories include

¶I am a feminist, but . . . my relationships with men are just fine, thank you.

¶I am a feminist, but . . . haven't you all gotten a bit soft on lesbians recently?

¶I am a feminist, but . . . women are *not* a minority group, so don't imply we have anything in common with minorities.

¶I am a feminist, but . . . why are you printing these uncompromising-sounding attacks on corporate power?

¶I am a feminist, but . . . last month you talked about sex! Please cancel my subscription.

¶I am a feminist, but . . . can't you express our views in a less alienating way? (Or, whatever has become of your sense of humor? Or, I love your goals, but I hate your tactics.)

Now read the list, absent prefatory disclaimer. *Ms.* has just been told by its readers not to mention the intimate oppression of women, heterosexism and homophobia, racism, capitalism, and puritanism—and to be more nice and liberal (and ladylike?).

I am a feminist, but . . . is this feminism?

Kitty MacKinnon
New Haven, Connecticut
August 1977 Issue

No matter how inclusive Ms. *tried to be, there was a media perception of feminism that made some readers defensive about the life choices they were making. In October 1975 we published a letter from Patricia Basu, who took issue with what she found to be "extremist politics" within the women's movement. One reader was surprised that we ran it.*

I found Patricia Basu's letter very interesting, not only for what she said but the fact that it was printed. I realized as I read it that I was surprised to find any deviation from what I, at least, considered the "party line." I would qualify as one of the reluctant feminists. To me, the key is individuality, the freedom and right to be what you want to be regardless of sex. So why am I a reluctant feminist? Because I don't think my personally chosen life style would meet with *Ms.* approval. I expect—perhaps wrongly—that you would be contemptuous of me, or at least condescending. You see, I've been *happily* married for twenty-five years. I find my husband a warm, interesting, good person. I've even had three children and enjoyed it. My daughter and I are close friends (she's twenty-four); my relationship with my sons (nineteen and twenty-one) is full of respect, equality, and plain old fun. I feel that before I could become an active feminist I would have to walk away from my family, apologize for my life; I would have to think of all males as "the enemy" and live a battle that only one sex can win. Is there room in the feminist movement for someone who doesn't want to judge everyone by their sex, but by their humanness, or lack of it?

Name Withheld
October 10, 1975

A July 1975 article by Vivian Gornick—"Feminist Writers: Hanging Ourselves on a Party Line?"—on the dangers of orthodoxy in writers identified with the women's movement, brought relieved response.

Gornick expressed quite well a growing frustration that I have felt lately—about stereotyping. As a feminist, I have become accustomed to stereotypic prodding by those who disagree with the women's movement. Though it disturbs me, I rather expect this unenlightened chatter. Lately, however, I have suffered a similar type of narrow-mindedness from other feminists who insist on "institutionalizing" feminist beliefs.

I refuse to relinquish the awesome gut feeling of my feminist enlightenment to a dogma that gets farther away from the "a-ha" moment of discovery and self-realization. As Gornick implies, dogma is the downfall of all ideas. I hope the feminist movement can continue to grow toward humanism rather than toward a narrow, castrating dogma.

Cathy Russell Smith
Lincoln, Nebraska
November 1975 Issue

As a feminist writer, I have long felt a sort of schizophrenic anxiety about my work. It's as if I have an ardent guardian angel peering over my shoulder whenever I'm working who asks, "Does this *really* reflect your political ideals?"

Thanks to Vivian Gornick, who put all those vague fears together for me, I'll *live* my feminism. Since writing necessarily reflects the writer's ideals, some of my politics are bound to overflow into my work. But I'm done with writing dogma.

Pat Kight
Sault Ste. Marie, Michigan
November 1975 Issue

Readers often seemed to consider Ms. *covers especially fair game. Since our covers were never tightly formatted, they varied enormously from month to month. One very successful cover in terms of newsstand sales, the August 1976 cover story, "The Truth About Battered Wives," brought this complaint.*

Ms., I congratulate you on your August cover, a new low in judgment. The battered wife as fashion model—bruised, maybe, but ever young and lovely, and with her eye makeup still intact.

Click, indeed!

Nancy M. King
Baltimore, Maryland
July 27, 1976

We explained in an Editors' Note that we had specifically picked a model that went against stereotypes of the expected victim of battering. In general, we tried to use models who looked like real, everyday folk for our covers, and with well-known cover subjects, we tried for realistic shots as well. Our October 1976 cover portrayed Lillian Carter.

I give Ms. a lot of credit for putting a sweet, wrinkled old woman on the cover. It was good to see a real person for a change, instead of perfect, youthful-looking models. Keep up the good work in breaking precedents.

Ruth L. A. Schissler
Jamaica Plain, Massachusetts
February 1977 Issue

I am not sure that I shall ever forgive you for the picture of Lillian Carter on the October cover. It is one of the most unkind photographs I have ever seen.

If *Ms.* is Lillian Carter's friend, she certainly does not need enemies.

Name Withheld
February 1977 Issue

Later, in an Editors' Note commenting on a feature in our Tenth Anniversary Issue (July 1982), we had a chance to share what Lillian Carter thought about the Ms. *cover story.*

Editors' Note: We were sorry that Miss Lillian Carter's comments for "Where Are They Now? Catching Up With Some *Ms.* Cover People" arrived after deadline. Here, then, is what our October 1976 cover person had to say about her *Ms.* appearance:

It doesn't matter a damn to me what all those women think—or men either. I've been doing what I want to for a long time. I got hundreds of letters after that cover. They're still in boxes somewhere around. I didn't know so many people subscribed to that magazine. And all of them were very positive and kind. Except I did hear from that woman, that one that goes on screaming about stopping ERA, her name is Phyllis something or other, but that doesn't mean a damn to me either.

November 1982 Issue

Lillian's son, Jimmy, made the cover in January 1978, with a story by Gloria Steinem, "Will Women Make Carter a One-Term President?" In honor of his famous "Life Is Unfair" statement explaining his position against Medicaid payment for abortions, we made him pregnant on our cover—something that a number of readers, but not all of them, thought a bit tasteless.

What a beautiful picture! Jimmy Carter pregnant. At least, he is making a contribution to the future, which a lot of us were suspecting he was incapable of doing. Little did we know!

Rosalyn will leave him, of course. Who needs a promiscuous man? A second term is now out of the question. A president with a baby? How too natural! At this point, our pregnant, "born again" president might even opt for abortion—as he watches the life he planned go down the drain. Life is unfair to those who get pregnant. It couldn't have happened to a better fellow.

Gina Allen
San Francisco, California
December 21, 1977

Another quite successful but controversial cover presented our special issue of September 1977, "Why Women Don't Like Their Bodies." Again we tried to explain ourselves with a lengthy Editors' Note. The cover pictured the full length of a woman's bare back with the title of the feature written as a tatto.

I was shocked that you would publish an issue probing into the reasons women don't like their bodies and then feature a skinny white woman on the cover. *That's* why women don't like their bodies—because we've been told we *should* look like the woman on the cover when most of us don't!

It's appalling that *Ms.* would stoop to a cheap method of selling magazines.

Robin C. McKiel
Alexandria, Virginia
January 1978 Issue

Editor's Note: We first tried a heavier woman with the cover line "Why Women Don't Like Their Bodies," but that conveyed a different, old-fashioned idea: that only fat women have a body-image problem. We also tried a darker-skinned women, but that conveyed a limited or racist message for the same reason. Using a supposedly desirable stereotype was the only way to say that, in a patriarchy, *all* women suffer from being identified totally by (and therefore being made to feel insecure about) our bodies. In addition, the woman's back was shown precisely so that we wouldn't be using "a cheap method of selling magazines." For that purpose, other magazines would have turned her around.

High-minded or not, the cover sold. One that didn't do so well was our special issue on the arts in December 1977. But it had never occurred to us that Mona Lisa would be offensive as a cover subject.

Please cancel my subscription immediately. When *Ms.* realizes that Dixie Lee Ray, Barbara Jordan, Rosalyn Carter, or a host of other important women are more appropriate to the cover than Mona Lisa, I will be happy to resubscribe.

Name Withheld
December 1, 1977

Our April 1979 cover subject for a feature on women in the work force— Jacqueline Onassis, who had gone to work in publishing—inspired poetry.

When Niagara falls.
When Virginia elects an intelligent United States senator.
When hell freezes over.
When Jackie Onassis appears on the cover of *Ms.*

Stephanie Selice
Charlottesville, Virginia
July 1979 Issue

If a pregnant president offended some, a pregnant woman dressed in what looked like a flag offended many more, as we discovered with our 1984 "American Way of Birth" cover story.

I am offended by the cover of the September issue that pictures a pregnant woman dressed in an American flag. If the intent was to convey the rights of pregnant women as part of their American heritage, I can understand and support the use of the flag somewhere on the cover. To use it, however, as an article of clothing, in my view, denigrates the symbolism inherent in the flag, namely, equality, justice, and freedom. I know it is common in this culture to misuse a national symbol. I'm disappointed that *Ms.* magazine thought it appropriate.

Karen Nyman
Minneapolis, Minnesota
December 1984 Issue

Editors' Note: The flag motif (though not the flag itself) was used to suggest the peculiarly American attitude toward childbirth. We only wish that Americans considered pregnancy at least as honorable as the flag— and certainly not a dishonor of it.

Coverage of love and romance in early issues of Ms., *especially in a cover story, was guaranteed to attract a number of dissenting votes. Here a critic lambastes the July 1974 cover feature—"Is Romance Dead?"—and the author comes to a spirited defense.*

Instead of "Is Romance Dead?" how about "Is the Women's Movement Dead?" Now that we've all been in C-R groups and we all know we can take care of ourselves, is our next step to trip out on a dose of "romantic love"? Will this help us all become better, more groovy lovers? Shall we all forget about our poor sisters in the slums, on welfare, on drugs, and in prisons and spin a web of escape fantasies into a romantic cocoon?

Romance is the opiate of oppressed women.

Laura McKinley
Berkeley, California
November 1974 Issue

I must respond to a letter in the November issue that castigated me for proffering "a dose of 'romantic love' " as an "opiate" to allow women to forget about "our poor sisters in the slums, on welfare, on drugs, in prisons." I fail absolutely to see the connection between loving a man and the selective amnesia that letter writer describes. I should think, quite to the contrary, that if one truly loves, one is truly loving. To love a man is not to blot out of one's consciousness the suffering of the oppressed; indeed, I think of romantic love as a consciousness enhancer, not a consciousness suppressor, as an illumination, not a lobotomy. I very much resent being charged with forgetting about my oppressed sisters; damn it, it ought to be possible to hold two things in your head at the same time—does it require such a terrible juggling act to love a man and love your sister, too? I don't think so. It is silly and *vulgar* to deny the truth of one's experience: I am not now in love with a man, nor am I now loved by a man; but I have been . . . and it's been generous and good, and I do not see that the cause of truth is served by censoring or denying romantic love. Am I not a feminist because I love my brother and my son and my father more than I love Clare Boothe Luce?

Sorry to be so unchic; but politics, I think, are in the head and the heart, the spirit and the will—not in the cunt.

Barbara Grizzuti Harrison
New York, New York
March 1975 Issue

In the eighties still, a cover feature on marrying late (March 1981) and another on "What Men Haven't Said To Women" (August 1984), brought their share of criticism.

What is the subliminal message you are trying to convey with this cover story? That the look of the eighties will be bridal white, with legal, nuclear, heterosexual couples always of common race; and that no matter how old you are when you wed, the man of your choice will be older?

I don't need *Ms.* to tell me this. I can get it from the Total Woman in the White House.

Sign me:

One Die-hard Spinster
February 1981

I've spent forty-nine years in "this man's world," dodging *their* rules and getting the short end of the stick, because they do all the measuring. And frankly, I don't give a damn about what they think about anything.

Eugenia D. Robertson
Abinton, Pennsylvania
November 1984 Issue

There were, of course, men we liked a lot. Male heros who were consistent advocates of feminism may have gotten a little overexposed in Ms. *as well as other media. Here two readers differ on a June 1981 cover story about Alan Alda.*

Am I alone in gnashing my teeth and tearing my hair whenever I pick up a magazine and find Saint Alan of Alda leering cutely at me from the cover, or reading yet another gushy article hyping his latest project? I'm sure he's a fine man, cheerful, courteous, and kind to his mother, but *enough* already. Just once I would like to read an interview where he staggers unshaven into the room, clad in a torn undershirt and bellowing at his wife to have dinner on the table in five minutes or he'll kick in her damned cello. Mr. Alda himself says in your article that he doesn't want to come off as "wise, saintly, or unnecessarily wonderful." Unfortunately, he seems to be the only member of the media to hold that opinion at the moment.

Please . . . have mercy in the future, and send the puff pieces where they belong—
People magazine.

Mary Z. Long
Baden, Pennsylvania
May 18, 1981

I have a wonderful idea: to hasten the "feminist revolution," let's replace all the men
with Alan Alda clones.

Name Withheld
March 4, 1981

Some complaints were earth shattering—at least to the reader making it.

*M*s. magazine complaints:

I am sorry to put in a complaint. But you have killed me. I am ten years old and live
in Claremont. My mother reads *Ms.* always, and in your December copy you had an
article on children's toys, and you talked about bikes and how boys' bikes are better.
Well, now I am stuck with a boy's bike, and if I ride it, I get teased by the boys. "Please,
write back."

Name Withheld
February 6, 1974

Valerie Monroe wrote her back, with what comfort she could muster.

*In a November 1977 article, "Hot off the Feminist Presses," a skeptical
Lindsy Van Gelder offended one reader.*

I was particularly upset at the misrepresentation of *WomanSpirit* magazine as some
sort of voice for the lunatic feminist fringe. In my close to three-year relationship with
WomanSpirit, and Ruth and Jean Mountaingrove, its caretakers, I have found the
magazine thought provoking, inspirational, and comforting.

The woman Van Gelder referred to as being a sort of final last straw is a personal
friend of mine who does indeed converse with trees, and two in particular are her
special friends. I have been known to talk with tree beings myself, and many other
women I know do also.

Once we open ourselves to the knowledge of the life forms with which we share this planet, the old mind-think of patriarchal culture no longer holds as much power over us.

Christina Pacosz
Portland, Oregon
March 1978 Issue

Lindsy Van Gelder Replies: Sorry, but on the scale of blows against the patriarchy, I fail to be deeply troubled by my inability to form meaningful relationships with mighty oaks and spreading chestnuts.

As always, another reader comes to the defense.

About the woman who converses with trees. Personally, I don't talk to trees, but I wouldn't think of doubting these women who do, and I would not question the value of their conversations as a blow against the patriarchy.

Name Withheld
March 2, 1978

Luckily, given all our critics, our readers let us know that Ms. *is a product with many uses.*

Last evening after I collected my mail (new issue of Ms. included), my male roommate and I commenced our nightly discussion about how things went with each of us that day. I related an incident about a particularly sexist comment that was made to me by one of our sales*men,* and my roommate laughed (and laughed and laughed). Already blue in the face from countless "discussions" concerning sexual harassment and women's liberation, I proceeded to use my new issue of Ms. in a novel fashion. I hit him with it until the magazine fell apart. He stopped laughing.

Name Withheld
January 22, 1981

I thought you and your readers might get a kick out of this.

While reading at my desk the other night I felt a sharp pain in my thigh, like something had bitten me. I screamed in fear and ripped off my nightgown. There was a large red welt where the pain was. My mom ran in to see why I'd screamed. By this time I had my gown off and she saw the big welt. She ran to get me ice and meat tenderizer (yes, you read it correctly, and it really works, too—make a paste out of meat tenderizer and water. But that's not what I came here to talk about . . .).

After my mom came back with my comfort measures, I had calmed down enough to look for the nasty beast who had so rudely interrupted my reading. When at last I found the bugger—a wasp—I grabbed my reading material, the August issue of *Ms.* magazine. Weapon in hand, I pounded the beast to death.

Score: 1 for feminism, 0 for nasty wasps.

Jacqui Glickman
Elkins Park, Pennsylvania
October 23, 1981

Milestones
Readers Live Fifteen Years of History

———————— ❧ ————————

With the twenty thousand letters Ms. *received in response to the Spring 1972 Preview Issue, an instant community was born. From all over the country, women wrote in—telling their life stories, delighted they weren't alone in the changes they were trying to make. We published many of these letters of discovery in our early issues.*

As the birth of Ms. *was the occasion for women to consider their own experiences, so were our various anniversary issues. And as events of national import occurred affecting the women's movement, readers would send in reactions to share with their* Ms. *community. The letters continued to record the advance of feminism in a very personal way.*

————————————

In high school, I ran like the wind, but there was no track for female students. All my life I loved the neat things my father did in electronics and printing. I failed at every "female" thing I attempted except having babies (there are five).

I've recently entered an all-male trade and love it. I'm into presswork and camera stripping. What a trip!

Ten years ago I knew nothing, nothing of the world but babies, a women's auxiliary, and a car pool. I'm happier now—but then, I'm not trying to be a woman anymore. I'm me.

Name Withheld
July 1972 Issue

For at least the last fifteen of my twenty-five years, I have felt uncomfortably different. Much of my early life was spent, blissfully, on a ranch in Texas. There I

207

learned to do men's jobs. I had no real choice in the matter, as the ranch was run solely (and very well) by my grandmother. Growing up as a tomboy was not an especially pleasant thing, but I was somewhat consoled by the fact that I could do anything as well as any boy I knew and many things that none of my peers could do.

My dreams of becoming a trumpet player and a veterinarian were stifled by age eight. (Men's jobs.) In my teens, I decided to become an actress. An unwise move, in terms of the society of a small Texas town. No matter how hard I tried, and there were times when I tried very hard, I could not seem to make wise moves. When, at sixteen, I fell in love with a boy, he and I both suffered untold horror for the simple reason that he, too, wanted to act. Anyone with that suspect idea was declared a homosexual and was treated as if he or she was a gangrenous armpit.

Well, sisters, I survived. I am an actress. I have only a few scars, and they are not, I think, unattractive. They may even give me character. Now I have been given the gift of membership in the Sisterhood of Woman. I am not alone. I no longer feel that I must disguise my quirks. I can sew and cook and garden and decorate without feeling smug, and I can build furniture, take karate, repair my car, and wear pants without feeling guilty. I am proud.

Name Withheld
July 1972 Issue

Our July 1972 first regular issue had Wonder Woman on the cover and an article by Phyllis Chestler, "Women and Madness," inside. Women who had paid a heavy price for resisting the roles society assigned to them responded immediately to the message that they weren't the ones who were crazy.

Last week i tried a shrink, the only nonmale one i could find, to get over the fear of looking for a job, getting away from marriage, even children (that i love). i cooperated and tried to trust her, because she was a woman, although old. take warning, my beautiful sisters. i thought i was getting better because i was struggling less. i was nearly killed, adjusted to slavery, I was nice to be with, when I came home from being told i was father searching, there was Wonder Woman (husband calls it *Ms.*-ery). what a day "women and madness" brought. like Lucy and Laura, i was beginning to think i was sick. last week i apologized to an old lover for giving him a hard time, because i was neurotic. now i've retracted the apology. one of the most difficult pits in the road is passed. i am proud to say that i am once again my bitch self, following my own way. everybody can go to hell who doesn't like it. i'm on the farm waiting for my sisters to rise up like wheat. i love you.

"Bernadette"
Romeo, Michigan
September 1972 Issue

One of the most important things that Ms. *readers shared, particularly in those early days, was their anger.*

I am a woman who, almost all my life, believed without question what I was told—women aren't as smart as men, women aren't happy being successful, to get ahead you should be pretty, witty, and secretly wise. I consequently floundered around in secretarial jobs for years, involving myself in work that was never challenging to me intellectually, work that never lit a spark in me. I tried to find meaning through the men in my life—fortunately for me I *was* pretty and witty. But I never wanted to marry, and whenever I looked forward to the rest of my life, I felt lost, because the thought of being autonomous by doing work I hated far, far into the future, made me panic.

Then I discovered the movement, both through a consciousness-raising group and through a heavy amount of reading. I realized that I wasn't the only woman who felt inferior, stupid, restless, underutilized, unused, intellectually underfed. That realization turned to anger, anger turned slowly to action, and action, eventually, forced me to change my life around. At the age of twenty-five, I started college on a full-time basis and finished my first semester with a four-point average and a small scholarship.

But I am still an angry woman. I am not angry for myself, for all the underutilized years, because things have turned out well for me in the end at a relatively young age. But I am angry for my sisters. I am angry for Ann, who has a master's degree and a brilliant mind—she has been made to think that men really *do* know more, and I have watched her flounder in debates with those men who are intellectually inferior to her. I am angry for Lucille, an artist, highly sensitive, who, rather than trying to find herself in her art, is trying to find it in her man—she's tried to commit suicide once so far. I am angry for Roberta, who drinks too much because she hates who she is. I am angry for Cathy, whose grandfather tried to rape her when she was seven; for Lydia, who is sixty and doing work she has been doing well for forty years; for Carol, who is sad about her lack of beauty; for Jan, who keeps looking for new men in the bars every Friday night; for Darlene, who is not afraid to love her six cats but is afraid to love anything human. I could go on. Almost every women I know suffers with her hidden or not-so-hidden scars. The joy I feel at having finally gotten a handle on myself dissipates, quite suddenly, when I take a half glance around me.

We have made a start, but it is discouraging to realize how very far there is to go. Discouragement = anger = action. We can only move forward.

Suzanne Rodriguez
Menlo Park, California
July 2, 1973

By sharing experiences and information—as in consciousness-raising— women helped each other, through the Ms. *Letters column, get beyond even terrible experiences.*

All my life I've been told, "Don't get raped." Which meant never put yourself in any situation where it might be possible. I have always been independent and done things by myself and gone places alone. And I still am and do. I refuse to give up my freedom and stay at home behind a locked door because there are rapists around.

Unfortunately, no one ever told me what to do if I was raped. I was totally unprepared for the agony I was put through after rape. From what I've read and heard, my experience seems to have been typical.

First of all, women should report all rapes to the police. Currently, only about one out of ten rapes is reported, mostly because of embarrassment and fear. No matter how bad the police are, reporting all rapes is the only way to have rape recognized by everyone as the large, serious problem that it is and to get more legal action against it. Every woman owes it to her sisters to report a rape, if it will perhaps take a rapist off the street before he harms another woman. (In my case, the rapist was out on bail for two other rape cases when he attacked me.)

All women should know what to expect from the police. Do not expect sympathy; policemen are *men* first. Expect to be questioned like a criminal. You must *prove* to them that you indeed have a case; they're not about to take your word for it. Be prepared to have to answer totally irrelevant questions about your personal life. Another thing—you must report a rape *immediately*, and you must then be examined by a doctor. The whole ordeal is a horrible experience to have to go through, but we must all do it, and do it with strength, if it will help another sister.

Then, if your case gets to court, that's a whole other story. Again, it is you—or more precisely your vagina—that is on trial. My case will eventually get to court. Expect everyone, including your best friends, to urge you to drop it all along the line, but do not give in. Dropping a case is condoning the rape. The police tell me my case is "weak" for two reasons: (1) I did not report the rape until the next morning, after I had seen my doctor; (2) I live with a man to whom I am not married, which is taken to mean that I have loose morals. I am not looking forward to meeting the defense.

Name Withheld
August 1973 Issue

One of the earliest organizing efforts of the current women's movement in this country was to encourage women to speak out about rape, to set up rape crisis hotlines, to reform laws so that a woman's sex life was less easily used in defense of rapists on trial, and to sensitize police and hospital workers who would be the first to come into contact with rape victims.

In December 1973 we published a special Letters section called "Dear Sisters." Introducing the feature, we reported that Ms. *was still receiving a minimum of two hundred personal letters a day and that the largest category "are intensely personal accounts of how one individual's life is changing."*

I am a member of the caught-by-surprise generation and wonder if someone might draw a little encouragement from these pieces of my own recycling project?

It's the late 1950s, and the kids are all under ten. When my husband washes the dishes and puts the kids to bed two nights a week so I can take math courses to keep my brain from turning to Jell-O, is he doing a job, or helping me with my job? (Hint: When people ask how I manage with four kids, I answer proudly, "My husband's wonderful; he helps a lot.")

It's the late 1960s, and the empty-nest syndrome may be a cliché, but it's no joke. I'm forty-three, and my job is phasing out. I never finished the M. A. in math; I decided I wanted to write more than I wanted to mathematicize. Now my writing is blocked. I have written myself out, and nothing new is coming in.

I read an article about a women's consciousness-raising group. Click. I look for more women's lib writings. I become a lib glutton. The clicks come in like a teletype. Bras don't bother me; wages haven't got to me yet; but *expectations*! Why have I never touched the world? Touched it, hell—grabbed it, shaken it, *changed* something.

I read the want ads. Oh, that liberal arts degree from 1947—with a thirty-five cent token it gets you on the subway. The walls of the house are moving in on me.

"I think I want to go to law school." I'm forty-five by now, still spending hours on the telephone.

"Uh, well, I've thought of finishing my degree," says my friend. "But by the time I finished, I'd be close to fifty."

"Sister," I say, "in three years I'll be close to fifty, no matter what I do."

But law school would be full time and then some. I'm not afraid of the brain work, but I'm not used to being out all day every day, and neither are the kids who are still at home. I should break in a little.

The Parents Association needs a president for next year, and I am approached. Panic. President? God, even in a junior high P. A., that's where the buck stops. Click. (Click? *Crash* is more like it.) It touches the world; it'll look good on my law school application (there's not a lot else, it seems to me); and, besides, it'll break us all in.

One year later that liberal arts B. A., that P. A. presidency, and a lot of other qualifications (that I hadn't recognized until I had to sell myself), and a thirty-five cent token get me on the subway, and when I get off, I'm starting my first year of law school.

I'm forty-six, and my hair is gray, and I don't color it. In November one of the professors smiles upon another female student (who is twenty-six) and me after class and says, "You girls will make good lawyers." I allow the predicate to cancel the subject and share my friend's euphoria. In March, I ask a law-firm partner if all New York law firms commonly refer to their female associates as "girls." I am treated to five minutes of jocularity. Never mind for now. At least, some New York firms *have* female associates. There's even a female partner here and there. They'll hear from me again.

It's July, and I have research to do in the library. My husband's summer-school teaching ended two days ago.

"What's for dinner?" he asks as I pick up my briefcase.

"I don't know," I say. "Look in the freezer."

The pork chops are just about done when I get home. He has got good at that job. I bake the blueberry pie. I'm good at that, too.

> Gretchen Sprague
> Brooklyn, New York
> December 1973 Issue

In 1973, the tennis match billed as the Battle of the Sexes, between the spokeswoman and star player of women's tennis, Billie Jean King, and the hustler Bobbie Riggs, seemed to start out as pure hype, but it turned into an event that united feminists into a national cheering section. And, it turned out, women weren't the only ones to cheer.

Yeah, I watched *that* tennis match. Like a whole lot of people, I was anxious as hell, looking forward to it. Every time Bobbie Riggs opened his mouth, I got madder. Sure, I know, most of his sounding was strictly promotion. But he was coming on too strong and uncool. Then I see this jive article about how the man really, in private, does not put women down and he didn't know there ever was such a thing as a women's movement. So, after all this nonsense, when it comes time for the match, I'm on the edge of my seat . . . digging Billie Jean's cool and ready for her to cream this cat. Now I got to admit that, deep down, there's that little doubt—can she really do it? After the first set—man, no more doubt. I'm yelling at the television. Real kicks! Billie Jean wins the second set, and I'm wild—shouting for a love set to really finish Mr. Riggs.

Then it hits me—something's happened to me. The fast heartbeat and the high emotion and the gulping beer without tasting it—damn! This scene I'm watching ain't just Billie Jean King versus Bobbie Riggs. I am busting with a too-familiar excitement. This is Joe Louis fighting Max Schmeling . . . Jackie Robinson against the baseball world . . . Sugar Ray fighting Jake La Motta . . . Althea Gibson playing

Darlene Hard, and Jim Brown trying to run over Sam Huff, and, well, damn—for two hours Billie Jean King is black!

Do you understand?

Mel Williamson
New York, New York
December 1973 Issue

The match had caught our imaginations, but Billie Jean King's successful efforts leading the fight for women in professional sports—for more money and better promotion—made her into a lasting hero. She was able to withstand even a bitter palimony suit years later.

My father has been a very conservative man for most of his life. He used to believe that a woman's place was strictly in the home and that the man was to be in control.

A few years ago I started to notice a change slowly coming over him. My older sister wanted to go to law school. My mother gradually prepared him for the idea that women lawyers were as good as men and that a bad woman lawyer was bad not because she was a woman but because she was a bad lawyer.

By the time my sister was ready to tell him of her decision to go to law school, he was ready to hear it. And, most important, he could accept it and be proud of it. Probably the most significant change I've noticed in my father is his views on homosexuals.

When homosexuals were beginning to come out in the early seventies, my dad's only response was "Disgusting." I never knew his attitude had changed on this subject until the palimony suit was brought against Billie Jean King. I thought Billie Jean would have one less fan. But to my surprise my very conservative father said, "I respect Billie Jean King more now than I did before." This personally was a great relief, since one day I will be telling him that I am a lesbian.

Name Withheld
July/August 1982 Issue

I am a Roman Catholic, married twenty-six years to the same man (never even been tempted to stray), have raised four children, and live so far out in the boondocks that only God and a good road map will find me.

I believe in women's rights, civil rights, gay rights, human rights, and Billie Jean King.

I do *not* believe in Phyllis Schlafly.

God bless us all.

Alice J. Norman
Edwards, New York
September 1981 Issue

Women were happy to be excluded from some national events.

To the dismay of many males, have you noticed which sex *isn't* involved in Watergate? That in itself is just great, but then, maybe the reason is because Nixon employed no women on his executive staff. Maybe he thought we couldn't keep a secret!

Chris Pfeffer
AuGres, Michigan
October 1973 Issue

Sometimes Ms. *itself took an active hand in organizing change. A Preview Issue article, "We Have Had Abortions," in the Spring of 1972 included a statement signed by fifty-three well-known American women. It grew into the American Women's Petition, a call to protect reproductive freedom directed at legislative bodies and public officials around the country and signed by tens of thousands of readers of* Ms. *and other feminist publications. A similar effort in 1975 produced the Petition for Sanity, which called for freedom of sexual and affectional preference, and these reactions from readers.*

We have no words that can begin to express our joy, our gratitude, and our love for the Petition for Sanity you ran in your February issue. For those of us who are only now developing the courage to "come out" in public in order to inform others about our life style, this petition is a rare gift from our sisters.

Some of us have suffered loss of jobs, loss of family love and support, and loss of legal rights. We have fought the heavy personal assaults as well as the legal ones, with little progress. But now, with the help of *all* of our sisters, there seems to be a light at the end of the tunnel.

The Lesbian Feminist Alliance
Santa Clara County, California
January 21, 1975

I certainly want to sign the Petition for Sanity. I am just the mother of a gay son in California. After he and his lover had "come out," his lover lost his job, and my son's job was threatened. They were forty-six and forty-eight and could take no more, so they went into their garage, sealed it, and turned on the motor. I lost both of them. Two more tragic casualties to bigotry and injustice.

Sarah V. Montgomery
New York, New York
June 1975 Issue

The current wave of the women's movement had begun in the sixties—growing out of the civil rights and anti war movements. Sometimes readers would reflect on differences between the sixties and the seventies. Here one reader responds to a September 1975 memoir by Robin Morgan, "Rights of Passage," and another to a June 1977 exposé by Letty Cottin Pogrebin on FBI surveillance of the women's movement.

I am reminded of 1969, when my efforts to start a day-care center were thwarted by the purist demands and more theoretical concerns of friends, without children, in our Students for a Democratic Society group. I was told to work for the revolution and wait. "But my children need care now, not after the revolution," I argued. "Besides, this isn't merely an individual need. We must deal with new ways to raise children, or our movement has no basis in real life. Making changes is what radicalizes people—changes in their own lives and neighborhoods."

Now, of course, we are living our politics. A female friend runs for the city council, raising consciousness if nothing else. Worker-run businesses thrive. It is happening in the worker's produce collective where my husband works (decisions are made by all; salaries are the same for each; men and women share the "shit work" equally) and in the alternative elementary school where I teach (run by parents but funded by the public-school system—a choice we won as taxpayers).

I know we are succeeding. An eight-year-old in my class criticized me for writing "lady" sheriff on a picture I had drawn of a woman riding in the Old West. "Why don't you just write sheriff?" she asked.

There's hope for the still hard times ahead.

Karin Miller Wiburg
Seattle, Washington
January 1976 Issue

I read with surprise, amusement, and indignation the rather lengthy list of "subversive" groups that the FBI has had under surveillance the past few years because of some link to the women's movement. I'm certainly glad that Mr. Hoover's boys were on hand to protect us from such subversive groups as the United Methodist Church and the Parents Aid Society. Why, that list read like a women's movement Who's Who! And I was certainly proud to see that we "uppity women" at the University of Kansas, Lawrence, were mentioned twice!

Jody Bitsche
Lawrence, Kansas
October 1977 Issue

*The women's movement of the early seventies was full of ambition and
replete with different styles of feminism, as readers would report from
different parts of the country.*

We would like to share our enthusiasm about a project we are beginning this
summer. We are making use of the facilities of a residential school—six hundred
acres in an Adirondack forest preserve, in New York State—for a women's retreat. On
July 1, we will open the facilities. Our concept is an unpressured atmosphere in
peaceful surroundings, where women can gain support from one another, share
feelings and ideas, pause to take stock of themselves, try out new skills, and simply
rest and do the things for themselves for which they never seem to have time.

The women will live in A-frames, domes, and in a beautiful log cabin. Most will
have their own space—a small area of privacy. They can eat meals communally or can
help themselves from a well-stocked pantry. There will be a trained counselor, who
will run daily women's groups as well as individual sessions. Some activities will be
weaving, pottery, photography, sauna, artwork, swimming, gardening, or reading. In
winter, cross-country skiing, snowshoeing, and tobogganing. A woman proficient in
Oriental foot- and body-massage and techniques of yoga and meditation will be in
residence. During the summer months, women will be welcome to bring their
children, who will be housed in a separate facility and supervised by a counselor, who
will provide recreation for them. In winter, however, the school will be in session, so
we won't have room for as many women, and we won't be able to accomodate children
from September to June.

We hope that our retreat will fulfill a need for women who are going through
periods of stress or changes in life style or who just need a place where they can
thoroughly be themselves. We are charging on a sliding scale, to make the retreat
available to as many women as possible.

> Marie Deyoe
> Women's Retreat
> Highland Settlement
> Paradox, New York
> August 1974 Issue

There are some beautiful, strong women out here in the Dakotas and other Western
states. Our problems are somewhat different from most of the problems you talk
about. We are much closer to the land and have to deal directly with an intensely
masculine society. We have the problems of dealing with cowboys and some of us
(myself included) have problems because we are Indians, especially in dealing with
our Indian men. With the recent upsurge of a return to traditionalism, we have a very
rough time deciding what is truly best for us as Indian women.

Still, I know women who are trying to develop an abortion-counseling service; women who break and train horses; women who dance men's-style Indian dances; a woman who is a lawyer on a reservation; and women who work to help bring political and legal changes in state and federal governments. There are also women trying to organize a feminist movement in states where the norm is still in the 1950s. We are backward out here, but we are growing and dealing with our own special problems and attributes.

For most of us, *Ms.* is our only contact with the feminist movement. We could use a little support from our sisters.

> Ellen L. Quick
> Pierre, South Dakota
> March 1974 Issue

The work of defining problems and issues had to come before solutions could be found. But more than one reader was impatient.

Every month while reading through *Ms.*, I experience such extreme frustration and hurt, for myself, for all of us who are hopeless victims of a sexist society, that I've stopped reading your magazine. Of course, I will always subscribe and support the movement, but right now, at this point in my life, it seems that the only way I'm going to survive emotionally is to avoid being confronted with more and more examples of what I already know, and can hardly bear.

What about solutions—what about action. How about some suggestions—some *help, Ms.*? I'm about ready to put my head in the oven!

> Elizabeth Woods
> Wilmington, Massachusetts
> July 15, 1974

In our first issue, Ann Scott predicted in "The Equal Rights Amendment: What's In It for You?" that the ERA would probably be ratified within a year. And there was reason for such confidence. After a fifty year battle, the amendment—which read, "Equality of rights under the law shall not be denied or abridged by the United States or by any State on account of sex"—had finally been passed by both houses of Congress and had gone to the states for ratification on March 22, 1972. The ERA was endorsed at the time by both the Democratic and Republican parties, and states rushed to be the first to ratify. By the time Ann Scott's article came out in

July, 1972, twenty states had ratified the amendment, leaving eighteen to go. By 1974, the rate of ratification had slowed considerably. Although progress was still being made, early warnings of backlash were sounded.

One of your readers recently warned of what she has observed to be the beginnings of a massive movement of repression throughout the country. I, too, believe this is happening. We are very much in danger of losing some of our hard-earned rights unless we begin to work to preserve them.

In my state, the Equal Rights Amendment was finally ratified this year, but only because of a technical maneuver by one of the senators. Another possibly temporary victory is the Supreme Court's decision concerning abortion.

We must stop congratulating ourselves and work more diligently than ever to preserve the ground we have just barely won.

Pamela J. Frizelle
Missoula, Montana
June 28, 1974

Another reader, responding to a July 1974 article by Susan Dworkin—"Is the Bicentennial Slowly Sinking Into the Potomac?"—reported a successful tactic in Indiana.

South Bend's Bicentennial plans have been largely centered around the opening of our new shopping mall, with outdoor entertainment, arts and crafts booths, and historical dramatizations.

In early June, a reenactment of five famous speeches of historic figures was scheduled. When I and other members of our local Women's Political Caucus learned that Susan B. Anthony was the only female figure to be represented, we offered to do portrayals of five other famous women: Abigail Adams, Sojourner Truth, Elizabeth Cady Stanton, Lucy Stone, and Eleanor Roosevelt, all speaking on various aspects of women's rights. Because Bicentennial programs are largely unfunded, program officials were delighted with our offer to volunteer our services. In effect, we took over the program with remarkable ease.

We are now writing and producing a brief documentary drama on the history of woman suffrage from its roots in the abolitionist movement to the introduction of the ERA. Perhaps this may be the most effective lobbying for ratification in Indiana.

We are planning a series of these programs and hope to have a full-length play by 1976. Although we are all amateurs, we are drawing in more and more women and

hope to establish a women's theater group, which would continue long after the
Bicentennial hoopla is over.

Pat Barrett
South Bend, Indiana
November 1974 Issue

*Women in Indiana were successful in their efforts, though it took until
1978 for the state legislature to ratify the amendment. Little did we know
that that state would be the very last to ratify the ERA—at least until it
is resubmitted. By the mid-seventies, however, readers in some states had
come to know the opposition.*

As the required number of states to ratify the ERA comes closer to the necessary
thirty-eight, antics in state capitols become more and more "far out." I was present at
the Arizona State Judiciary Committee hearing in Phoenix the latter part of January.
Approximately seven hundred women were there, many carrying anything from anti-
ERA signs to babies, home-baked apple pies, and American flags (i.e., you are anti
American if you support the ERA)! The whole experience was very upsetting—we
have got *such* a long way to go!

Name Withheld
February 7, 1975

*The right to choose to have an abortion, guaranteed by the Constitution
as a matter of privacy between a woman and her doctor according to the
United States Supreme Court ruling in Roe v. Wade, January 1973, was
also being challenged by the mid-seventies. The polls consistently showed
a majority for choice regarding abortion but, as one reader warns, the
antics were well-orchestrated. Another reader tells how difficult the issue
was for her.*

I work on Capitol Hill for one of our better-known political figures. My boss is fairly
moderate. While he doesn't like abortion personally, he does believe that each woman
should have the right to make that decision by herself. We come from a fairly
conservative district. Every time he goes back there, he is hit by the pro lifers. I hope
people realize that the right to abortion is rapidly being chiseled away in votes on the
House and Senate floors.

Our office has been deluged with mass mailings from pro lifers in the past few
months. My boss, and others of similar ilk, are going to get bludgeoned into voting to
ban abortions unless women are made aware of the terrible danger we are all in.

We recently received a letter from one of our leading Catholic lay leaders, haranguing us for not signing the pro life petition. He went on to affirm his support for all forms of life, lashing out at IUD devices and morning-after pills. He announced that it has been proved that "psychologically it is better for a woman rape victim to be counseled into bearing her child." Believe me, with Neanderthals like this around, we are all in big, big trouble.

We need help here in Washington. Unless women actively support the Supreme Court decision, in 1975 I fear a new age of repression will be upon us.

Name Withheld
January 1975 Issue

Another mid-seventies discovery was that sisterhood was not such a simple byproduct of consciousness-raising. In a classic article in April 1976, an early women's movement activist and writer using the pen name "Joreen," explained about " 'Trashing'—The Dark Side of Sisterhood." She described how the feminist ideal of sisterly support in some cases did not survive the political and organizational fights of a growing movement. Readers welcomed the discussion.

"Trashing" sounds like a new name for an old game. When trust makes one vulnerable, trashing's effectiveness and power is thoroughly devastating.

Until women in the movement can recognize and "own" their feelings of envy and jealousy, admit their competitiveness, and discover their hostility, this "dark side of sisterhood" will continue to exist. Perhaps we have been lulled into thinking that consciousness-raising, support, and trust are sufficient to achieve personal liberation.

As members of a church-affiliated women's support group, ranging in age from thirty to sixty, we've discovered that it isn't quite that easy. In fact, the search for more authentic and honest ways of being human is a time-consuming, difficult, and quite often painful process. We've been meeting for over six years and have learned that it is much harder to confront the enemy within us than to do battle against the enemy without. Nevertheless, until we can discover our own dark side, how can we expect to create a more positive way of coping with our feelings, each other and the world?

Our thanks to Joreen for airing some of the self-destructive dirty laundry which needs to be examined more closely.

Audrey Vincent
Margaret K. Wilson
Laurie Chisler
Bets Gourley
Marjorie N. Leaming

Teri Rhodehamel
Pat Babcock
Members of the Santa Paula, California
Unitarian Universalist Church Women's Support Group
May 12, 1976

I started going to NOW meetings in the Quad Cities (a forty-mile drive), because Clinton doesn't have any organized feminist group. They're wonderful! I just wanted everybody out there in the big bad world to know there are good (sisters)—and they far out number any bad ones they might find. If nothing else, come join my sisters and me.

Happy in Sisterhood
Name Withheld
August 30, 1976

Another reader had very specific expectations of sisterhood.

I have been a feminist for about six years, and worked on a feminist paper for three years. Recently, I decided to rent a house with four other women who appeared to share my views on equal pay for equal work and nonexploitation of women.

Our only agreement on work duties was that each would do her own dishes. With four people leaving "just a bowl and spoon" or "only a plate and fork" and "maybe a glass now and then," the sinks were overflowing. Several nights I did dishes after midnight just to have utensils to fix breakfast the next day.

So I have learned a valuable lesson. Many sisters are also *pigs*. Pig sisters! Clean up after yourselves. Sisterhood certainly is powerful. Sometimes the stench is overwhelming.

Name Withheld
July 21, 1976

Whatever the organizational problems, the issues that faced feminists were too immediate for the women's movement to disintegrate over a few sisterly problems. A main concern that continued to emerge in the mid seventies was violence against women. First organized around the issue of rape, groups learned from British feminists how to confront the issue of spouse abuse by organizing battered wife shelters. Many who were organized against such violence enlarged their concern to include the issue of pornography. And women who had survived early experiences of molestation and incest organized support groups. The interrelation of these violence issues was explored and debated by feminist theorists, but the first step, as always, was for women to share the truth about their lives.

Ms. features on battery and incest were followed by Letters Forums on these issues, in "Unforgettable Letters From Battered Wives," December 1976, and in "Incest: Personal Testimonies," September 1977. Other readers would simply write as part of their way of dealing with frightening and painful experiences.

No one except someone who has experienced rape can know the late night, quiet playback and the thousands of stirring memories ready to rear up their ugly heads at the slightest incitement. Even almost a year later, as the "anniversary" draws near, I can feel all of my original reactions once again full force, and they are something which will not recede in time. Only women who have spent lonely nights such as this one trying to exorcise the ghosts can truly comprehend the insolence and hideousness of rape. And our number is growing, faster all the time. We must stop it! There are enough of us already.

> Joanne Pilgrim
> Wantagh, New York
> January 1975 Issue

I am fifteen years old, and last summer I was raped by the closest friend of my boyfriend. I did not consider it rape at the time, because I knew the guy relatively well, and I didn't think you were raped by your "friends." I felt like a whore and a piece of trash; but worse than that I felt used. I felt that I had no one to turn to for help, or even someone that I could tell. It was all because I felt that I had done something to make him want to have sex with me.

After school started, a woman from WOAR [Women Organized Against Rape] came and spoke to my class about rape. I realized that women can be raped by anybody, friends, neighbors, strangers, whatever, and if the woman is unwilling to commit the act, then it *is* rape, even if it's her husband. Although I still felt I had no one to turn to, at least I had a name for my hurt, and someplace to direct it and my anger.

> Name Withheld
> February 24, 1976

Ever since I was a little girl, I remember my grandmother telling me never to get married until you were really sure he was the man you want to spend the rest of your life with. She married a *wife beater,* which I shall never forgive my grandfather for. In the beginning of their marriage, he slapped her around, and gave her a black eye once. She went home to her father, and he told her to go back to my grandfather. Well, she went back and stayed for forty-three years, and just a year and three months before she died, he pounded her up to the wall. Then my grandmother got out of that house and came to live with my family until she died. Thank God for woman's lib and guidance centers and abortion clinics and many a hotline number to call for help. If my grandmother had been born into a century when all these things were available, she would of had a chance to get a *good education and support herself and not be afraid.*

Name Withheld
June 6, 1977

My best friend has been my lover for almost three years now, and we were good friends before we became romantically involved. But there were conflicts to overcome, as is natural. I had never really loved anyone so deeply before, and I discovered that I felt really sick at the thought of his collection of porno magazines. I'd thought of myself as pretty liberal and "with it," I guess, with my little pile of *Playgirls,* and I suppose even thought it made me *liberated.* But that was before I knew about the beauty of making love, with someone you care for, such a far-apart idea from the representations in porno magazines, where clothes are torn off and poses struck for the pleasure of a stranger.

The subject came up about five months into our relationship, and I ended up by flipping through one of his many magazines. I couldn't take it. I felt filthy, debased. I really had not seen an actual "dirty" book since I was a little kid, stealing quick peeks at the *Playboys* my uncle had left my father. Not that I was surprised, but I felt stung.

Finally, when I confessed how degraded the books made me feel, my lover admitted that he felt a little jealous of the "perfect" bodies in my *Playgirls.* But he was not quick to fully understand. How can a man be expected to understand immediately how we as women feel after being bombarded by sexist material everywhere, whether visually or even by the commonplace dirty joke? There was many a tearful debate trying to get my frustrated view across. Finally he agreed to throw them out, and I mine, and that would be the end of it.

About eight months later, waiting for him to come back from the store, I casually looked into his bottom drawer. And there they were, dozens and dozens. I took twelve Valiums. I paced and shook and waited for his return. I didn't have to tell him what I had found. I thought I would never want to make love with him again. But time assuaged, as we never think it will, and he finally understood, as much as a man can be expected to. He was truly sorry and upset about it, but it took at least a year for my trust to emerge.

I became very angry at the pornography littering our billboards and stores. I began to hate myself, to think I was a puritanical freak, living in the wrong time. Some days I get so weary of averting my eyes it seems I pull armor around me till I see nothing and feel nothing for a long time.

I have never told anyone this story, but it was important for me to let it out.

Name Withheld
November 10, 1978

I recently went to a movie by myself. I arrived a few minutes early and took my seat. Soon after the movie started, a man sat down next to me. My immediate response was to move over a seat—putting at least one seat between us—but then I decided that I was being too sensitive. So I settled in to enjoy the movie.

After about fifteen minutes the man took off his coat and hat and put them in his lap, periodically lifting them on the side next to me. I realized that he was exposing himself, masturbating, and hoping that I would watch. I quickly said, "When I get up to leave, I'm going to report you." He replied, "Well, then, I think I'll move," and he got up and left. When the movie ended, I didn't report this incident to anyone except friends.

I am very angry at myself for not taking more aggressive action against this man. I should have reported him, and I am ashamed that I didn't.

When I was in fifth grade, I was picked up by a man who said that my parents had asked him to take me home. I was running, because I was late, and as I lived in a small city, it never crossed my mind that he wasn't a "nice" man. I got into his car and answered questions as he drove toward my house, but he kept going straight instead of turning onto my street. By this time, I realized that I had goofed. I became hysterical, tried to jump out of the car, and pleaded with him. He exposed himself and played with himself, but I was lucky, because he didn't rape me or beat me up or kill me.

Finally, he stopped the car and said that he would let me out if I promised never to tell anyone about this incident. Of course I promised, and I jumped out and ran home as fast as I could. I never told my parents about the incident because I was sure the man would kill me if I told anyone. About five years later, I told my older sister about the incident. She told my parents. I'm sure that they never took me seriously, because I was an imaginative, dramatic child.

I guess the main reason for this letter is to get this all off my chest. I have only recently told people about my fifth-grade abduction. I wonder if other people have similar incidents in their backgrounds, which they have repressed for years as I did. I also wonder how many women would have taken the same easy path that I did recently in the movie theater. I have always believed that I would have the guts to turn in a pervert, and I only hope that next time I *do* live up to my estimation of myself.

Mary E. Forsberg
Philadelphia, Pennsylvania
May 1977 Issue

The letter from Mary E. Forsberg has prompted me to tell my story. At age ten, my next-door neighbor sexually molested me on several occasions, the last time culminating in actual penetration. It was always "our secret," as he explained, and no one must ever know. No one ever did know, but not because it was our secret, but because of the tremendous guilt I experienced. To make a sordid story short, my sexual relationships were more often for punishment than for pleasure. Finally, through a better understanding of myself as a person and a woman, I decided that I had served my "sentence" for my "crime" and could live a better life.

I know from experience that guilt is a horrible, vicious emotion, and one that is too often experienced by women. You can feel guilty for saying yes, you can feel guilty for saying no; you can feel guilty for not being married, you can feel guilty for being married; you can feel guilty for neglecting your family for your career, you can feel guilty for not having a career. Sometimes you can feel guilty for just being female. Well, no more for me. I'm glad I'm a woman.

As far as the man who molested me, he still lives next door to my parents, and when I go and visit them and see him in his yard, I just stand there and stare at him. He always turns quickly away and goes into the house. So what if he feels guilty, that's his problem.

Name Withheld
April 18, 1977

In a November 1981 article, "A Rational Look at the Oldest Taboo," Elizabeth Janeway analyzed issues of dominance and power involved in incest. A reader recognized a pattern from her own life.

As a former victim of incest, I totally agree with Elizabeth Janeway. I think that male pleasure and dominance is definitely part of the dynamics of incest. At least in my situation it was. In the six years that the incest took place, my feelings about it never counted: my fears and pain went unnoticed. I'm certain my father felt pleasure from it (his physical responses proved it), and he would threaten and physically abuse me to establish in his mind the position of power he thought he should have. He needn't have bothered. I became such a passive child that I easily gave him all my power—and still do—even though he's been dead for eight years. He dominated my life then, and I continue to let him do so. Trying to have some sense of control in my life, of feeling my own power, is one of the issues I'm struggling with in coming to terms with the incest, especially since I have a tendency to give my power away to whoever wants it. I feel my father betrayed my trust. I loved him, but I hated his behavior. He used me, and my love and trust, for his own pleasures and it makes me extremely angry—at him, at myself, and at all men in general.

As long as we continue to live in a patriarchal system, men will continue to use women, and little girls, for their own pleasures. I firmly believe this.

And somehow, knowing that I'm not alone, that there are other former victims struggling also, makes me more enraged than comforted. . . .

Name Withheld
November 11, 1981

With such pain to deal with, it's no wonder that some activists experienced burnout.

I wonder how many feminists feel as I do—like one of the "walking wounded"? It's not that I feel that my efforts have not been productive, because I have tangible evidence that they have been, in a small way.

But other personal efforts have not been so successful: battling to get my book published, running for public office, trying for another radio gig, getting my course on sex-role stereotyping accepted in the school system in the way that I want it. My reputation as a feminist has not helped any of these projects. I won't back down on that, so it seems to be a draw. My "independence" has been hard won, and it is maintained at some personal damage to my psyche, because I put up an assertive front. I have a razor-edge tongue, well developed through working for the movement. It causes the male sector to tread cautiously. But I have the feeling that I'm battling every step of the way not only for the cause of women's liberation (a new rape bill; women over forty) but for my own survival.

Maybe the trouble is just that at sixty the old energy clock is running down; I feel too tired to fight any longer at the barricades. Are these typical conclusions of other burned-out women as they retire to lick their wounds?

There is also a curious phenomenon out there. One year out of the activist front, and the movement passes you buy as though you had never existed. The least they could do is put up a small plaque commemorating those of us who have fallen in battle.

Perhaps there should be a veterans' hospital, where burned-out leaders in the movement can heal—a place to overcome fear and discouragement. A place to be nourished, as we have nourished; to be loved, as we have loved; to be consoled, and to learn to accept reality with grace.

Jane Mace
Milwaukee, Wisconsin
April 1977 Issue

Our Fifth Anniversary Issue, in July 1977, seemed very much the time to look at how far we had come in the women's movement and to plan future strategies. Gloria Steinem set a framework for this purpose in her essay "Now We Are Five."

The four questions posed by Gloria Steinem really hit home. For example:

Where are you now? A doctoral candidate in higher and adult education.

Where were you five years ago? A forty-five-year-old women with a thirteen-year-old daughter. The highlight of my day was when she returned from school in the afternoon.

Where would you like to be in the future? Peer counseling and doing research on the displaced homemaker.

How should we work to get there? Work together for legislation. Control our own grants, i.e., those grants that filter down through the educational bureaucratic jungle are still controlled by men and most often go to men. We should see that funds earmarked for research in the area(s) of women are designated for women researchers.

Five years ago I did not even have an undergraduate degree. Now I have completed a B.A. in psychology and an M.A. in counseling, and I am working on a doctorate. This is what the women's movement and *Ms.* have done for me. The sexism and ageism I have encountered are appalling, but I'm where I want to be in spite of it all. Thanks for raising my consciousness.

Please withhold my name. When the doctorate is in my hands, all will be told!

Name Withheld
November 1977 Issue

The Ms. *fifth-birthday year was also the year of the National Women's Conference in Houston in November 1977, and the state conferences organized out of International Women's Year (I.W.Y.) funding that led up*

*to Houston. The plan for women to gather and set priorities in every state
and then convene in Houston to set a national women's agenda was
largely the accomplishment of Bella Abzug, who managed to win Congres-
sional approval and funding for the proposal in her last year in Congress.*

*The Houston Plan of Action, which eventually emerged from the na-
tional conference, is a remarkable document that covers issues ranging
from the ERA, abortion, women's employment rights, and child care to
concerns about domestic violence, "displaced homemakers," racism, disabled women, poverty, sexual preferences, and peace. And the state
conferences brought women from all sides of issues together in mammoth,
democratic community meetings. Issues at many of the state meetings
were hard fought, as one reader reported in response to an article by Lisa
Cronin Wohl, "The Mormon Connection? The Defeat of the ERA in
Nevada" in our Fifth Anniversary Issue.*

When I saw the article about a Mormon movement to block the ERA, I confess to
thinking *Ms.* a little paranoid. As I read the well-documented article, I thought
perhaps you were all on to something. After a weekend at the Washington State
Women's Conference, I will never again take *Ms.*'s articles so lightly.

At that conference, non-Mormons realized that an immensely well-organized
minority could effectively take over—and therefore dictate—restrictive, narrow policies that the majority of us would have to live with.

Thank you, *Ms.*, for your efforts. My only regret is that we in Washington fell so
easily into the old trap of thinking it'll never happen here.

Gail M. Shackel
Everett, Washington
November 1977 Issue

The incredible number of thirteen thousand women attended the recent I.W.Y.
conference in Salt Lake City, from a total state population of just over a million, of
which approximately 60 percent are Mormon. (Out of sixteen million Californians,
six thousand attended their state conference.) Nine thousand Utah women attended
preconvention briefing sessions called by the church and addressed by a male
Mormon bishop. The strong presumption that the women were instructed to attend
the convention and vote "right" was borne out by the results, which were overwhelming votes against ERA, abortion in any form, day-care centers, sex education in the
schools, federal aid to developing countries and the United Nations, to name a few.
Non-Mormon participants were frustrated, dismayed, and appalled by the hostility,

rigidity, and conservatism that enveloped the convention. Dissenting views were literally shouted down.

The only good thing is that the ruthless power of the Mormon Church is now out in the open for everyone to see, and from some indications it has been a real and horrifying eye-opener for a lot of its members. Also, maybe some of the Mormon women who went to the conference saw or heard *something* that might start them thinking for themselves.

Alice G. Hart
Logan, Utah
July 29, 1977

Despite the experience of women in Utah and other states, the elected delegates to Houston turned out to be overwhelmingly feminist, and the "spirit" of Houston affected women all over the country, who responded to media accounts and the final Houston conference report.

I want to say thank God for women like Gloria Steinem after watching her on the TV program *Good Morning America* from Houston, Texas, at the National Women's Year conference.

If only my mother were alive to see the woman telling about their beatings from their husbands and the woman telling about the self-induced abortion of her friend.

I can still see my mother's tear-stained face after a beating from my father and hear her words of helplessness when me and my sisters begged her to leave him. "Where would we go, and what would I do for a living?" She had a third-grade education, and if she asked the police for help, they didn't want to be involved in a "family fight." I prayed my father would die, and he did at age forty-seven, and I wasn't sorry!

My mother limited her family with self-induced abortion until a doctor finally tied her tubes when she nearly died from infection as a result of her third abortion.

She never dreamed to hear the things I heard on TV today, as she was too ashamed to speak of these things in her time and told me after I was grown. The pain she kept to herself!

For the first time in my life, I am proud to have been born female!

Name Withheld
November 18, 1977

But the next year, in response to an article by Lisa Cronin Wohl in February 1978, "Are We Twenty-five Votes Away from Losing the Bill of

Rights . . . and the Rest of the Constitution?"—on the dangers of a right-wing plan to call a constitutional convention to force through an anti abortion amendment—we heard a different assessment of Houston.

As a member of Eagle Forum, I hope the Con-Con goes through. It would be our answer to the Houston National Women's Conference—and we'll pay for it with our own money! Meanwhile, I wonder how much longer you will indulge in the conceit of calling yourselves the "women's movement," now that *Good Housekeeping* has found the "right-wing leader" Anita Bryant the world's most-admired woman? Bella Abzug doesn't even make the list!

Lee Kuivinen
Mount Prospect, Illinois
June 1978 Issue

The Houston conference, with its sweeping mandate for long-term reform and its success in incorporating a wide range of concerns, was an exhilarating experience for thousands of feminists. It also, for the first time, brought many of us face to face with women who were organized to oppose these changes—women who welcomed the ultra-right's focus on issues such as the Equal Rights Amendment and abortion. And despite our success in Houston, the ERA ratification effort remained stalled, needing five more states to ratify by 1979.

The ERA was defeated today here in North Carolina on a twenty-six to twenty-four vote. Two of the men who voted no had promised support of the ERA during their campaigns. Those two men cost us the ERA. I am not expecting it to become a part of our Constitution. It has succeeded in turning women against each other. The opponents of the ERA did their work well. They placed home-made cakes on the desks of the men, and spread rumors, such as "rape laws will be abolished," et cêtera. A recent poll here showed that 63 percent of males were in favor of the ERA, but only 51 percent of the females supported it. Still, though, 51 percent is a majority, but thanks to the senators (one of whom told reporters, "I am one senator who still puts women on pedestals, no matter what the opposition says," while his wife smiled proudly beside him), we have been slapped in the face. I am very disappointed in North Carolina. By the way, I'm not "a loudmouthed, bra-burning homosexual," as supporters of the ERA have been called. I'm a quiet, happily married, unemployed woman. If only we could all unite. . . .

Name Withheld
March 1, 1977

I deeply resent women who try to stop the ERA's passage. These women who fight to keep *me* from getting the ERA, who fight to keep me from becoming a totally free and independent person, I resent their ignorant interference.

I do not resent the woman who wants to be a mother, a homemaker, a good wife; I do not oppose her desire to have the doors held open, the cigarettes lit; she has as much of a right as I do to live the way she chooses. The woman I resent is the one who wants to tell me how to live, who decides that *all* women want to live as mothers, wives, and mistresses—the woman who denies my rights to live as a full and equal person in my own country. I despise the woman who wants *my* rights taken away along with hers! She is the enemy, she is the tyrant. She is the one who will destroy the democratic process, because her life style will be imposed on all women. She is so totally heinous she would have all women be one thing, fill one role in life, live one way, demand a narrow path, fill only one gap.

Name Withheld
November 2, 1977

One reader, who told us she was a businesswoman in the music field, wrote to explain her problems with the amendment.

I believe that if the ERA is passed, the men of our society will lose a lot of respect for women, it will induce homosexuality, and if just one publicly known woman fouls up after the law is passed, the rest of us will have to suffer.

Women want equal rights; for what? If they had any confidence in themselves at all or used their knowledge that God has given them, they will find the answer right in front of them without this law being passed. Women are the backbone of this world and don't even know it. We have come so far already without this law.

I believe that women should have the same opportunities as men, not rights. She should be able to try to do the same things as a man, and if she doesn't succeed, then pat her on the back and send her on her way. If I do something as effective as is expected of a man, I receive a lot of praise and *respect!* If I do the same thing after this law is passed, it will be looked on as just a job well done. Respect is the key for the woman of our society. If you carry this with you, baby you can do anything!

Name Withheld
July 15, 1978

Although the state legislatures refused to budge, the ERA still enjoyed wide national, bipartisan support. As it became more and more likely that the five necessary states would not ratify before the original seven-

year time limit ran out in 1979, women's movement leaders gathered to reassess strategy. Some thought that limited resources of both time and money had already been overspent on the ERA. Others thought the battle too critical to lose. The strategy that carried the hour, largely due to its passionate presentation by Eleanor Smeal, president of the National Organization for Women, was to mobilize national support and push Congress to extend the ratification deadline. In a May 1978 article, "A New Lease on Life for the ERA," I argued that the seven years allowed for ratification was an arbitrary decision of Congress and not mandated by the Constitution and that since the ERA was still an unresolved issue and a current controversy, Congress should extend the time limit for another three years. One reader responded with a memory of the suffrage leader and author of the ERA, Alice Paul.

Alice Paul dedicated her life to passage of the ERA. Miss Paul (as she was invariably called, even though she had earned her doctorate) was frequently difficult, always demanding, a brilliant legislative analyst, and a hard-driving lobbyist. I had the honor and privilege of working with her from her headquarters at Belmont House in Washington, D.C., and it was her firm conviction that the only way the ERA would be enacted into our Constitution was when we united to give *sole* priority to the measure, setting aside other inequities until women were recognized under the Constitution.

Barbara Ireton
New York, New York
September 1978 Issue

The culminating event in what was to be a successful drive to extend the deadline was a march on Washington, in which women's movement organizations were joined by civil rights, labor, and church groups to bring together 100,000 people near the steps of the Capitol on an unbeliev- ably hot but cheerful day. As one reader noted, however, members of the news media seemed more interested in women pitted against one another than in that massive outpouring of support. It was an assessment that we at Ms. could appreciate, having had the tiresome experience of being asked time and time again by the national media to suggest interview subjects who were against the ERA and other feminist issues.

On Sunday, July 9, 1978, at 7:00 A.M., my daughter and I boarded a school bus at Philadelphia's Thirtieth street station bound for Washington, D.C., to demonstrate for the ERA. The waiting, the heat, the lack of sanitary facilities, the expense of money and energy was shared by 100,000 other people.

When we returned home, nearly midnight, my husband told us how NBC radio had covered the historic event: not with Gloria Steinem, Bella Abzug, Betty Friedan, or Ellie Smeal, but with Phyllis Schlafly, who claims to represent a nonexistent majority in opposition to the ERA.

It is true, violence was not anticipated. It is true, no one threatened to burn any bras. True, also, that efforts to pass the ERA have been going on since 1923. However, 100,000 demonstrators, albeit peaceful, are newsworthy.

Name Withheld
July 10, 1978

The extension was won, and the Equal Rights Amendment remained the top priority of NOW and many other women's groups. But other issues demanded immediate attention as well, particularly reproductive freedom, since the Congress and state legislatures were chipping away at a woman's right to choose abortion. In a June 1978 review of Linda Bird Francke's Ambivalence of Abortion, *Barbara Grizzuti Harrison argued that feminists needed to reclaim the moral perspective in the abortion debate. One writer's morality, however, didn't fit a reader's life experience.*

Barbara Harrison tells us that she is appalled at the idea of abortion as "a frivolous lifestyle choice." One of the examples she gives is the desire not to defer a graduate degree.

Permit me to clue you in on some facts about graduate school. We women who are planning professional careers in nontraditional areas, particularly the sciences, are a dedicated, hard-nosed group of people, because we have to be. In most cases, the department, our families, our colleagues, our society are rooting for us to fail. We are passed over for fellowships and scholarships, our aspirations are not taken seriously, and we have no wives to provide us with psychological or financial support.

Five of the graduate and faculty members at my university have had abortions due to contraceptive failure. All but one was single. The question was simple: Do you want to be a scientist—yes or no? There are no mothers in my department, because a graduate degree takes all or nearly all of one's time, energy, and money. There is nothing left. Period. A woman must leave the program to have a baby, and that—realistically—means an absolute minimum of five years lost. The most successful scientists in terms of research opportunities, salary, and promotions are the ones who receive their doctorates in their twenties and at the latest in their early thirties.

Insisting that a woman cancel or seriously cripple her life goals because of contraceptive failure is not, in my view, a "moral" position.

M. J. Lyle-Smith
Scottsdale, Arizona
October 1978 Issue

Especially vulnerable in the abortion battle were poor women who depended on federal funds in the form of Medicaid to pay for their health needs. In a January 1979 article, "Investigation of a Wrongful Death . . . The story of Rosie Jimenez," Ellen Frankfort and Frances Kissling told of a woman who had suffered the consequences of the Hyde amendment, which forbade the federal funding of abortion and set poor women back to the pre-1973 era of dangerous back-alley abortions. In proof of the fact that Rosie Jimenez depended on federal funds, Frankfort and Kissling told how she had had other safe abortions paid for by Medicaid. The reaction to this information by several readers showed just how complicated our feelings about abortion rights were.

I read with great concern your story about Rosie Jimenez—a needless tragedy due to archaic abortion laws. My sense of outrage came to an abrupt halt, however, at the line "Rosie had twice before . . . used Medicaid funds for legal abortions."

I stopped and reread it several times, trying to make it coincide with the image of Rosie that the story had put forth up to that point. How, I asked both myself and the article, could a woman so independent, so intent on fulfilling the promise of a productive life, so close to achieving her hard-fought goals, be undergoing her *third* abortion? Why was a woman so determined to alter the course of her life so blind to the reproductive part of it?

It is, of course, a searing personal tragedy that Rosie Jimenez died a painful, needless death. But the larger tragedy lies in the fact that in 1977 an intelligent, progressive woman used abortion as a means of birth control and not as a last, desperate attempt, as it should be. Cases such as Rosie Jimenez's serve only to add fuel to the fire of right-to-life narrow-mindedness and to add color to the image of abortion as thoughtless, wanton "baby killing."

Abortion on demand *is* a woman's right, but only when *all* women use the right responsibly will *all* receive it.

Miriam A. Botkin
Pittsburgh, Pennsylvania
May 1979 Issue

Rosaura Jimenez's life was not unusual. I know—her story could have been mine. In 1975, like Rosie, I had my first abortion. I was receiving federal aid at the time but was too ashamed to ask if there were funds available to help me out. I was lucky enough to be able to borrow some money and healthy enough to be able to go hungry for a month or two. I asked for a tubal ligation, but no doctor would perform that type of surgery on a twenty-one-year-old.

My second abortion, like Rosie's, was in 1977. It was more traumatic and lonely. Like most Mexican-raised Catholics, I was guilt ridden. *Again*—I found myself with no money, and this time feeling bitter and desperate and wondering *why*, goddamn it? I used birth control both times. I was in graduate school with a grade average of three-point-eight and a teaching assistantship.

I borrowed more money for another legal abortion and applied for food stamps. "Just another year and this depressing circle will end," I'd tell myself.

Well, it's a year and a half since my second abortion. Rosie didn't make it, but I did, thank God. I own my own store now, am making money, and would be glad to give some of it to federal Medicaid funds. Abortion should be available to the poor, the rich, and to the struggling—like Rosie and me.

Name Withheld
May 1979 Issue

The issue of controlling one's reproductive life—including the right to choose or choose not *to have an abortion as well the right not to be sterilized against one's will—became even more of a heated political battle in the eighties. And readers continued to struggle with their own personal choices.*

I am a feminist—I am a physician—and less than six months ago I had an abortion. The first two statements are ones that I am proud of—the third I would give much to take away. Don't misunderstand—I would never wish to deny a woman the right to a safe abortion or to take that decision away from her. For some women, at some times, I believe the decision to be right—for me it was not. And I protest the system that made it so easy to do this thing. The reflex "single woman-abortion" is as dangerous to our right to choose as any other reflex concerning our reproductive potential.

I am deeply sorry that the society of which I am a part is one where every pregnancy cannot be welcomed—where the response to a positive test is as often "Oh, shit," as "Terrific." Our ability to give life should be a good and joyous thing.

So I end with a plea to my colleagues: Ask! Not what she feels she should do, not what her mother or lover or husband wants—but what *she wants*. Take the time to find out! Find out why she got pregnant—for abortion is always a failure, of contraception, of education, of trust—then do what you must.

Name Withheld
May 25, 1981

Webster's: "abortion—n. 1. the expulsion of a nonviable fetus . . . 2. MONSTROS-ITY. . . ."

And so it goes on that way. As a subscriber to *Ms.* and a mother of two I find myself in constant conflict on this issue. I was not married when I became pregnant with my son; luckily his father and I knew each other well. Before the pregnancy test, I vowed an abortion; my life was going too well to be complicated by a baby. Five seconds after I heard "positive," the thrills that began in my toes were winging out my head. Why was that? I was the same person; could this new person inside of me be responsible?

So we married, and I continued working until this past year when my daughter was born. I stay home and watch Phil Donahue and *The Edge of Night*, garden, bake, sew. My kids are a continual source of laughter and frustration. I expect that had I continued in my job childless and single, the good and bad would average out the same. Life consists of trying to successfully deal with changes.

My latest problem is an unsigned letter in your June 1981 issue [See "Parenting: Bringing Up 'Free' Children," page 53 from a birth mother who relinquished her child for adoption. The letter writer says that there is nothing satisfying about carrying a child you cannot love. Of course not. I can think of few things worse. But is abortion the answer? It tears at my insides to imagine it.

Why isn't the "choice" you are constantly referring to, the choice of the Pill or the diaphragm? Or have your tubes tied if you know you'll never want children; it's a simple operation.

So then, after the fact, the pregnancy happens anyway, the woman knows her life is ruined. I had that feeling, briefly. And the pregnancy is so brief in retrospect. A perhaps uncomfortable feeling at times, but still not that hard of a lesson, if learned correctly.

I am only trying to be honest with my feelings to you, and I'm sure there are many feelings I'll never understand. I will be glad when we are all at peace on this issue.

Name Withheld
May 17, 1981

Did you know that rape of young foster girls in Ohio was so common twenty years ago that when young foster girls were suspected of being pregnant, abortions were performed on them? No questions were asked, no pregnancy tests administered. At a time when even the women who had taken thalidomide were denied abortions on "moral grounds," young girls were forced to undergo abortions or be jailed.

The reasons for these illegal operations were simple. Any girl who was a ward of the state (sociological orphan) was likely to be forced to undergo a trial in juvenile court and name the person responsible for the pregnancy. Obviously, forcible abortion was preferable to dirtying the reputations of "decent" men. It was also cheaper to kill the fetus of an already unwanted child than to let it live.

How do I know? Easy—from the age of six until the age of eighteen, I was a ward of the state's Division of Child Welfare and Catholic Charities. At the age of ten, my foster mother took me to a doctor, an old woman whose only function as far as I could figure it, was simply to set up abortions for wards of the state.

It is a matter of record that an abortion had been set up for me. It is also a fact that I didn't need one and managed to avoid it. No sexual assault occurred, but the speed in which this operation was being obtained was enough to convince me that forced rape and abortions were too damned common.

Name Withheld
January 1, 1981

By the mid-eighties, issues of reproductive freedom were complicated by incredible new advances in birth technology. In "The Ethics of Choice," April 1984, sociologist Rayna Rapp dealt with some of these issues in telling her personal story of choosing abortion after finding, through amniocentesis, that the fetus was afflicted with Down's syndrome.

Thanks to Rayna Rapp for piercing her private pain to share with us her heartbreaking experience. She also pierced my own pain, eight years buried, which I found amazingly accessible after all this time.

No one can doubt the particularly devastating agony in terminating a pregnancy at five and a half months rather than at five and a half weeks. The movement within a woman's body is a constant reminder that the fetus is indeed a baby, with arms and legs in motion. Our image of the child we carry is quite tangible. Compound that agony with the longing and love and anticipation for that child to be and with the horrors of trying to justify to yourself, your husband, and your other children how you plan to cope and care for (or not cope and care for) a Down's syndrome child. In the end, my husband and I chose to abort.

I wish I could write that there are no regrets and that time has shown our decision a wise one. There are even periods of time when I don't think about what our lives would have been like had we chosen to bring a Down's syndrome child into the world. There are days now, too, when I am glad my own children, who are just beginning private, independent lives of their own, will not have to take over the care of their sister in the event that we could not. I continue to be outraged that society is still so little prepared to care for such a child.

Nancy Keil
Grand View, New York
August 1984 Issue

Few things make me feel more utterly desolate and abandoned than the women's movement's resolve to support the choice to abort "deformed" fetuses. Yes, I know all the arguments. I am pro choice, too, I say. Yet I am severely disabled. Deformed. My mother would have aborted me, too, if she could have.

My movement, the disability-rights movement, is no match against either the pro choice movement or the pro life movement, both of which are better organized, and neither of which really understands what it feels like to be one of that group that everyone else is glibly fighting over. We still have no voice. Sometimes, lying in bed at night, executive job and all be hanged, I simply cry about this.

We can't say it's okay to be disabled, and mean it, and not want to bear a disabled child. It's simply a contradiction. We have to resolve this issue first. The way we're resolving it now allows no room to make a better world for people with disabilities. For the hope, conscious or not, is that maybe, someday, there will be none of us left.

Name Withheld
August 1984 Issue

While the abortion-rights fight was being waged in the streets, in the courts, and in the legislatures, there were other emotional battlegrounds. In an April 1979 reassessment, "A Year Later: The Lure of The Women's Room," *Lindsy Van Gelder talked of her own and a number of feminists' first reaction to Marilyn French's classic novel: that many of us felt, or needed to feel, that we had worked ourselves beyond the raw anger portrayed by the French characters. The book's immense popularity had caught some by surprise, and a reader reported that the book's impact could be just as strong for a man.*

I am a man, and I believe that *The Women's Room* has become one of a very few books I would call pivotal in my life. My first reaction on reading it was one of tremendous sadness. Guilt? Yes, but the deeper more overwhelming feeling was sadness. My wife had brought the book home and after reading a short portion was not able to continue—her feelings were so strong. I needed no other urging to pick up the book and read for myself.

No woman had ever before been able to communicate so well what it meant to be "a woman in a male-dominated world." To give you an idea of how dramatically the book has affected me: recently while undergoing "minor surgery," I found myself commenting to my doctor—who was poised ready for surgery with knife in hand—that he might profit a great deal from reading this nonfiction novel.

> Reverend Donald R. Niswonger
> Naperville, Illinois
> August 1979 Issue

In her excellent article on *The Women's Room*, Lindsy Van Gelder wrote that Marilyn French touched a vein of anger in all women that feminists learned to channel several years ago. Maybe it is time for feminists to get back in touch with that raw anger as motivation for the uphill struggle to get the ERA ratified and to prevent the chipping away of our rights by the swelling tide of conservatism.

> Cecelia Barton
> Fayetteville, North Carolina
> August 1979 Issue

If French's fictional characters seemed all too real for many women, the case of Jean Harris, the respectable, middle-aged headmistress of a girls' school accused of murdering her famous lover, Dr. Herman Tarnower, also touched a deep nerve. A Ms. article, again by Lindsy Van Gelder, discussed what seemed a questionable defense mounted by Harris's lawyer at her trial.

Jean Harris, the alleged murderer of the Scarsdale Diet doctor, is claimed by Joel Aurnou, her attorney, to be "a classic victim—a one-man woman hopelessly in love with a cad who couldn't handle commitment."

This attorney insists that women are helplessly "fascinated by men with interesting careers, money, and success," and he implies that we are unable to be responsible for the outcome of our infatuations. So, praise be this attorney, he is going to save us— "Jean Harris won't be the only one on trial." All things considered, this attorney isn't helping the women's movement; he is merely perpetuating the myth of feminine helplessness—of our inability to control our own destinies.

> Barbara Griss
> Denver, Colorado
> December 1980 Issue

As it turned out, of course, Aurnou wasn't enough help to Jean Harris either. But even after she went to prison, more than one angry reader identified with her.

It seems to *me* that Jean Harris should have gotten off on self-defense. I went through much the same thing many years ago, with my husband of twenty years and his young mistress. We had had a successful and social life, but after he divorced me he tried to prevent me from seeing any of our old friends, or going to the same places, or even from going to the children's school. His mother and I had continued to be friends, but when she lay dying, he kept me from seeing her and even returned a farewell letter I had sent to her . . . unopened. It occurred to me then that divorce . . . or what Jean Harris went through . . . is a kind of murder, whereby you try to forcibly remove someone from your life not only emotionally but socially and retroactively; to erase even the memory that a relation ever existed.

It is easy to say that she (or I) should simply have walked away from the whole sordid mess, but I remember all too well the panicky disbelieving feeling of being systematically removed, of inexorably being forced over some invisible cliff into extinction, while your erstwhile friends are being told lies behind your back and the whole episode and twenty years of your life are being quietly buried (*my* husband never even admitted there was another woman, publicly). I can only thank God that I did not find him, the night I went after him with a gun. I doubt if anyone on that jury quite understood what Mrs. Harris had endured, to react as she did . . . in self-defense.

Name Withheld
February 25, 1981

In my very small social environment (I'm "just a housewife"—not a joiner), I number Jean, the doctor's wife; Marge, the lawyer's wife; Delores, an engineer's wife; Terry's mom; Chris's mom; my high-school classmate Pat; who—when faced, at over fifty years of age with the divorce court's decision that since their husbands no longer wished to support them, they should "get a job" (after many, many years of homemaking and child rearing)—suicided.

My husband, also, after thirty-eight years of marriage has asked me to divorce him and, in the wake of my inaction to comply with his request, is plotting very carefully to leave me destitute at fifty-eight. He will succeed; it is not that difficult.

I too will have little choice but suicide. Welfare—thirty dollars a week for everything—is just a slower, more painful suicide than the car motor left running in a closed garage, the gas jets turned on, plus sleeping pills.

No, at fifty-eight, no one is going to hire me for anything—my bottom dentures don't fit and wigs only seem to call attention to an indecent expanse of bare scalp shining through—result of stress, my doctor says. "You bet."

At any rate, I have a fantasy alternative to suicide. I call it the Jean Harris Memorial Movement. If every about-to-commit-suicide-because-of-no-alternative displaced homemaker were to take with her one of those big, strong protective —— males— that's activism where it counts. Taking hubby with you into "that good night" is a temptation. But to really achieve any divorce-law reform, judges, legislators, or at least divorce lawyers would be more effective. How long do you think it would take before we would get some kind of legal reform?

How about it gals? I'm about to become a joiner. I want to be a charter member of the Jean Harris Memorial Movement. What the heck, we might even decide not to suicide afterwards—like Jean, live on the state in the penitentiary.

A divorce-law authority figure to whom I spoke recently about our only alternative being suicide said, "Well, we've all got to die sometime."

Name Withheld
January 27, 1982

One lesson learned from the ERA stalemate was that sympathy with feminist issues by a majority of Americans, shown consistently at the polls and expressed through the public's reaction to "The Women's Room" for example, did not translate directly into an active enough political constituency. Widening this constituency became a concern of the eighties, as NOW and other groups stepped up their fund-raising activity on behalf of the ERA. One reader responded to a July 1979 essay in which Catharine R. Stimpson took to task people who would say, "I'm not a feminist but . . ." and then go on to proclaim support for equal pay for equal work or some other feminist goal.

I was glad to see the story about the "I am not a feminist, but . . ." people. This has been my pet peeve for years. It bothers me because the women who say it seem to be implying that old bra-burning, man-hating image of feminists. They don't want to be identified with women's liberation, yet they are reaping the benefits made possible by the movement.

I can't think of what I personally have done to help liberate women except join NOW and subscribe to *Ms.* (what a hero!), *but* I am a feminist.

Trixie Kelleter
Springfield, Virginia
June 20, 1979

Another reader explained how, for her, the fact that feminists seemed more willing to air internal debates and differences made the women's movement more inviting. It was a trend that she saw in a number of Ms. articles, including Lindsy Van Gelder's "Cracking the Women's Movement Protection Game" of December 1978.

Lindsy Van Gelder's article along with "Trashing," "Phallic Imperialism," and June Jordan's article "Second Thoughts of a Black Feminist" [" 'Trashing:' The Dark Side of Sisterhood," by Joreen, April 1976; "Phallic Imperialism," by Andrea Dworkin, December 1976; and June Jordan in February 1977] herald a feminism finally on the threshold of a tolerant and unified philosophy. Although I have been a loyal reader of *Ms.* since 1973, as a single-black-woman-lawyer-mother-et cetera, I have of times been disillusioned by a certain absence of color—and culture—consciousness in *Ms.* When I have read a piece by a nonwhite, non-rock-steady middle-class-oriented woman, I have felt that it was a token act to woo us, as a significant segment of womankind, into a movement that historically *more* privileged white women have defined. "Cracking . . ." faces this *j'accuse* squarely.

When feminism first reached me as a high-school student in the late 1960s, along with the anti war, anti capitalist "movements," young, self-righteous, "99 percent of the time white" proselytes dubbed me either unenlightened or heretical for not adhering to *the line,* such as it was. At the same time, I was barraged from other quarters by black revolutionists-nationalists calling my understanding and commitment into question. And so I remained outside the pale of both movements *formally* but participating at their nerve centers all along.

Orthodoxy is the most anti life force of all, for it has provided the justification for all of history's carnage. It is possible that we heretics can now be embraced as of the fold. If so, truth is surely gospel!

Name Withheld
April 1979 Issue

A letter from the National Organization for Women arrived in the mail today with a strategy for defeating the New Right. One tactic suggested was to send missionaries to the Mormons. Are they kidding? Why don't they send missionaries to the outposts like Florida, where there are women with energy, drive, ambition, ideals, in short, everything the women's movement needs but money? Why don't you organize a system of mobilizing us?

You're never going to win ratification, never going to win the fight for violence shelters, round-the-clock government-funded day-care centers, or anything else unless you aim at somehow mobilizing the women in places like Florida. I am familiar with the scene down here. In four years, I have not met another woman whose goals resemble mine. But somewhere down here others must exist.

I am angry and disgusted. I realize the women's revolution is taking place right where it started: in my daughter's and my living room; and until I find some way, on my own, of raking in a huge wad of money, I might as well hang up any notions of aiding the women's movement. Can it be you glorified career women up there don't even realize we *exist*? Get real!

Name Withheld
February 9, 1981

In response to a February 1982 article by Cathy Cevoli—"Is There Anything a Twenty-Eight-Year-Old Can Teach Her Teenage Sister (That She Doesn't Already Know)?"—a reader who described herself as "a Ms. reader since the first issue, published when I was thirteen years old" warned that older feminists were turning off her generation.

As I see it, blindly following the dictums of a dead counterculture is no less tragic than embracing the current preppy fad and its accompanying conservatism. Sixties nostalgia has also become a form of "dopey normality." As long as "punk" feminists like myself are universally ignored or condemned by second-wave feminists, there can be no third wave of feminism. It's a shame, because as a third-generation feminist (my grandmother was a suffragist), I know how much I owe my predecessors. We could learn from each other, but not until we put our prejudices behind us.

Deborah K. Lazaroff
Orinda, California
June 1982 Issue

Yet another article by Ms. contributing editor Lindsy Van Gelder, who had a long-developed expertise at measuring the pulse of the women's movement, discussed a disturbing phenomenon. "Burn-Out: What Happens When the World Won't Change," May 1982, brought this response.

Lindsy Van Gelder has great insight into burn-out, but I wonder if she appreciates the fact that in many small towns feminist burn-out can equal not just feminism's depression, but its death.

I live in a rural town, where a few of us last fall started a local chapter of the National Organization for Women—quite jolting for this conservative farming community. Since then, husbands, children, and friends have consistently resented our feminist gatherings, no more radical than garage sales and monthly public meetings. Many of the stores in town won't display our announcements, and some of our members could lose their jobs using our new-found strength in speaking out. Living in a town where there are only fourteen feminists out of sixteen thousand people, I am often pushed toward burn-out. But I fight it. If I "went under," what would happen to our infant movement? Clearly, for us *not* burning out is the greatest feminist challenge.

I hope that sisters elsewhere who are on the verge of burn-out may find strength and courage from our example. For renewed optimism, keep reminding yourself what a life-and-death situation it can be for small-town women merely to say, "Keep the faith," and how radical it is for them to do it.

Leslie Jacobs
Connersville, Indiana
October 1982 Issue

"Renewed optimism" was certainly needed, for in 1980 the Republicans adopted a party platform that not only included an anti-abortion plank but withdrew the GOP's longstanding support for the ERA—much to the dismay of loyal Republican feminists, such as former party co-chair Mary Crisp, who walked out of the convention. And the nation elected a president who was only too happy to run on that platform—though Ronald Reagan himself had endorsed the Equal Rights Amendment when he was governor of California. The amendment had acquired some powerful enemies, but it still seemed like simple justice to us, simple enough for a child to understand.

Recently my nine-year-old son and I were looking around the house for a ruler for his homework assignment. I observed to him that when I was growing up, most rulers had the golden rule printed on them. "What's that?" he asked. "Do unto others as you would have them do unto you," I replied. "Oh," he said, "I know where you got that. You got that at all those ERA meetings." Click!

Betsy Brinson
Richmond, Virginia
August 1980 Issue

I offer the following excerpt, taken from a school assignment written by my seven-year-old grandniece, as evidence of the future good health of the feminist movement:

"George Washington's brother had died. In those days women did not get to own there own home. So George Washington's sister did not get the house. George got the house. . . . He became the first president. And then he was put on a nickel."

Name Withheld
March 11, 1979

I have just finished reading your January articles on Reagan and the ultra-right. It's very depressing. But what am I to do? I don't like involving myself in local organizations and scheduling my life with meetings, fund raising, and events. So I sat down and thought up some ideas for people like myself.

¶ Give friends and relatives subscriptions to *Ms.* magazine and other feminist publications or membership in some effective women's organizations (such as the National Organization for Women).

¶ Send periodic post cards to federal and state senators and representatives with your message.

¶ Send periodic contributions to a feminist group or organization.

¶ Arm yourself with well-written materials and pamphlets on the ERA and other issues—especially if you are not a very good debater, like myself. Some good material is available from the League of Women Voters.

¶ Keep informed!

Brenda Theyers-Wilson
Kodiak, Alaska
May 1981 Issue

As time was again running out on the ERA, tactics, which included a travel and convention boycott of unratified states, became more creative—and more desperate.

This year, when we decided to get married, we decided not to get married. We feel that until the Equal Rights Amendment becomes a legal part of our Constitution, marriage in America will remain a sexist institution. We live now as husband and wife but without benefit of clergy or justice of the peace. When the ERA becomes law, we will officially legalize our marriage, but not until then. We are protesting symbolically; but symbols, as the civil-rights movement and the anti war movement proved, can be powerful.

Brenda Mann and Daniel Bloom
Corvallis, Oregon
August 1981 Issue

At work, I throw into the trash all catalogs and requests for business from companies in unratified states.

Name Withheld
August 7, 1981

Personally, I think the best thing you could do to help the ERA would be to print the text of the amendment on your cover, bold red letters on a white field and a blue border. It seems the time is nigh for a multimedia push. A simple, forceful approach, much the same as that used to sell millions of dollars' worth of tooth-rotting Coke is needed.

Women, I say put your amendment everywhere you can (have a sympathetic friend write it on a men's room wall) and people will buy it on its own simple merit.

Yours in effective marketing,

Name Withheld
July 13, 1981

The fate of the ERA in some state legislatures drove home a lesson: feminists needed to run for local office and win in larger and larger numbers. This had been the mandate of the National Women's Political Caucus since its founding in 1971, and the numbers of women in office at the local level had increased dramatically, but feminist politicians still felt isolated in many instances.

I was the first elected woman county commissioner in Bay County, Michigan, and also the youngest. I fought the political machine and won, upsetting one of the good old boys. It was an uphill battle all the way, because very few people took me seriously. My own father said (after I had waged an extensive door to door campaign), "If the right man ran against Ernie, he could probably beat him." We were all surprised when I did win.

The next two years was a consciousness-raising experience for me. It was during that time I became a feminist. I went through a number of sexist situations, including having the chair close the meeting twice while I had the floor and also having one commissioner continuously refer to me as "the boob." I had to work much harder than any of the other twenty members of the board. I never got up and talked unless I had my facts and figures in front of me. I just couldn't take the chance of being labeled "a dumb broad."

While serving, I introduced a resolution asking the commissioners to limit county travel to only ratified-ERA states. This was like opening Pandora's box; the next National Association of Counties Convention was scheduled to be in Las Vegas, and very few commissioners wanted to miss that trip. I read everything I could on ERA and contacted as many organizations and individuals as I could. I even started a petition drive to let the other commissioners know what kind of support there was in the community. I felt very disappointed at the lack of support from the local chapters of the League of Women Voters and the National Organization for Women (this chapter of NOW was not based in our county, where a chapter has since been organized). When it finally came to a vote on the floor of the commission, there were only two other women in the room. The debate lasted three hours on a hot, humid August day. I was hit from all sides by all different questions and arguments. I equated the boycott to the Boston Tea Party and the plight of women to the plight of blacks. Of course, nothing worked, and the resolution was not passed, but to my surprise by a slim three-vote margin. I quietly left the room, went into the bathroom, and had a good cry. Making sure that nobody could tell what I had just done, I went back to the commission floor with my head held high and continued with a business-as-usual attitude, but I felt defeated and very alone.

Afterward, I realized that I had done some good. Several commissioners told me that they were much more aware of the problems women face and also aware of what ERA stands for (many thought it was some leftist, radical women's group). They also began to see me as a person and began to respect my views and opinions.

I didn't make my reelection. I feel the conservative community that elected a timid housewife the first time was not ready to elect an assertive feminist the second time.

During my term as commissioner, I found a sympathetic ear and support from the Bay County Women's Center. I realized that I wanted to help other women and give them the support they needed, so I am currently serving as vice-president of the center.

Susan C. Gotfried
Bay City, Michigan
April 29, 1981

Since 1970, feminists had been celebrating the anniversary of suffrage on August 26, with marches and demonstrations. In 1981, a year before the extended deadline for ratification, August demonstrations were focused on the Equal Rights Amendment. One of our most faithful correspondents celebrated the anniversary with one of her many "post cards" to the Editor.

Celebrating the Anniv. of the day we were "given" the vote.

Today, after seventy-five years of hard work, & "suffering the slings & arrows of outrageous fortune," I am late, but a part of, women's amazing courage from day one. I do not know why God requires so much more from women than men, unless he *knows* that eventually, "we can take it, we can make it," all over the world.

To the death of sexism!

When I am dead, I'll have a proud smile on my face, because I'm so HAPPY to be a humble member of this "gallant company of women." I *know* that ERA will prevail OR THIS JUST *IS NOT* AMERICA ANYMORE.

> J. Chally
> Morris, Illinois
> August 16, 1981

In another message some months later, the same letter writer told us something about her own role model.

My great-grandmother is such an inspiration, she lives and will never die as long as she is remembered. Way back, there were rude, ignorant men & boys hooting at the suffragettes & "some housewives who shouted surprising things, they were jealous because they feared to join us" (my grandmother said). Grandma said there were bad moments but also a lot of real gentlemen who were fair & just & equal to giving women the vote. I doubt that any of these women regretted it. Indeed, they were proud. And why not? To ask for justice is a rational thing among rational people, & to defraud us of justice is the work of *poltroons*. Some men are fearful of losing place & never did play fair or honestly. These men are the *repressors*. But we *will* be in the Constitution of the United States sooner than some think.

> J. Chally
> Morris, Illinois
> May 2, 1982

One reader wrote to tell what happened on her way to the ERA march in Portland, Oregon.

I live on the Oregon coast in the country. On Saturday morning, August 22, 1981, there was an ERA march in Portland, a two-and-a-quarter-hour drive from here, and I had planned to go.

Because women are the first laid off in depressions, I am unemployed. And because I have never made much money—again due to my sex, not a lack of skills or ability—my unemployment check amounts to ninety-six dollars per week, which usually arrives on Friday. I live alone and my only means of support is that ninety-six dollars per week plus ten dollars per month in food stamps. Out of that must come mandatory insurance payment, mortgage payment, food, medicine, water, telephone, electricity, and fuel for house and car, and whatever other necessities arrive on my threshold.

The food stamps will vanish pretty soon due to our concerned president—concerned about his own interersts.

Already because of federal cuts to state unemployment funds, the state of Oregon has closed our local unemployment office, and some people must drive over thirty-five miles a week to sign up for benefits and seek work. There is no public transportation in this area. What kind of way to save energy is that? And with rapes up alarmingly high, hitchhiking isn't too safe unless you want to pack a .44.

To add to my woes, my unemployment will soon expire. Although I have made a diligent effort to find work, none is forthcoming. Some days I have had as many as six interviews in Portland. They either tell me I am overqualified or subtly indicate they want a sweet, young, sexy thing. Sometimes I send out ten résumés a day to blind newspaper boxes, and not one has replied.

There is no welfare in Oregon for able-bodied persons without minor children. What are older women and others to do in this very materialistic society without a source of income? Shoot ourselves when the unemployment runs out or when we reach thirty-five to avoid further aggravation and hassles? Or should we who always paid our taxes organize and oust that piker millionaire president who doesn't pay taxes and exhibits other brutal un-American behavior?

Well, Friday, August 21, came, and due to some bureaucratic blunder, my unemployment check did not arrive; thus I had no money for gas to drive to the ERA march in Portland.

So on August 26, I sat down and wrote some boycott letters to businesses in states that have not ratified the Equal Rights Amendment. When I had finished writing the first three letters, I began to sob uncontrollably. I could not complete any more that day. Every time I started to think that in over two hundred years this country cannot even grant women their basic rights, I started crying. And we promote ourselves as being the land of the free. No wonder men accuse us of being too emotional. We are, and for good reason!

Jody I. Robindottir
Lincoln City, Oregon
September 5, 1981

Another reader sent what she called "an open letter to Phyllis Schlafly" in response to a revealing interview we published in the January 1982 issue.

In your interview with Henry Schipper, you stated that the reasons people want the Equal Rights Amendment are "to give funding for abortion, to give homosexual privileges, to give massive federal child care, and to force us into a gender-free society." If you truly believe these are their reasons, I think you are oversimplifying the position of ERA proponents.

As a happily married wife, mother, and grandmother, I want the passage of the ERA for completely different reasons: for career opportunities for myself, my daughters, and my daughter-in-law; for the right of protection in the inheritance laws that differ from state to state; for the satisfaction that I am sharing the load with my husband; and for my own self-esteem as a woman. I think there are many other women like me, in the age bracket of thirty-five to fifty-five years, middle of the road politically, economically, and socially, who support this concept of equality and who will continue to support it whether or not the current amendment reaches passage.

When I look at the years of struggle women had to endure simply to secure the right to vote, I realize that any change in the social climate requires a period of time for acceptance and adjustment. Perhaps it takes radicals to bring about these changes, radicals on both ends of the spectrum. But when the pendulum swings to the middle, after all the haranguing has been done, I feel there is going to be widespread support for the idea that women are indeed deserving of equality. I hope you will give my views the same courtesy of consideration that I have given yours.

Jean Skog
Iowa City, Iowa
May 1982 Issue

The last day for ERA ratification was June 30, 1982, and the deadline passed fairly quietly.

Only in recent years have I begun to learn the women's history that was never taught in any of my history textbooks: the *millions* of women murdered in Europe as "witches," the worship of Goddess-Mother before the introduction of God-Father, and the countless contributions of women in art, literature, and science that were credited to men. *How could it have all been erased?*

Last month, watching cable TV's HBO, "The Year That Was: 1982," I finally understood. I saw Princess Diana's first child, Henry Fonda's death, the invasion of the Falkland Islands, sports events, unemployment lines, and a host of other Major Events. But I did *not* see or hear one thing about the end of the ERA-ratification deadline. Our struggle for women's rights had been wiped right out of history.

Name Withheld
February 16, 1983

June 30, was a disappointing day for us, but I felt that I received a special gift when my boyfriend (a conservative, middle-aged man) called from work and told me of watching the six o'clock news with his male colleagues on the defeat of the ERA.

Several of them were rejoicing and making the usual remarks about keeping women in their place when he whipped out his ERA card [with the ERA printed on it] and said his piece, as he has done several times before. Most uninformed persons are amazed to see how simply the ERA is worded.

Kaye B. McLeod
Anchorage, Alaska
July 3, 1982

On June 6, two days after the North Carolina legislature failed to ratify the ERA, I attended the ERA rally in Raleigh. Later that day I went to a restaurant with my family. There I met a nine-year-old girl, her hair in pigtails. She looked at my green ERA-Yes buttons and white dress, and said, "You must be for the Equal Rights Amendment. Did you go to the rally?"

"Yes," I answered. "Did you?"

"No," she said. "I couldn't go because I had a softball game. We got creamed, as usual. I probably couldn't have gotten anyone to take me anyway. I have real dumb relatives who don't believe in equal rights."

Then, very tentatively, she asked, "Have we ever had equal rights?"

I answered, "No."

"Will we ever have them?" she wanted to know.

Who will answer this child?

Name Withheld
August 25, 1982

I'm twelve years old, and for my civics class I had to do a project, so I decided to do mine on the ERA. I handed out a questionnaire asking what the students wanted from the ERA and if they wanted it anyway. About half the boys wanted the ERA, and the other half either didn't or didn't know. Quite a few of the boys who didn't want it said that the reason women want the ERA is pride. *Pride,* I thought to myself! All my life I've been brought up by a woman, no man. I suppose the fact that my family has lived on "peanuts" all our lives had something to do with some man thinking that the only reason my mother wanted a job was because of pride—nothing to do with the fact that we have to eat and wear clothes! It makes me sick! Half the girls who did want the ERA didn't know why. That was it. But I know one thing—I'm not going to be one of those women stranded and relying on a man to pay for my way in life. Oh, no! Not me!

Justine Angelis
New York, New York
December 1982

As one reader made clear the next year, ERA proponents and opponents were a long way from understanding one another.

Although I'm not a feminist, I subscribe to *Ms.* because it tries hard to portray the whole woman and generally refuses to link femaleness simplistically with home, garden, fashion, sex, family, or career. And although I basically consider *Ms.* a propaganda rag, every month or so I find a good article that is both enlightening and true. I do wish more of my Mormon sisters would be broad-minded and read *Ms.* and display it publicly in their homes alongside church periodicals.

May I explain my doubts about the ERA? I've concluded that the traditional American male is, in general, characterized by several puzzling practices: excessive competition and profit seeking; exclusion or dominance of the weak; preoccupation with outside work and neglect of household, family, and civic responsibilities; inability to be patient, attentive, thoughtful, open, loyal, or humble; and belief in the utility of angry words and brute force. In my simple view of the world, the ERA would facilitate the adoption by women of traditional male standards of behavior. Do we women really want every person in this country growing up to act like traditional American men? If so, World War III is on its way.

However, I must confess to you a change in heart and mind about one important issue in the debate over the ERA; I've decided that financially independent, self-reliant women make independent, healthy families, and because I firmly believe healthy families make for healthy government and a strong nation, I would actively support with time and money a constitutional amendment of some sort granting women explicit rights. Healthy families will continue to disappear until all women, feminist or not, are given constitutional rights to develop self-reliance.

Catherine Hammon Sundwall
Silver Springs, Maryland
July 1983 Issue

It was lucky for our state of mind that the Ms. *Tenth Anniversary double issue and celebration came on the heels of the defeat of the ERA. This anniversary brought more than the usual batch of reader reflections: we had asked readers to contribute their thoughts for a special anniversary feature, "What's Been Happening to You in the Last Ten Years?" (July/August 1982). They complied with characteristic generosity.*

One of the most delightful offshoots of divorce (after twenty-five years), and a move to a strange town to return to college was the reaction of my children. They gleefully insisted that college was corrupting me. It helped to move into an apartment without a washer-dryer hookup. My son says that the first hint of corruption showed in my laundry habits. For years, I was aghast that my college student children would wash underwear with dirty socks, or jeans with white sheets. What a surprise to discover it was not only possible but, on my limited income, quite necessary. I learned that everything comes out relatively clean (relative to other students anyway). My son was shocked at my new attitude, but had the presence of mind to say, "I told you so!"

My daughter raised her eyebrows when I told her I had asked a man to go out with me. I met him at the Laundromat between the wash cycle and the add-the-softener cycle.

During the first introductions, she kept a straight face (she does act), and then dragged me into the kitchen saying, "Good God, Mother! I was expecting a business type around your own age!" I tried to explain to her that he was the only person I'd met who liked plays. So what if he is fifteen years younger than I am? At that, he was the oldest person I'd talked to in weeks.

Katherine Lepthien
Hilo, Hawaii
July/August 1982 Issue

Sixteen to twenty-six, a decade of amazing turbulence in my own self-history. At one end point, a pudgy guilt-wracked teenager (too tall, too fat, too smart), and at the other, a lieutenant in the United States Navy, navigating the rocks and shoals of a very traditional hierarchy. Learning at last how to be a worthy friend to another woman and not canceling our dinner together because a man called. Losing men I have loved because they couldn't or wouldn't accept, in the end, a resourceful, assertive, *leanable-on* woman. Finding a strong man who gladly accepts me as his partner, lover, friend. All these things have shaped me in my girl-woman decade; I cannot complain.

Lieut. Mary Josephine Sweeney, USN
New York, New York
July/August 1982 Issue

In 1972, my husband of five years felt very liberated because he "helped with" housework and child care when it was convenient for him—but refused such hard-core tasks as cleaning bathrooms and ironing. In 1982, he answered the door on a Saturday morning, his pink rubber gloves dripping; when his colleague from work asked what on earth . . . he replied, "Cleaning the toilet—doesn't everyone?"

In 1972, our entertaining routines and family holidays left me exhausted from doing *everything*. In 1982, I do the grocery list and cooking—he shops, cleans up, and refuses female help in the kitchen. Once in the heat of battle he shouted, "Your 'fem' crap is ruining our lives!" My " 'fem' crap" saved the marriage.

Then, our life was a battlefield—I kept one eye on the apartment-for-rent ads and my suitcase (and the kids') mentally packed; today I can hardly remember what a *big* fight feels like. But I do know what love feels like—a warm contentment, inspired by justice. Now that the principles have been established, mercy on both our parts has replaced abiding by the strict letter of the law, and we have long since abandoned formal schedules.

An unsettling footnote to this picture of bliss is that most of our, and my, friends are divorced, as are most of the women I meet and like best. With only one marriage of fifteen years, I have the distinct feeling of being out of sync. The camaraderie I felt and shared with other women in 1972, when mutual bitching bound us together, is now gone; I don't miss the bitching, but I do miss the camaraderie.

I guess in 1982, I'm looking for a feeling of community and a wider sense of purpose. I feel somewhat unsettled right now, but not unhappy. Writing this, I wonder what I'll be saying in 1991—who will I be? I *like* being unable to predict that!

Nancy Spohn
Beaverton, Oregon
July/August 1982 Issue

And in response to that feature, some other readers sent their thoughts.

In 1972 I asked, "What's wrong with me?" Now, at thirty-three, I ask "What the hell is the matter with them!"

Kathryn A. Olsen
Park Forest, Illinois
November 1982 Issue

[Ten years ago] when my daughter was born in the Ozarks, there were no midwives who would come out to a country birthing, so we did it ourselves. Now we also have, as well as a number of competent midwives, a women's trucking collective, a large cooperative food warehouse, a battered women's shelter, a women's health collective, alternative child-care facilities, and a feeling of sisterhood among alternative country and city women.

I am still dealing with small rural school systems, a lack of transportation, poverty, and men who haven't heard of women's rights, but at least now I know that these problems are common to many women. The feeling that the circumstances of my life are hopelessly out of control has left me.

Kathi Barnhart
St. Paul, Arkansas
November 1982 Issue

Another "up" was Sally Ride's launching as the first woman in space, in April 1983. Our January 1983 cover story on Sally Ride, "The Making of an Astronaut" by Sara Sanborn, brought this response.

The article on Sally Ride was the most uplifting story I have read since my copy of the first issue of *Ms.* arrived. While doing my dissertation on curriculum resources for women in science, medicine, and technology, I discovered that women in the 1960s were not allowed to be jet pilots and therefore could not qualify for astronaut training in this country. What a difference to have Dr. Ride and her colleagues.

I am now the science consultant for the school district of the city of Highland Park, Michigan, and plan to supply reprints of the article to the thirty science teachers in my district. NASA should do a poster of Sally Ride!

> Dr. Shirley Kyle
> Highland Park, Michigan
> April 1983 Issue

One young reader hadn't waited for Sally Ride to form her own dreams.

When I saw that in my spelling book they had "the Queen is the wife of a King," I got really mad. Even though I'm only nine years old, and only in the fourth grade, I've written five poems. One from the five I thought you might want to put in *Ms.* Here it is:

> If you think I'm going to slave
> in the kitchen for a man who is
> supposed to be brave,
> Then I'm sorry to say,
> but you're wrong all the way,
> Because *I'm* going to be an
> astronaut.

> Anita Buzick II
> Killeen, Texas
> June 1975 Issue

A reader commented on another 1983 "event": a photograph of Gloria Steinem that appeared in another magazine.

I was kind of surprised to see Gloria Steinem in a bubble bath in *People* magazine. But, what the heck, I guess it's as good a way as any to appear in *People*. At least she must have felt cleansed afterward.

Remember when they used to say "heck," Gloria?

Nancy MacDonald Ornstein
West Orange, New Jersey
December 9, 1983

Peace activism had always been a strong component of the current women's movement—with groups such as Women Strike for Peace, founded in 1960, leading the way. In the eighties, the women of the Greenham Common peace encampment in England, where demonstrators set up a permanent camp outside the U.S. Air Force base to protest nuclear weapons, inspired activists here.

I am an American living in London. Two hours ago I returned from Greenham Common, a military base an hour by train west of London. The base is used by the U.S. Air Force, and all personnel currently serving there are Americans. By December of this year, ninety-six cruise (first strike) missiles are scheduled to be sited at Greenham Common.

For two years women, thousands of women, have focused on Greenham Common in their protest against nuclear weapons. Holding hands, women stand vigil at the main gate to the airfield. They camp outside the grounds. They climb over the fences and link arms, encircling the silos. They lie in the paths of the military personnel, forcing the men to step on their bodies in order to get into the base. They are dragged away by British police and dumped into vans, vans which cannot move because other women lie down in front of the wheels.

Does all this sound chaotic? It is not. The only violence comes from the police dogs, the patrolling officers, and the menace of the air base itself. The women sing. They smile. They come with flowers and tea and even knitting; it is, after all, a long siege.

Yesterday, fourteen women "in breach of the peace" (the irony!) were carried away from the main gate by police officers. They were dragged by their shirts, their hair, even their ears. One of the officers was a woman. She pulled at us roughly, feeling all our eyes on her. "Please stand up. Please stand up," she begged to the middle-aged woman she pulled by the arms. "Please, you sit down," responded the woman being pulled away.

Later a friend and I saw this female officer standing behind a parked police bus. She was standing by herself, crying. I hugged my arms and cried over the madness of a system that tears women apart, not only from one another, but from themselves.

Name Withheld
August 15, 1983

In December 1983, we published a report by veteran peace activist, poet, and writer Grace Paley of the peace camp that summer at a Seneca, New York, military base—not far from Seneca Falls, where the historic 1848 first national women's convention adopted a call that included the demand for suffrage. Grace Paley had been particularly grateful for the minority of local women who turned out in support of the protesters.

As a resident of Waterloo, New York, I read with special interest Grace Paley's thoughtful and moving account, "The Seneca Stories: Tales From the Women's Peace Encampment." The story is all too true. The ugly name calling, the vicious signs, the potential mob violence were all there. These tactics are all too familiar to those espousing any cause whose time has not yet come to the provinces. And not just the provinces either. I remember construction workers attacking peace marchers during the Vietnam era, while police turned their backs and Nixon applauded. This happened on Wall Street, in New York City. Ignorance and tolerance are frequent partners.

I was privileged to be among a small handful of local women demonstrating at the fairgrounds in support of the incarcerated women. If we helped make their day, you can believe they sure made mine. All the self-righteous flag wavers have surely been given something to think about besides their misplaced pride in how they faced up to "outsiders." I hope those thoughts will include the knowledge that if this earth goes up in smoke, that means "me, too."

Grace Clary
Waterloo, New York
March 1984 Issue

Also in 1983, the New Bedford rape case made national headlines—with a trial televised on cable. Readers responded to a memorable essay by Mary Kay Blakely, "The New Bedford Gang Rape: Who Were the Men?," for our July 1983 issue, in which she discussed the climate that permitted such a thing to happen in a crowded bar.

My husband and I were traveling south on I-35 to Oklahoma City. I had just read Mary Kay Blakely's article and had taken over driving. I gave the article to my husband to read, which he did. As he finished it, he looked at me very soberly, and then he glanced out the window. At that precise moment, I was swinging out to pass a car that we noticed had a bumper sticker. My husband exclaimed, "Oh, no! I don't believe it! That sticker said: Don't Argue With Your Wife—Dicker!"

Any thoughts he may have had about Blakely overstating "Who are the bystanders, and how did we come to tolerate them?" were wiped out in the instant he read that bumper sticker. It became obvious. The bystanders are all around us, and so are those who tolerate them.

Tommy Haas
Grinnell, Iowa
August 17, 1983

I am married to a wonderful man who lives his life based on feminist principles. We share equally the mundane duties of everyday life; he supports my work as a counselor at a battered women's shelter, and I support his as a physician. Yet he has never been outspoken about his feminist philosophy. I have always found that particularly frustrating.

Not long after our first child, a daughter, was born, we found ourselves in the middle of a discussion of the New Bedford rape trial with my family. Someone made a disparaging remark about the woman involved. My usually soft-spoken husband rose to his feet and began an angry discourse on the cruelty of the remark, on rape and the fear most women are forced to carry with them, and on the general injustice of "the system" and our society where women are concerned. As my family sat stunned, he said finally, "What if it had been Rebekah (our daughter)? Would you still be so callous and unfeeling?" I felt like applauding.

When we watched Walter Mondale pick Geraldine Ferraro for his vice-presidential running mate, the excitement was overwhelming. My husband told four-month-old Rebekah what the nation had been told: "If you want to, you can grow up to be president."

Thank you, Rebekah, for helping your dad find his voice and for setting him free.

Darlene Furey
Abington, Pennsylvania
November 1984 Issue

Toward the end of 1983 a reader told the story of the terrifying violence that had hit his family.

This morning my mother called to tell me that my sister has been murdered in a probable rape attempt. Twenty years after "having to get married," raising three kids, drifting through three marriages, discarding her academic goals, and earning her keep as a part-time waitress, Carol was walking alone in the wrong place at the wrong time. Why did a man stab and gash and puncture her skull with a screwdriver? Was it simply that she was there? All women are "there"; are all women fair game? The man accused of this murder must think so: he was on parole after nine years in prison for the murder of his wife and has also been charged with the June stabbing murder of *another* woman.

Why does any man believe he can do this to a woman? What is wrong with a "civilization" that allows a man to even contemplate an attack on a weaker being without feeling an overwhelming sense of the community wrath descending upon him? Why do we make it easy? Where is the power of our two-hundred-million good souls? Why is society so impotent? And why does it expend its precious energy on denying a pregnant seventeen-year-old the abortion that will keep her from wasting twenty years?

For the past few years, Carol had been working toward a dream of social worth and self-sufficiency. She was doing excellent work at New Mexico State. At age thirty-nine, my sister was beginning her life—the real one. Carol will never be born. Please tell me how we can stop this waste. How can we teach our children that people are not there to be used however we want? How can we keep violent criminals from returning to the streets? Would death by screwdriver truly be a cruel and unusual punishment? How else can we put fear in the hearts of those whose hearts are devoid of humanity?

Even if these questions were answered, I doubt the right people would listen. After all, it's still a man's world, isn't it?

Dan Geminder
Winnipeg, Manitoba, Canada
December 1983 Issue

When I read Dan Geminder's letter, it scared me. It made me cry, and it made me angry as hell. I am so sick and tired of our judicial system releasing rapists, child molesters, and murderers who go back on the street and commit the same crime— over and over again! I am tired of hearing *why* men rape, as though they weren't responsible for their actions! Until feminists get involved in *all* lawmaking and enforcement areas, women will continue to be powerless and preyed upon.

I *hate* feeling the way I do every time I hear stories like Geminder's and of children who are raped and murdered. I feel like starting a "hit back" group to stop the offenders our courts release—and I am not a violent person. What can I do to make a difference, as one person who cares?

My heart goes out to Dan Geminder. I hope he can learn to deal with it when they release his sister's murderer—and I'm afraid the chances are good that they will.

Name Withheld
March 1984 Issue

In 1984, Ms. commissioned a Louis Harris poll to survey American women and men on a broad spectrum of issues. One of the most surprising results, published in the July 1984 issue, was that when asked to choose whether they believed the women's movement had peaked, was on the decline, or had just begun, 57 percent of the women surveyed said they believed that the women's movement had just begun. A women's studies teacher offered her explanation.

As a women's studies instructor in a women's college, where I am continually experiencing the journeys of young women into feminist thought, I was surprised to find that 57 percent of the Harris Poll's resondents felt the women's movement had just begun. So many young women I encounter regard it as a thing of the past. While these young women feel very grateful to feminists of the past for giving them certain freedoms, they also feel a nostalgia for "good old days" when women were not burdened with the responsibility of choosing a career or making important decisions. I suspect that the 57 percent of us who believe the women's movement has just begun have only recently realized the magnitude of the task of revising our daily lives—increasing our power with lovers, friends, families, co-workers, bosses, and all other people we encounter. These relationships have always meant more to us than the abstraction of national politics.

Leslie Miller
Columbia, Missouri
October 1984 Issue

A reader who had written in the year before confirmed a theory often put forth by Gloria Steinem—that radicalism, far from a characteristic of young people, increased with age.

Inasmuch as I will become thirty this year, I thought it was time to write and tell you that you have been right all along. I was initially skeptical about the relevance of feminism to my life. In high school, I was one of those who said I didn't know what I needed to be liberated *from*—and in truth I have very supportive parents, and I found no barriers to academic achievement. But now, after the experiences of being a law student, the first woman lawyer in a law firm, a wife, and a mother, I can say, with A. E. Housman, "And Oh, 'tis true, 'tis true."

Thank you, *Ms.*, for the courage your existence has given me to carry on and be happy with myself (if not always with the world in which I live).

Linda Biehl Molyneaux
Davenport, Iowa
November 1983 Issue

For our October 1984 issue, our cover absolutely had to be Geraldine Ferraro, who had that summer been nominated for vice-president by the Democratic convention to run with Walter Mondale.

I am writing just moments after watching history being made: Geraldine Ferraro has been nominated for vice-president of the United States! I happily admit I cried throughout the announcement and speeches. I cried because I was filled with gratitude, hope, and pride.

To me, the outcome of the election is almost irrelevant, for now I *know* that more great, pride-filled moments such as this one lie ahead for *all* Americans and that, as Gerry Ferarro suggested, more and more of those heavy old doors will be opening.

Lucy Allen
St. Louis, Missouri
October 1984 Issue

In June 1985, at the National Women's Political Caucus convention at Atlanta, Lynn Cutler, of the Democratic National Committee, was asked whether she thought Gerry Ferraro's campaign had been "good for women in politics" even though the ticket lost in a Ronald Reagan landslide. "Just think what the campaign would have been like without Gerry Ferraro," she answered. That's certainly how we felt when making Ferraro one of our women of the year for our January 1985 issue.

Honored along with Gerry Ferrro as a Ms. woman of the year was ten-year-old Charity Grant, a spunky kid from Iowa City, Iowa who had refused to accept a "good reading" award because it was offered by a club that didn't allow women members. For the January 1987 women of the year issue, Charity, in turn, interviewed another young heroine who was among the awardees, Sarabeth Eason. Sarabeth, an eleven-year-old from Toledo, Ohio, had signed a newspaper advertisement supporting a woman's right to choose abortion. She was expelled from her Catholic school when she refused to "desist" from publicly taking that stand. Sarabeth and Charity, in discussing how kids can really think about issues and make their own decisions, gave us all hope for the future.

The interview of Sarabeth Eason by Charity Grant moved me to tears. It brought me back with a jolt to my own childhood. I could have used friends like Charity and Sarabeth when I argued for "girl's rights" at age eleven. I, too, had my mother's support, but kids looked at me as though I was a freak, and adults acted as though it was just a phase. I felt helpless and lonely.

I am now twenty-four and on my way to becoming an ordained minister, hoping someday to help kids like Charity and Sarabeth express themselves openly and without fear. I have discovered other women who have struggled with the same issues and felt the same pain. I have been enveloped by women's support groups and by friends who are brutally honest and always loving. I still feel lonely sometimes, but believe me, Sarabeth, Charity, it gets better.

Arlene M. Franks
Claremont, California
April 1987 Issue

To prepare for our Fifteenth Anniversary Issue of July/August 1987, we asked readers to tell us what part of feminism most changed their lives and what part made them most uncomfortable. We received many thoughtful answers, but the self-affirming connection women feel to one another clearly remains the great strength of the women's movement.

What a fascinating task you have given us, your readers! It will take our wisdom, pain, and humor to give you accurate answers. To honor us all, I make the attempt.

The aspect of feminism that has most changed my life has to be the magical, healing essence of female affirmation. It goes way beyond feeling that I'm "okay" as a woman (or in spite of it) to real belief that I and all females are wonderful in ourselves. This has allowed me to take all manner of risks over the years, from rock climbing for the first time at twenty-nine years to openly discussing feminist politics and theories in the public classroom. To be rid of all the damn "givens" I grew up with and explore life with new courage and unlimited options is the very best thing feminism has given me. I work daily to pass it on to everyone I know.

The part of feminism that has made me unhappy and uncomfortable is when we allow ourselves to be divided from each other for all sorts of reasons. We have so much more in common as women than we have as any subgroup that we *must* keep together. We must honor the bond all females have the world over and continue to get strength from each other. Thanks to *Ms.* for providing the forum to do just that.

Meleta Murdock Baker
Milton, New Hampshire
February 21, 1987

AFTERWORD

❦

by Eva Moseley

Like *Ms.*, the Schlesinger Library is a phenomenon in women's history. It was founded as the Women's Archives in 1943, when Radcliffe College accepted a large gift of books, papers, photographs, and memorabilia of the woman's suffrage movement from Maud Wood Park, an alumna of the class of 1898.

But I see the roots of the library as reaching back at least to 1840. That year saw the first World's Anti-Slavery Convention, held in London and attended by many American delegates. Among them were several female abolitionists. When they arrived, the women learned that, even though some of them were delegates of their anti-slavery organizations, they had to sit in the gallery and could neither speak nor vote. All good *Ms.* readers can hear the CLICK echoing down the decades. Elizabeth Cady Stanton, Lucretia Mott, and the others didn't use this word but the effect was the same, and eight years later Stanton and Mott were two of the leading organizers of the first Woman's Rights Convention, held at Seneca Falls, New York, in July 1848. Here Stanton first suggested the revolutionary idea that women demand the vote. Hence, the suffrage movement, which would triumph (after 72 years!) in 1920.

While building on its suffrage collections, the library has increasingly stretched its collecting philosophy to make it more inclusive. Of course the library always wants papers of notable women who have made major contributions to American society. But we are just as concerned with acquiring a representative record of the ordinary lives of women, with the struggles, triumphs, frustrations, boredom, the work, family, and personal obligations, satisfactions, and trials that all of us experience one way or another.

From the beginning, the library emphasized the importance of collecting unpublished materials: the personal papers of individual women (such as letters, diaries, speeches, writings, school papers, photos, drawings, and scrapbooks); family collections, generally with papers of several generations; and archives of organizations. Such archival or manuscript materials are the raw material of history. The library has also emphasized acquiring contemporary materials. Many will disappear if not collected quickly; and we know that history is being made *now*.

The *Ms.* letters, most of them unpublished, fit in here very well, providing illuminating, poignant, behind-the-scenes glimpses into the lives of many American women and girls, few of them well-known. Although the Schlesinger Library is almost thirty years older than *Ms.*, the library has experienced its greatest growth during the years of the magazine's existence. Both owe their vitality to the "second wave" women's movement. With 250 research visits in 1969–70, there are now about five thousand each year. Women's history is here to stay, accepted as a discipline in many quarters, and influencing more and more the ways in which traditional history is perceived and written. So the library daily welcomes students and scholars, sometimes school-children, often journalists, teachers, or the curious, helping to spread the word about women's true place in history, which many dimly realized all along but few dared to assert: women have always been there, always active though often oppressed, an essential half of the historical picture. When women are left out of history, that history is a distortion.

With the ongoing and vital support of Radcliffe College, the library is able to build and care for its collections, serve the public (it is open to everyone), and sponsor events to make its holdings and women's history better known. The women who have written to *Ms.* can themselves become researchers, reading the many letters to the magazine that were not published or any of the other manuscript collections, the books, pamphlets, or periodicals that document women in America. (Note: The letters at the Schlesinger Library are protected by privacy provisions. With the exception of letters concerning the Equal Rights Amendment, they are closed to all but those to whom they are addressed—the *Ms.* editors—for ten years from the date of their writing. When they are open to research, readers must agree not to use the names or correct initials of the letter writers, and unpublished letters may not be photocopied for fifty years after the date of their writing.)

When a former colleague, Kathy Marquis, and I sorted through the files of letters at the *Ms.* office, she came across a letter from a classmate in junior high school. Not everyone will find someone she knows, but for all there will be many echoes of their own stories. The reality of which these stories are a part must not be forgotten when the history of our time is written. The Schlesinger Library, with the help of the staff and readers of *Ms.* and countless other women, intends to make sure that it is indeed remembered.

Eva S. Moseley
Curator of Manuscripts
Schlesinger Library
Radcliffe College